Between Desert and River

Hohokam Settlement and Land Use in the Los Robles Community

ANTHROPOLOGICAL PAPERS OF
THE UNIVERSITY OF ARIZONA
NUMBER 57

Between Desert and River

Hohokam Settlement and Land Use in the Los Robles Community

Christian E. Downum

CONTRIBUTORS

Douglas B. Craig
John E. Douglas
Keith Katzer
John H. Madsen

THE UNIVERSITY OF ARIZONA PRESS
TUCSON
1993

About the Author

CHRISTIAN E. DOWNUM is Director of the Anthropology Laboratories and an Assistant Professor of Anthropology at Northern Arizona University in Flagstaff. Previously he held positions as Archaeological Specialist with the Arizona State Museum and as Adjunct Professor in the Department of Anthropology at The University of Arizona, Tucson, earning his Master's (1981) and Doctoral (1988) degrees from that institution. He has participated in and directed large-scale survey projects from Wupatki National Monument on the Colorado Plateau to the Tucson Basin in the Sonoran Desert. While engaged in research to investigate the functions of *cerros de trincheras* in the United States and Sonora, Mexico, he served as co-director of the Cerro Prieto mapping project from 1983 to 1986. His efforts in protecting and preserving the trincheras features at Cerro Prieto have resulted in the nomination of the Los Robles Archaeological District to the National Register of Historic Places and the designation of the Cerro Prieto and Pan Quemado sites as a future Arizona State Park. His broad research interests include Prehistory of the Southwest, Evolution of Sociocultural Complexity, Archaeology of Prehistoric Landscapes, and Development and Application of Ceramic Dating Techniques.

Cover: Archaeologist Glenn D. Stone records attributes of a rectangular stone structure on the slopes of Cerro Prieto, an early Classic period *cerro de trincheras* of the Los Robles Community (see Chapter 4).

THE UNIVERSITY OF ARIZONA PRESS

This book was set in 10/12 Dutch Roman
∞ This book is printed on acid-free, archival-quality paper.
Manufactured in the United States of America.

97 96 95 94 93 7 6 5 4 3

Library of Congress Cataloging-in-Publication Data

Downum, Christian E. (Christian Eric). 1957-
Between desert and river: Hohokam settlement and land use in the Los Robles community / Christian E. Downum ; contributors, Douglas B. Craig ... [et al.].
p. cm. -- (Anthropological papers of The University of Arizona; no. 57)
Includes bibliographical references and index.
ISBN 0-8165-1375-9 (alk. paper)
1. Hohokam culture. 2. Land settlement patterns, Prehistoric--Arizona--Los Robles Wash Region. 3. Los Robles Wash Region (Ariz.)--Antiquities. 4. Arizona--Antiquities. I. Craig, Douglas B. II. Title. III. Series.
E99.H68D69 1993
979. 1'7--dc20 92-44964
CIP

Contributors

Douglas B. Craig
Department of Anthropology, University of Arizona, Tucson

John E. Douglas
Department of Anthropology, University of Montana, Missoula

Keith Katzer
Department of Anthropology, University of Arizona, Tucson (Deceased)

John H. Madsen
Arizona State Museum, University of Arizona, Tucson

Contents

FIGURES

TABLES

Preface

In Hohokam archaeology, the past decade or so has been an exciting time of discovery. This has been especially true for the zones between and around the edges of major river valleys. As the Central Arizona Project (CAP) canal and other massive construction plans have forced Hohokam archaeologists to investigate desert zones that were not watered by perennial streams, it has become evident that the prehistoric cultural landscape was more continuous and interconnected than previously believed. As a result, the Hohokam world has become considerably more complex and interesting. Today, most Hohokam archaeologists would probably acknowledge that traditional cultural labels and concepts need revision in light of new discoveries, and all surely would welcome the opportunity to assimilate and synthesize the overwhelming amount of new information that has been generated by the past decade's archaeological field studies.

The chance to catch one's breath, however, has receded into the distant future. The pace of Hohokam archaeology appears actually to be quickening as new and ever-larger projects are underway (such as the U.S. Bureau of Reclamation's ongoing Lake Roosevelt studies, and recent freeway expansion work in Phoenix). Thus, any new grand syntheses of Hohokam prehistory will probably need to wait at least until the current round of major field investigations and associated analyses are properly reported. In the meantime, we must be satisfied with watching pieces of this puzzle emerge, and with taking time properly to savor the archaeological details that someday will be enriched with interpretive significance.

This report presents both a piece of the regional Hohokam puzzle and an initial account of some of the details of Hohokam existence in an area intermediate between two major perennial streams (the middle Santa Cruz and Gila rivers). Based largely on a recent U.S. Bureau of Reclamation-sponsored survey and the Cerro Prieto mapping project, this volume describes Hohokam, protohistoric Piman, and recent settlement patterns and land use across a broad portion of the Los Robles Wash area in the lower Santa Cruz River Basin. Much of the work is devoted to an extensive set of Hohokam sites, and in particular the *trincheras* site of Cerro Prieto, that appears to have been integrated into a coherent community of interacting and apparently cooperative and politically unified settlements. Like a previous publication in this series on the Marana Community by Suzanne Fish, Paul Fish, and John Madsen (1992), this report provides an initial portrait of a large, nonriverine Hohokam community in a so-called peripheral area. Far from being marginal or irrelevant to the overall course of Hohokam cultural developments, such communities now seem to have forged significant links in a system of regional interaction stretching from the Phoenix Basin southward to the Sonoran Papaguería. As such, they must be regarded as integral parts of the Hohokam regional system, and they illustrate the cultural and behavioral variability encompassed by that system.

As with so many Hohokam investigations in the 1980s, the field work upon which this report is based originated with a massive development project, in this case the CAP canal. Between 1981 and 1989, three systematic archaeological inventories were made by the Arizona State Museum to document patterns of settlement and land use around several Classic period Hohokam mound sites in the lower Santa Cruz River Basin (P. Fish, S. Fish, and Madsen 1989). These surveys were conceived and sponsored by the U.S. Bureau of Reclamation (USBR) to provide a broad research context for Hohokam sites excavated prior to construction of the Tucson Aqueduct of the USBR's Central Arizona Project. The broad-scale areal and temporal patterns revealed by these surveys enhance and complement the detailed excavation studies conducted along the Tucson Aqueduct and its various lateral canals and pipelines.

One of these three projects, the Los Robles Archaeological Survey conducted in 1985 and 1986, explored the prehistoric community associated with the Los Robles Mound Site, an early Classic period settlement on the west bank of Los Robles Wash about 10 km south of Picacho Peak. The survey was under the general supervision of Paul and Suzanne Fish of the Arizona State Museum. It was organized by ASM archaeologist John

H. Madsen and executed by field supervisor James M. Bayman and a team of two to five survey crew members. Over the course of many months, the Los Robles survey documented some 145 new archaeological sites, and revisited or restudied 31 sites that had been recorded previously. In addition, hundreds of isolated artifacts and nonsite artifact concentrations were discovered and recorded, and the geomorphological and vegetational zones of the survey area were mapped. Site numbers in this report are Arizona State Museum Site Survey designations unless otherwise indicated; R- refers to preliminary Robles Survey Site numbers.

Fortuitously, the Los Robles survey overlapped with the Cerro Prieto mapping project, an independent research endeavor conducted by Douglas B. Craig, John E. Douglas, and me, all of whom were at the time graduate students in anthropology at The University of Arizona. This project was conducted on weekends and vacations from March of 1983 to April of 1986. Using volunteer labor and financial support provided by The University of Arizona, and private donations, we mapped most of the houses, terraces, and other major rock constructions at Cerro Prieto. The result of this study has been a much clearer understanding of this remarkable trincheras site, now known to have been a major early Classic period Hohokam settlement, of its potential role in local and regional settlement systems, and of its function in the Los Robles Community.

As often happens, modern events had a strong impact on our research plans. In July, 1985, a Marana-based development corporation announced its intent to lease portions of State Trust lands surrounding the Cerro Prieto and Pan Quemado sites for the purpose of building a "combination guest ranch, shooting range, military arms museum, and flight school" (*Arizona Daily Star*, 7-13-85). According to the corporation partners, this facility was to cater mostly to Japanese tourists seeking training in the use of firearms and desert survival gear. A state-of-the art electronic shooting range, to be situated on the south slopes of Pan Quemado, was intended for use by "the National Rifle Association, various local law enforcement officials and the U.S. Olympic team." It was also promised that the range would feature "a Gatling gun... available for firing" (*Tucson Citizen* 7-13-85).

These announcements provoked a swift reaction from Tucson-area archaeologists, who mounted a campaign to protest the lease applications filed by the corporation with the Arizona State Land Department. Protest took a number of forms, including individual letters, an organized tour of the sites sponsored by the Arizona Archaeological and Historical Society (*Arizona Daily Star*, 9-1-85), a recommendation of lease denial by the Arizona State Historic Preservation Officer, a resolution passed by the 1985 Pecos Conference, and letters from various archaeological organizations, including the Society for American Archaeology. All of these actions attracted the attention of the Arizona State Parks Board, which advocated that the Cerro Prieto and Pan Quemado sites be authorized as a future Arizona State Park. This recommendation was added to a 1986 State Parks authorization and funding bill, H.B. 2498, and lease applications were withdrawn by the corporation. In April, 1986, H.B. 2498 was passed by the Arizona legislature and signed into law by then-governor Bruce Babbitt. Thus, the area described in this monograph is now protected and eventually will be developed as a State Park.

The geographical and cultural context of the Los Robles Community and a history of archaeological research in the area are presented in Chapter 1, followed by a review of the environment, which is crucial to understanding the variety of subsistence opportunities available to the early Hohokam (Chapter 2). The enumeration in Chapter 3 of the kinds of sites located during the survey further demonstrates the diversity of land use practiced in prehistoric times and illustrates some of the many petroglyphs appearing on rock outcroppings. The trincheras site of Cerro Prieto is described (Chapter 4), along with rock cairn and open pit features near the lower Santa Cruz River (Chapter 5). The concluding chapter summarizes land use patterns and the temporal patterns of settlement in the Los Robles Community, and places the Community in the larger context of Hohokam development.

Acknowledgments

Many institutions and individuals contributed to the success of the Los Robles Survey and the Cerro Prieto mapping project. The U.S. Bureau of Reclamation supported the survey financially through a cooperative agreement (No. 4-CS-30-01380) between the Bureau, the Arizona State Museum, and the Arizona State Land Department. The original inspiration for the platform mound survey project came from Gene Rogge of the USBR, who desired to place USBR-sponsored excavations of sites along the Tucson Aqueduct in a regional context. After Gene's departure from the Bureau, the project was ably administered and enthusiastically supported by USBR archaeologists Tom Lincoln and Kathy Pedrick. Their continued commitment to publishing the results of the platform mound surveys has made this volume possible. Additional financial assistance for the Los Robles survey was provided by Arizona State

Historic Preservation Office grants SP8315 and SP9314. The nomination of the Los Robles Archaeological District to the National Register of Historic Places was made possible by SHPO grant 10735. Bob Larkin of the Arizona State Land Department and Theresa Hoffman of the Arizona SHPO were of special assistance during the National Register Nomination effort.

Major institutional support was given by the Arizona State Museum (ASM) and the Department of Anthropology at The University of Arizona. Raymond H. Thompson, Director of the Arizona State Museum, provided unwavering backing and encouragement of the platform mound survey project. Particular thanks are also extended to Paul and Suzanne Fish of the ASM for inviting me to join their ongoing survey and excavation projects in the northern Tucson Basin, especially investigations of *cerros de trincheras* sites. The Fishes have provided the methodological and intellectual foundation for much of the research reported in this volume. John Madsen of the ASM provided logistical assistance and information about the Los Robles survey and many other matters, and his help is gratefully acknowledged. ASM archaeologist Jim Bayman should be singled out for his contributions to the Los Robles Archaeological Survey. Jim brought to the survey a rare level of archaeological skill and devotion, and a large part of this report has come from the survey data that he so expertly collected. Survey crew members also deserve special thanks, especially John Field, Karen Harry, Tina Lee, Jim Lombard, Miriam Stark, Chris Powell, Barbara Roth, and Jim Vint.

The Department of Anthropology at The University of Arizona donated financial assistance to the Cerro Prieto mapping project through the award of multiple Comins Fund fellowships. Mike Schiffer, Jeff Reid, Paul Fish, and Norm Yoffee provided important letters of support for these fellowships. Pima Community College, through the generous assistance of David Stephen and J. R. "Buff" Billings, made available the mapping equipment used at Cerro Prieto. The financial support of Elizabeth Boggess and Archaeologists Unlimited, Inc., and Margarita Bischoff, is also gratefully acknowledged. Without their help, the Cerro Prieto mapping project would not have been possible. I also thank the Department of Anthropology at Northern Arizona University, Flagstaff, for support during the final editing of this report.

Volunteers were an essential part of the Cerro Prieto mapping project, and dozens of people contributed hundreds of person-days to the effort. Jeff Bentley, Buff Billings, Al Dart, Kelley Hays, Fred Huntington, Frank Kinney, Joan Lloyd, Paris Manfredonia, Adrianne Rankin, Kay Simpson, and Glenn Stone were among the regular contributors, and they deserve special thanks. Barbara Harper took and donated valuable color aerial photographs of Cerro Prieto. Henry Wallace and Jim Holmlund are acknowledged as the individuals who introduced me to the site of Cerro Prieto.

The production of this volume benefitted from the efforts of many people. Stephanie Whittlesey classified the Los Robles survey ceramic collections. John Field and Jim Lombard studied the area's geomorphology. Karen Reichhardt mapped and interpreted local vegetation and plant communities. Helga Teiwes produced field and artifact photographs. Henry Wallace has also contributed several photographs. The aerial photos that appear in Figures 2.4, 2.5, and 4.5 were obtained from Cooper Aerial Photo, Inc., of Tucson. Figures 4.7 through 4.9 and Figure 4.33 are the work of Charles Sternberg. The remaining line drawings were drafted in final form by Ron Beckwith. The text, illustrations, and general appearance of the book have been immeasurably improved by the editorial skills, wisdom, and general publishing artistry of Carol Gifford. Though perhaps not obvious, her contributions to the work are many, and she has patiently guided it from rough draft to final product.

On a more personal note, my colleagues and close friends Doug Craig and John Douglas also deserve special recognition and thanks. Without them the Cerro Prieto mapping project never would have begun and certainly could not have been completed. The lost weekends spent on the slopes and summit of Cerro Prieto, which we all thought would never end, are now cherished memories. Throughout the heat, fatigue, cicada serenades, gnat swarms, stuck vehicles, flat tires, broken equipment, dead batteries, lost forms, lost features, bad coffee, bad lunches, hot drinking water, snake surprises, falls, scrapes, bruises, and assaults from the local flora, I cannot remember a single cross word or expressed regret. Thanks also to Denise, Becky, and Linda for bearing our weekend absences and general obsession with Cerro Prieto.

I also thank all who visited Cerro Prieto and contributed ideas regarding this site and its possible role in the Los Robles Community. These include, but certainly are not confined to: Jim Bayman, Mary Bernard-Shaw, Buff Billings, Doug Craig, Bill Doelle, John Douglas, Paul Fish, Suzanne Fish, Bill Hartmann, Gayle Hartmann, Julian Hayden, Emil Haury, Jim Holmlund, Fred Huntington, Keith Kintigh, Carol Kramer, Steve Lekson, Jim Lombard, John Madsen, Randy McGuire, Adrianne Rankin, Jeff Reid, Mike Schiffer, Chet Shaw, Glenn Stone, Elisa Villalpando, Henry Wallace, David Wilcox, and Norm Yoffee. All posed questions or made comments that have shaped my interpretations, though of course any excesses or deficiencies in the views expressed herein are entirely my own stubborn fault.

Finally, many individuals and institutions contributed to the efforts in 1985 and 1986 to protect the sites of Cerro Prieto and Pan Quemado from development, and to preserve these places as a future Arizona State Park. Among the institutions lending support were the Society for American Archaeology, the Arizona Archaeological and Historical Society, the Arizona State Museum, the Arizona State Historic Preservation Office, the Arizona Archaeological Society, and the Cochise County Historical and Archaeological Society. More than a hundred people wrote letters of support to the Arizona State Land Department, the Arizona State Historic Preservation Office, the Arizona State Parks Board, Governor Bruce Babbitt, and the Arizona State Legislature. Although space limitations and incomplete knowledge do not allow me to list individual names, I would like all to know that I am sincerely grateful. Without your help, Cerro Prieto and Pan Quemado would be quite different today.

CHAPTER ONE

Archaeological History and Cultural Context

One of the most exciting aspects of recent Southwestern archaeology has been the expansion of knowledge about the Hohokam, a term for the people who lived in the desert regions of southern and central Arizona between about A.D. 200 and 1450. Previously, our understanding of Hohokam prehistory came primarily from intensive excavations at a mere handful of large sites, most of which were concentrated in the Gila and Salt River valleys. These drainages were believed to constitute a demographic and cultural center for the Hohokam, from which people and ideas spread into the peripheral areas of the Hohokam world (Fig. 1.1). The most dynamic of these so-called peripheries were thought to have been centered on the major streams such as the Verde, Agua Fria, and Santa Cruz rivers. Areas intervening between the Hohokam core and its peripheries, if considered at all in regional models, were traditionally believed to have been sparsely populated and ultimately of little importance to the main line of Hohokam cultural development. A pervasive component of such thinking was that the Hohokam could flourish only in those areas with perennial streams. Outlying areas, watered by secondary, seasonal drainages, were considered inhospitable and culturally impoverished (for example, Gladwin and Gladwin 1929: 127–129; Wormington 1947: 142–144). This dichotomy was formalized in 1950 by Emil Haury, who recognized a division between "Riverine" and "Desert" branches of the Hohokam (Haury 1950: 546–548).

Over the past 15 years or so, these concepts have been radically altered not only by important theoretical shifts in Southwestern archeology, but also by the data from a series of large-scale archaeological studies, most of which were conducted in a cultural resource management (CRM) context (Gumerman 1991; Crown 1991a). The largest and most influential of these were undertaken in connection with the U.S. Bureau of Reclamation's Central Arizona Project (CAP), which involved the building of a massive canal designed to divert water from the Colorado River to southern Arizona's farms and to the cities of Tucson and Phoenix. Because this remarkable construction is engineered to carry water *uphill*, it cuts a swath across the desert irrespective of the courses of natural drainages. Consequently, environmental studies required by canal construction have taken archaeologists into many previously unsurveyed, unexcavated, or otherwise poorly understood areas between the major river valleys. The result has been a dramatic increase in our knowledge of Hohokam prehistory, and a much deeper understanding of the resilience and complexity of the Hohokam regional cultural system.

We now know that the Hohokam regional system encompassed many more subtle shadings of environment than can be captured by the opposing classifications of desert and river. As demonstrated by S. Fish, P. Fish, and Madsen (1992), intermediate areas drained by secondary washes sometimes supported substantial populations organized into extensive communities. Riverine settings and irrigation agriculture, therefore, can no longer be identified as prerequisites for Hohokam organizational complexity. Although nonriverine Hohokam communities typically incorporated fewer residents and were spread over greater areas than their Phoenix Basin counterparts, they were nonetheless dynamic and complex systems. Lacking irrigation agriculture, individual settlements of nonriverine Hohokam communities apparently were bound by an ethos of shared subsistence risk (S. Fish, P. Fish, and Madsen 1992: 97–105). Thus, the variety of agricultural strategies practiced by nonriverine Hohokam populations, including floodwater farming, planting in hillside terraces, and cultivation in rockpile fields, appears to have been a major strength, provided that these strategies could be integrated into a single, cooperative community. Archaeological evidence for community integration is provided by a number of measures, including recognizable boundaries for the settlement system, hierarchical differentiation of settlement types, and the presence of public architecture such as ballcourts and platform mounds.

This volume is devoted to an examination of the long-term archaeological history of one such nonriverine Hohokam community located along Los Robles Wash in northern Pima and southern Pinal counties, Arizona.

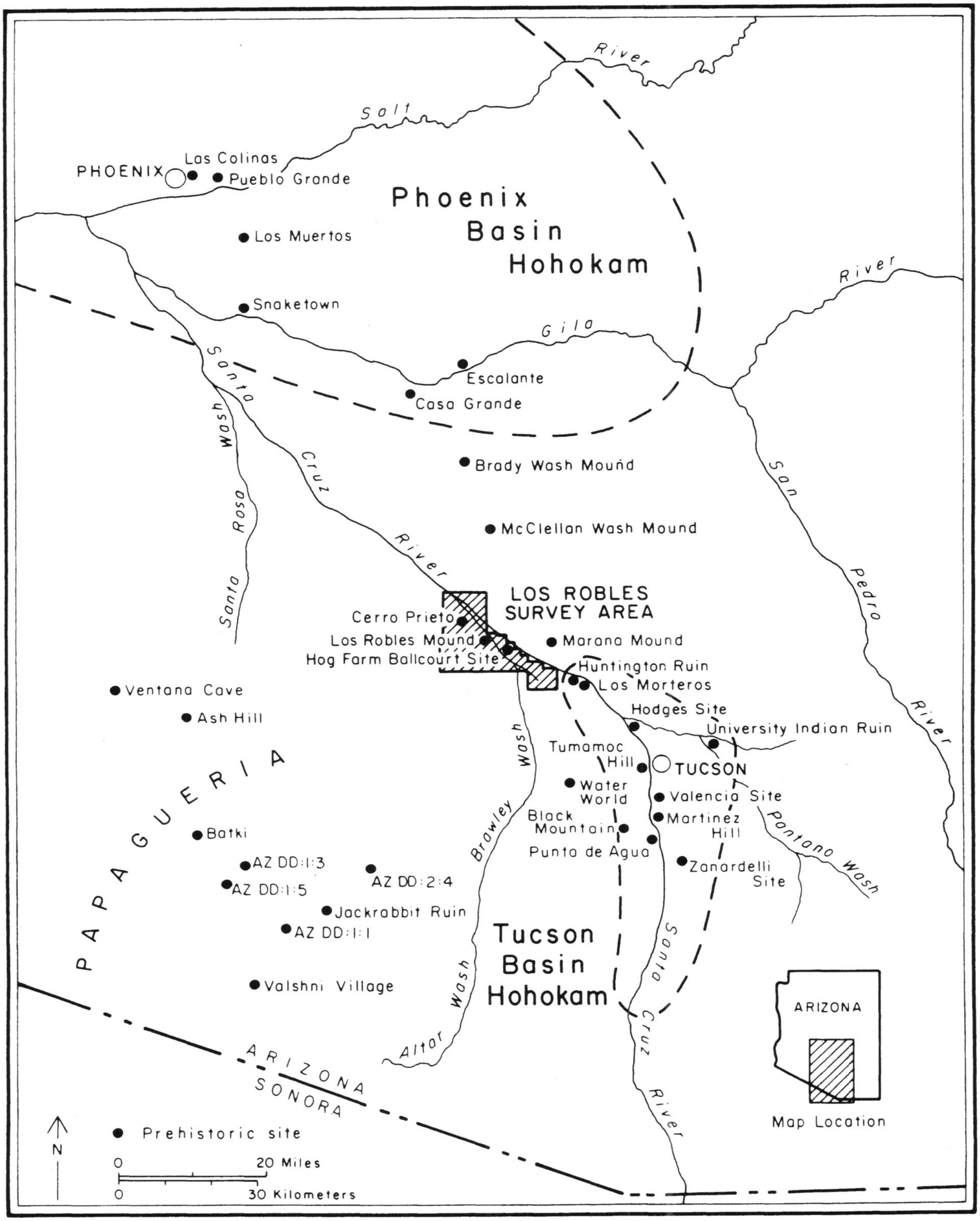

Figure 1.1. Regional setting of the Los Robles survey, showing selected modern cities, drainages, and archaeological sites.

A.D.	Major chronological subdivision	Period	Phoenix Basin Phase Sequence (Dean 1991: 91)	Tucson Basin Phase Sequence (Dean 1991: 91)	Papaguería Phase Sequence (McGuire 1982: 181)
1500					
1400					Sells
1300	CLASSIC	CLASSIC	Civano	Tucson	
1200			Soho	Tanque Verde	
1150					Topawa
1100		SEDENTARY	Sacaton	Rincon	
1000					Vamori
900		COLONIAL	Santa Cruz	Rillito	
800	PRECLASSIC		Gila Butte	Cañada del Oro	
700			Snaketown		No local
600			Sweetwater	No local	phase
500		PIONEER	Estrella	decorated	sequence
400			Vahki	pottery*	identified
300					
200			Red Mountain		
100	LATE ARCHAIC	LATE ARCHAIC	LATE ARCHAIC	LATE ARCHAIC	

* The Tucson Basin Pioneer period recently has been subdivided into the Tortolita phase (A.D. 450–700), including red ware ceramics (Bernard-Shaw 1990: 209–213), and an earlier phase with only plain ware pottery dating between A.D. 200 and 450 (Bernard-Shaw 1990: 215; Huckell and others 1987: 293–296).

Figure 1.2. Hohokam periods and phases for the Phoenix Basin, Tucson Basin, and Papaguería.

Here, from the late Pioneer through early Classic periods of the Hohokam cultural sequence, there arose an extensive community spread from the floodplain of Los Robles Wash to the eastern flanks of the Samaniego Hills. Like the nearby Hohokam community at Marana (S. Fish, P. Fish, and Madsen 1992), the Los Robles Community provides important new evidence on the nature of Hohokam settlement, subsistence, and organization in a setting intermediate between the major river valleys and interior desert.

THE LOS ROBLES ARCHAEOLOGICAL SURVEY

A particularly informative CAP-related study has been the Los Robles Archaeological Survey, which provided much of the information reported in this volume. The genesis of the Los Robles Archaeological Survey may be traced to early 1985, when the Los Robles Mound Site (R-138, AZ AA:11:25 ASM) was discovered by two amateur archaeologists from Tucson, Paul Hughes and Merry Austin. Hughes and Austin promptly reported their find to personnel at the Arizona State Museum (ASM), and archaeologist James M. Skibo visited the site and mapped it. On the belief that the Los Robles mound was probably a platform mound of the Hohokam early Classic period (about A.D. 1150–1300; Fig. 1.2), Skibo incorporated it into a platform mound reconnaissance survey then being conducted for the ASM archaeology section (Skibo 1986). Shortly thereafter, in the summer of 1985, the ongoing platform mound survey was shifted to the area of Los Robles Wash.

Although originally this survey had not been slated to cover the Los Robles Wash area, the shift in coverage had several advantages. First, the nearness of the Los Robles mound to Tucson alleviated a number of logistical problems and costs associated with surveying areas farther to the north, allowing expanded survey coverage. Second, because the Los Robles mound is located directly across the Santa Cruz River from the Marana platform mound (AZ AA:12:251 ASM), survey of the Los Robles Wash area provided an excellent opportunity for the comparison of two contemporaneous early Classic period mound communities located in similar environmental and cultural settings. Furthermore, coverage of an area surrounding the Los Robles mound allowed a very large, contiguous area on both sides of the Santa Cruz River to be filled in with complete survey coverage. The shift to include the Los Robles community also permitted an even greater contiguous area to be connected with systematic survey transects. Finally, the large trincheras and petroglyph site complexes at Cerro Prieto and Pan Quemado had recently been mapped and recorded by two independent research projects (Downum and others 1985; Wallace and Holmlund 1986), thus enhancing the possibility of better understanding the structure and function of various settlements and site types in the prehistoric Los Robles Community.

Together, the Los Robles survey and the Cerro Prieto and Pan Quemado mapping projects have filled in a large gap in our understanding of the prehistory of southern Arizona. These efforts disclosed an impressive array of prehistoric settlements and specialized activity sites paralleling the course of Los Robles Wash, an area traditionally conceived as a marginal zone between the better-defined subareas of the Hohokam world: the Phoenix Basin, Tucson Basin, and Papaguería. A more limited number of sites was discovered by sampling the upland environment west of the wash. The prehistoric occupation represented by these remains primarily spanned the late Pioneer (about A.D. 700) through early Classic (about A.D. 1300) periods (Fig. 1.2), with population evidently reaching a peak sometime during the thirteenth century. In the Preclassic, settlements along Los Robles Wash were centered on and probably organized around a large ballcourt village, the Hog Farm Ballcourt Site. During the early Classic, the settlement system seems to have been reorganized. The Hog Farm Ballcourt Site apparently lost its preeminent status, and the focus of the community shifted to the north. Two new types of settlements appeared in the form of the Los Robles Mound Site and a large *cerro de trincheras* (terraced hillside village) at Cerro Prieto. These villages signal new forms of organization and ceremony, adopted during a prolonged period of ideological adjustment and settlement change following the demise of the Hohokam ballcourt system. Like the Marana Community just across the Santa Cruz River, the early Classic period Los Robles Community appears to have been a socially, politically, and economically linked settlement system dependent on a variety of subsistence strategies practiced in diverse environmental zones. There are hints that inhabitants of some settlements also engaged in various craft specializations, including the manufacture of ground and chipped stone tools. The closeness and contemporaneity of two large but different villages featuring public architecture, the Los Robles mound and Cerro Prieto, suggest that during the early Classic period Los Robles was a complex and dynamic community.

A lack of Salado polychromes or other late Classic period ceramics within the surveyed area indicates that the Los Robles area was abandoned by the Hohokam sometime around A.D. 1300 or perhaps 1325. Reasons for this particular exodus remain as elusive as an explanation for the general collapse of the Hohokam regional system a century and a half later. Widespread changes in the Hohokam world at the onset of the fourteenth century suggest that the Los Robles Community, like its neighbor at Marana, succumbed to processes enacted at a regional, and not local, scale. Enigmatic caches of post-Hohokam ceramic vessels and scattered occurrences of sherds resembling Whetstone Plain reveal a Protohistoric reoccupation or reuse of the Los Robles survey area. These finds signify that the upland zone of the survey area was the hinterland of a Piman settlement system, perhaps one associated with the lost village of St. Catarina, believed to have been located along the Santa Cruz River somewhere south of the Picacho Mountains. A few late nineteenth- and early twentieth-century Native American sites have also been documented; some of these may have been associated with the now-abandoned mining town of Sasco, which flourished from 1907 into the early 1920s.

HISTORY OF ARCHAEOLOGICAL INVESTIGATIONS

Until recently the Los Robles survey area had been largely ignored by both professional and amateur archaeologists. Although surrounding ruins were visited, mapped, and described by early explorers such as Adolph Bandelier (1892), Frank Russell (1908), Jesse Walter Fewkes (1909), and Ellsworth Huntington (1913, 1914), all seem for some reason to have missed visiting the area encompassed by the Los Robles Archaeological Survey. Fewkes and Huntington came quite close. Fewkes (1909: 418–419) visited the site of "Chakayuma" (Los Morteros, AZ AA:12:57 ASM), at the northern tip of the Tucson Mountains, and observed several ruins in the vicinity of the Picacho Mountains, just a few kilometers north of the survey area. Huntington (1913, 1914: 53–58) spent a considerable amount of time mapping and recording both the "Charco Yuma" (Fewkes' "Chakayuma") and "Nelson's Desert Ranch" sites (the Marana Mound Site, AZ AA:12:251 ASM), located about 10 km due east of the Los Robles mound.

Explorations by The University of Arizona and Gila Pueblo

Probably the first significant archaeological fieldwork within the survey area was undertaken by University of Arizona archaeology professor Byron S. Cummings and a group of students, including Emil W. Haury, for many years the Head of the Anthropology Department of the University of Arizona. In a conversation with Haury in 1983, he indicated to me that Cummings led a small party of students to the site of Cerro Prieto (AZ AA:7:11 ASM) in October of 1925, an occasion that marked Haury's first fieldwork in the U.S. Southwest. Several masonry rooms, terraces, and other features were excavated during a single weekend of work. As with other weekend projects of this period, Cummings' purpose was probably two-fold: to give students first-hand experience in excavation, and second, to secure a sample of Tucson-area artifacts for the collections of the Arizona State Museum. Such artifacts would have been considered illustrative of a peripheral area of the "Lower Gila" culture, as defined by Kidder (1924) in his just-published synthesis of the archaeology of the Southwest.

Unfortunately, there are virtually no records of the 1925 excursion to Cerro Prieto. The only remaining evidence of this and other visits by Cummings to the Los Robles survey area are a few of his snapshots. These pictures, on file at the Arizona Historical Society Museum in Tucson, show close-ups of petroglyphs from a location described as "Black Mountains . . . about 10 miles south of Casa Grande Highway at Red Rock" (Arizona Historical Society Library, Cummings photographic collection, Box 6, File 5). This would place the petroglyphs in the general vicinity of Cerro Prieto and Pan Quemado, but precisely where on the slopes of these two hills cannot be ascertained, because the photographs do not show sufficient landscape details to orient them to major topographic features.

In April, 1929, representatives of the Gila Pueblo Archaeological Foundation in Globe, Arizona, visited Cerro Prieto, recording four sites (Arizona J:7:1–4 GP) and photographing numerous petroglyphs, stone houses, and other features (ASM Photo Archives, Negatives 71.506–71.510; ASM Site Files). Initials on the photographs and site cards are "F.M.," probably those of Frank Mitalsky (who later changed his name to Frank Midvale). Artifacts were collected from all four sites, but there evidently were no excavations. Although no record can now be found of the exact plots for these sites, it is clear from photographs and descriptions of the sites that Cerro Prieto was assigned site numbers J:7:1 GP (summit of the hill) and J:7:2 GP (north slope), and perhaps the remaining two site numbers as well.

Interestingly, one of the 1929 Gila Pueblo photographs (Negative No. 71.510) depicts the earlier excavation activities of the 1925 Cummings party. The photo shows a neatly excavated stone room, with a partially reconstructed stone wall. There is no doubt that this is the same room recorded by the Cerro Prieto mapping project as Feature 55; individual wall rocks visible in the 1929 snapshot (Fig. 1.3) match exactly with those of a 1982 photograph (Fig. 1.4). According to ASM photographer Helga Teiwes in 1988, when shown a contemporary photograph of Feature 55, Emil Haury distinctly remembered it as one of the masonry rooms excavated in 1925.

Investigations from 1929 to 1979

Following the visits by Cummings and Midvale, the Los Robles survey area was largely unexplored for more than 50 years. This is indeed curious, considering both the density of archaeological remains here and the level of contemporary archaeological activity in other areas of the Southwest. However, from 1929 through 1979 archaeological investigations were confined to a few, brief visits by archaeologists from the Arizona State Museum, a few scattered surveys and excavations conducted by amateur archaeologists, and limited test excavations by a University of Arizona graduate student.

Only recently, with attention forced upon the area by the CAP-related surveys and excavations, has it been widely recognized that the territory between Phoenix and Tucson is a rich archaeological zone with a long and substantial prehistoric occupation (for example, see Wilcox 1984; Doyel 1984: 152). Thus, in spite of the evidence recorded by early explorers like Bandelier, Fewkes, and Huntington, for nearly half a century secondary drainages like Los Robles Wash were not viewed as significant components of the prehistoric settlement systems of southern Arizona. Consequently, the lower Santa Cruz River and its adjacent drainages may have been perceived as archaeologically unrewarding, resulting in a self-fulfilling prophecy about the research productivity of such "marginal" environmental zones (McCarthy 1982: 33, 39).

One of the few important efforts in the Los Robles Wash area during this period was undertaken by ASM archaeologists William W. Wasley and Alfred E. Johnson. At the request of ASM Director Emil Haury, on 30 November 1961 Wasley and Johnson inspected and recorded a petroglyph site (the Inscription Hill Site, AZ AA:7:8 ASM) and two unspecified habitation sites (perhaps AZ AA:7:9 and AA:7:10) on a property then known as the King Ranch, near Pan Quemado. After their visit, Haury sent a memorandum to the Arizona State Land Department, detailing the significance of the petroglyphs and other features of Inscription Hill, and recommending that the site "be protected by fencing, against the possibility of eventual destruction" (memo by Emil Haury, 6 December 1961, ASM Site Files). Evidently the fencing was never installed, but Wasley and Johnson did return to the site and erect signs warning against damage to the petroglyphs. (These signs are visible in photographs taken in the early to mid-1960s, and remnants of the signs could still be found at the base of Inscription Hill in 1989.) Probably during their return visit Wasley and Johnson also recorded Cerro Prieto (AZ AA:7:11 ASM), because the original recording date for the site is 1962.

Shortly thereafter, there were two investigations by amateur archaeologists in the Los Robles survey area. As reported to me 27 June 1989 by Carl Halbirt of Northland Research, Inc., in 1963 Yjinio Aguirre, a local

Figure 1.3. A 1929 Gila Pueblo photograph of the north wall of Feature 55, Cerro Prieto Site. (ASM photograph 71.510, by Frank Midvale.)

Figure 1.4. A 1982 photograph of the north wall of Feature 55, Cerro Prieto Site. (ASM photograph 86824, by Christian E. Downum.)

rancher, and his family conducted excavations at an unidentified site on their ranch near Red Rock, just west of the Cake Ranch Site (AZ AA:7:3 ASM). According to Aguirre (1983: 127–133), one large adobe room was completely uncovered, several rooms were tested, and a few cremations were removed. A large compound wall, at least 56.7 m (186 feet) long, was also observed. Aguirre (1983: 128–132) provides several photographs of the excavations in progress, the architecture that was unearthed, and the artifacts that were recovered. One of the vessels pictured (Aguirre 1983: 132) appears to be either Casa Grande Red-on-buff or Tanque Verde Red-on-brown. This jar, and an apparent absence of Salado polychromes, indicates an early Classic period date for these features.

A second amateur archaeological effort was a 1965 survey by free-lance author Stan Jones. Jones' survey was apparently conducted in the Samaniego Hills on and around the site of Cerro Prieto. This effort resulted in a *Desert* magazine article about Cerro Prieto, entitled "Mystery of the Hohokams" (Jones 1965). In this article, Jones proposed that numerous stone houses and features at Cerro Prieto had been constructed several centuries ago by a wayward tribe of Norsemen, who had run aground and wandered across North America, ending up finally in the Sonoran Desert near present-day Red Rock, Arizona. Evidently, while conducting field research for his article, Jones recorded two prehistoric sites: AZ AA:7:13 ASM and AA:7:14 ASM.

The first formally documented and reported archaeological excavations in the survey area were conducted in the early 1970s by University of Arizona anthropology graduate student V. K. Pheriba Stacy. Stacy's dissertation research was concerned with the function of trincheras sites in southern Arizona, including Cerro Prieto. To test the idea that some trincheras features might have been used as agricultural terraces, Stacy excavated a few test trenches in unspecified rock features at Cerro Prieto for the purpose of collecting pollen samples (Stacy 1974: 96). Although no pollen from domesticated plants was recovered, Stacy (1974: 195) nonetheless concluded that some of the terrace features at that site would have been suitable for growing crops.

Contract Archaeology and Private Research Projects, 1980–1986

Partly because of public and private development projects, but also because of an expanding avocational and academic interest in the archaeology of the territory between the Tucson and Phoenix basins, archaeological research in the Los Robles survey area accelerated dramatically in the early 1980s. The factors behind this trend are many and interrelated in complex ways, but the underlying cause is unquestionably the population boom and related developments that transformed Arizona in the 1980s. During this period, federal archaeological legislation passed in the 1960s and 1970s decreed archaeological and environmental studies that had not been required during previous growth periods. Thus, the expansion of transportation and utility networks, construction of the CAP canal and its delivery systems, and creation of new residential areas in southern Arizona were accompanied in the 1980s by a proliferation of archaeological survey and excavation projects, some of which were of unprecedented magnitude and scope. In the process, many formerly "peripheral" areas, including that encompassed by the Los Robles survey, became the subject of new or renewed archaeological scrutiny and debate. Although the Los Robles survey area was not among the most intensively developed zones in the 1980s, it, too, was affected by the research projects and attendant changes in archaeological perspectives taking place during that time.

A complete review of all mitigation-related projects is beyond the scope of this report, but a few of the major efforts deserve brief mention. Among these, perhaps the most important were powerline surveys for the Tucson Electric Power company conducted in 1980 and 1981 by John P. Wilson. From this work Wilson (1981, 1985) developed the proposition that some of the sites, principally a set of small trash mounds and artifact scatters near the mouths of alluvial fans along the west bank of Los Robles Wash, represented seasonal *ak chin* (floodwater) farming settlements. Wilson further proposed that these settlements might represent a prehistoric system of double-cropping, with an early spring planting at the arroyo mouths supplementing a mid-summer planting (compare Nabhan 1983, 1986; Gasser 1990).

A second CRM project was the mapping and recording effort of Frederick Huntington and James Holmlund in June, 1986, which concentrated on the Hog Farm Ballcourt Site (AZ AA:11:12 ASM). This team mapped and recorded archaeological features within the right-of-way of a Western Area Power Administration transmission line that passes through the site. During a week of fieldwork, Huntington and Holmlund (1986) made observations on artifacts at two loci (A and B) previously identified by the ASM Los Robles Archaeological Survey, reported under the Hog Farm Ballcourt Site (p. 27). The efforts of Huntington and Holmlund remain the most intensive work yet conducted at this important site, believed to have been at the center of the Preclassic settlement system along Los Robles Wash (Chapter 6).

Additional small surveys were instigated by the construction of facilities such as sand and gravel pits, powerlines, or other small-scale facilities. These projects are recorded in the site survey files of the Arizona State Museum. Generally, the limited geographical scope of such studies precluded regional conclusions, but a few small sites were discovered and reported to the ASM site survey inventory.

Not all recent projects in the Los Robles area have been mandated by CRM legislation, however, and a number of small-scale, privately funded efforts have contributed significant information. The Arizona Archaeological and Historical Society conducted a rock art course at the southern end of Pan Quemado in 1980, directed by Madeleine and Juel Rodack of Tucson. This work resulted in a collection of petroglyph photographs now in the archaeological site files of the Arizona State Museum.

In 1980 and 1981, Tucson archaeologists Henry D. Wallace and James P. Holmlund (1986) conducted a privately funded archaeological study of Pan Quemado. Their research involved mapping, recording, and photographing a large sample of the petroglyphs at the sites of Inscription Hill (AZ AA:7:8 ASM) and Pan Quemado (AZ AA:7:43 ASM), using a computer-coded attribute system. More than 1,800 petroglyphs, from an estimated total of 2,700, were inventoried.

In the spring of 1981, a University of Arizona archaeological field class, under the direction of Paul Fish of the Arizona State Museum, conducted limited test excavations of a stone house and large terrace at Cerro Prieto. This work was part of a larger program to investigate the functions of Tucson area sites through mapping, excavation, and experimental cultivation (S. Fish, P. Fish, and Downum 1984; Downum 1986; Reichhardt 1989a). These excavations resulted in the recovery of several ground stone tools, partially reconstructible early Classic period ceramic vessels, a chipped stone assemblage, and other artifacts from the floor of the house. A badly disturbed cremation and other items came from the terrace. These excavations are reported in Chapter 4.

In March of 1983, University of Arizona anthropology graduate students John E. Douglas, Douglas B. Craig, and I began a mapping project at Cerro Prieto. Preliminary results of the work, finished in 1986, were reported in papers presented at the 1983 Hohokam Symposium (Downum and others 1985) and at the 1984 meeting of the Society for American Archaeology (Craig and Douglas 1984). Mapping results are reported in Chapter 4.

GEOGRAPHICAL AND CULTURAL CONTEXT OF THE LOS ROBLES AREA

The Los Robles survey area lies between the Phoenix Basin, traditionally identified as the "core" area of the Hohokam world, and the Tucson Basin, usually considered a "peripheral" geographic zone but one nonetheless having a lengthy and complex occupational sequence. This area, therefore, may represent a transition zone, where cultural identities of individuals, corporate groups, or settlements were dynamic, varying with time, space, or specific extralocal kinship, political, or exchange ties (Wilcox and Sternberg 1983; Wilcox 1991b: 122–124). Populations residing in the Los Robles area thus might have been critical links in a chain of regional interaction, connecting the Hohokam core area of the Phoenix Basin with more peripheral Hohokam groups to the south. Ultimately, it may have been through groups such as those residing in the Los Robles area that the Phoenix Basin Hohokam maintained interaction with groups residing along the northern Mesoamerican frontier.

Because few excavations have been conducted within the survey area, there are still insufficient data to categorize the Los Robles sites in terms of traditional cultural labels or specific interregional relationships. Some preliminary evidence, in the form of surface inventories of Colonial period pottery from two Los Robles sites, suggests that the survey area was at the far northern limits of the territorial range of the Tucson Basin Hohokam (Wallace 1988: 326; see also Dart and Gibson 1988). Such a conclusion is based on an apparent predominance of sherds from the Tucson Basin brown ware series over Phoenix Basin buff ware sherds. However, sherds collected during the Los Robles survey from a large sample of sites show more complicated mixtures of brown and buff ware ceramics, so more information is needed to evaluate the cultural affiliations and exchange relationships of particular sites.

The geographic position of the Los Robles survey area suggests that it may indeed have been a well-traveled zone, for it is strategically located with respect to probable prehistoric transportation routes (Fig. 1.5). Because the survey area encompasses the juncture of three major drainages, Brawley Wash, Los Robles Wash, and the Santa Cruz River, it straddles the intersection of three likely avenues of prehistoric travel and exchange. From the Los Robles area, the Santa Cruz River may be followed north, to its junction with the Gila River and on into the heart of the Phoenix Basin, or south, into the Tucson Basin and beyond, toward southeastern Arizona and ultimately into the Casas Grandes area of northern Chihuahua. Los Robles Wash may be followed south, into the northern end of the Avra Valley; from there, Brawley Wash leads into the central Avra Valley and beyond, to the Altar Valley of southern Arizona and northern Sonora. This last route may have been a particularly significant regional connection in the Classic period, linking the major platform mound communities

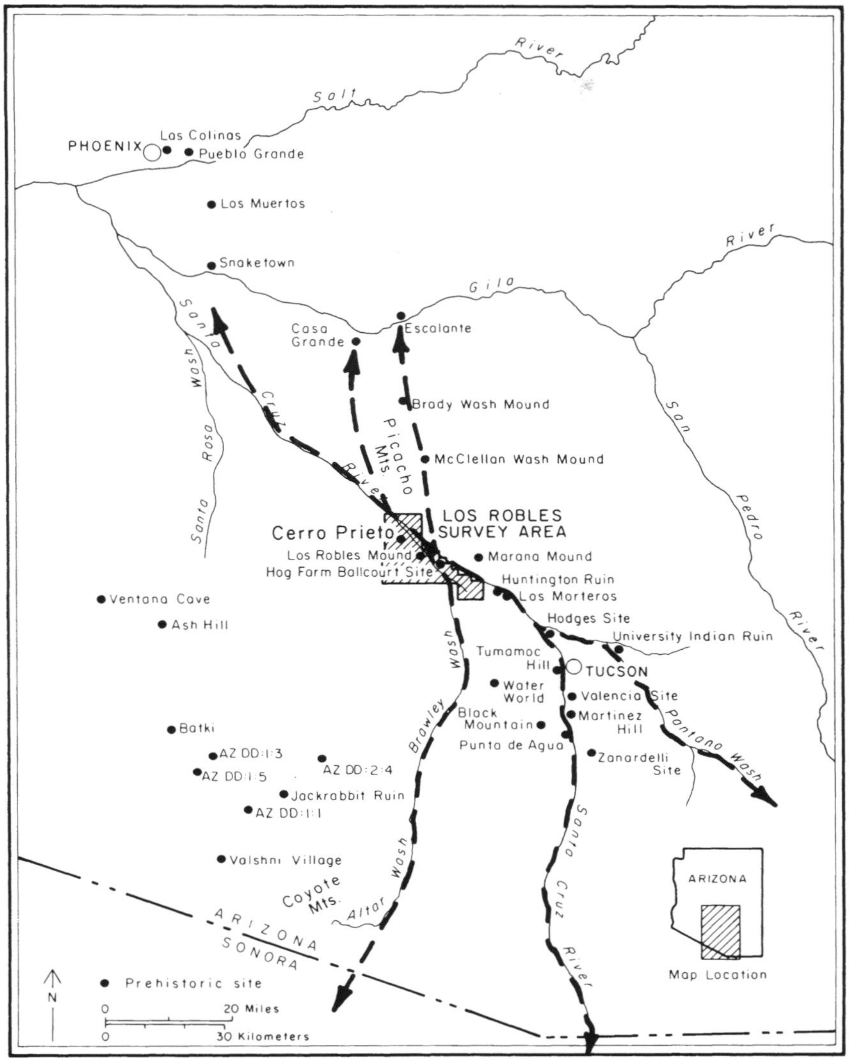

Figure 1.5. Postulated prehistoric routes of trade and travel in southern Arizona.

of the Phoenix Basin with a set of apparent platform mounds and surrounding villages along the east slopes of the Coyote Mountains, near the International border (Downum and Madsen 1989; Dart and others 1990).

The Los Robles area probably had considerable influence in more localized sociopolitical and exchange systems. The presence of a Preclassic ballcourt village (the Hog Farm Ballcourt Site) and the later development of a mound community (centered around the Los Robles Mound Site), strongly suggest that the Los Robles area maintained the status of an important economic and political place for a period of several centuries. The precise factors leading to these developments remain to be investigated, but at present there are several reasons why this area might have achieved prominence within a local set of communities.

The brokering or redistribution of extralocal exchange commodities might have encouraged the growth of particular settlements here, leading to the early rise of one or a few as centers of exchange, ceremonial activities, and social and political decision-making. Once such a center emerged, perhaps initially at the Hog Farm Ballcourt Site, the area might have attracted immigrants from a number of nearby settlement systems, most likely those that were already in place in the northern end of the Tucson Basin (Bernard-Shaw 1989a, 1989b, 1990;

Bernard-Shaw and Huntington 1990) or along the southern flanks of the Picacho Mountains (Downum and Dart 1984; Wallace and Holmlund 1986; Ciolek-Torrello 1987; Ciolek-Torrello and Wilcox 1988).

Whatever factors led to the initial foundation and expansion of settlements (see Chapter 6), it is likely that the Los Robles area was able to maintain and expand such settlements through continued agricultural success. Several attributes suggest the area was an exceptionally productive agricultural zone, with excellent opportunities for floodwater agriculture. The periodic flooding of Los Robles Wash, because of the enormous extent of its upstream drainage basin, insured the continued fertility of agricultural soils. The alluvial fans of local arroyos, originating in the Samaniego Hills, provided a second set of productive field locations, periodically replenished by loads of sediment and organic material washed down from upslope (Gasser 1990; Field 1992). The extensive mesquite groves and upland cactus forests of this area were a reliable source of wild plant foods and a significant buffer against population-resource imbalances that might have plagued other settlement zones.

The well-watered soils and relatively low elevation of the Los Robles area also could have offered an unusual combination of moisture and temperature parameters that could have allowed double cropping. As suggested by Wilson (1981), there is some evidence in the ethnohistoric record that Piman populations living in this area were able to grow two crops of beans, squashes, and perhaps corn in a single year.

A final possible factor in the local prominence of the Los Robles Wash settlement system may relate to craft specialization, notably during the Classic period. Ground and chipped stone tools, particularly tabular knives fashioned from the Cerro Prieto quarry material, were especially important exchange commodities after about A.D. 1100. During the early Classic period in the Tucson Basin, these knives were a critical part of the tool assemblage used to harvest and process agave. As discussed by S. Fish, P. Fish, and Madsen (1992), agave cultivation became an important economic activity for some Tucson Basin Hohokam communities during the early Classic. Evidence for the growing of agave is found in many bajada areas, particularly on the lower west slopes of the Tortolita Mountains bordering the Marana Community, which is immediately east of the Los Robles survey area. Here, there are literally thousands of rockpiles and stone alignments, accompanied by roasting pits and specialized chipped and ground stone tool assemblages, including abundant tabular knives. Considering the fact that Cerro Prieto and other sites may have controlled some of the most important sources of raw materials for tabular knives, craft specialization involving the manufacture of these tools may have been a consequential factor in the economic success of the early Classic period Los Robles Community.

CHAPTER TWO

Environment and Resources of the Los Robles Survey Area

The Los Robles archaeological survey covered an area along the lower Santa Cruz River near the Pima and Pinal County line in south-central Arizona, approximately 65 km (40 miles) northwest of Tucson and 110 km (68 miles) southeast of Phoenix (Fig. 1.1). The project was so named because the most prominent archaeological remains surveyed are located along or near the banks of Los Robles Wash, a large, seasonal stream that is tributary to the major through-flowing drainage in this area, the Santa Cruz River (Figs. 2.1, 2.2). The survey also sampled a more limited area surrounding the lower reaches of two other major desert drainages, Blanco and Brawley washes, both of which empty into Los Robles Wash in the southeast portion of the survey area.

PHYSIOGRAPHY AND HYDROGRAPHY

The Los Robles survey area is a roughly L-shaped parcel covering approximately 282 square kilometers. Elevations range from around 526 m (1,725 feet) on the floodplain of the Santa Cruz River, to 821 m (2,693 feet) at the summit of an unnamed peak in the Samaniego Hills. Cerro Prieto, the highest point in the vicinity of Los Robles Wash, reaches an elevation of 820 m (2,690 feet).

Although the survey parcel is squarely within the Basin-and-Range physiographic province of Arizona, the precise delineation of a "basin" here is problematic, and meaningful natural limits for a prehistoric settlement system are difficult to identify. The survey did intersect a number of important geological and hydrological features, and presumably these were important physical markers and orientation points, if not actual boundaries, for the prehistoric inhabitants of the area.

On the southwest, the survey parcel was bounded by the extreme northeast slopes of the Silverbell Mountains, a relatively high (1,295 m, or 4,249 feet) and extensive volcanic range that is a major barrier between the Santa Cruz drainage basin and the interior desert of the Papaguería to the west. The southeast corner of the study area is just north of the northern tip of the Tucson Mountains, a feature that marks the northern extent of the Tucson Basin. The northern boundary reaches to the southern end of the Santa Cruz Flats, a broad, alluvial basin where the Santa Cruz River begins to lose its distinct channel. Although the Santa Cruz Flats are not an obvious physical boundary, ceramic evidence indicates that this area underwent a somewhat different settlement history than that of the Los Robles area, with the occupation of Los Robles terminating at least a century prior to that of the Flats. Hence, the Los Robles settlement system may not have extended as far north as the Santa Cruz Flats.

The eastern boundary of the survey area is the Santa Cruz River. Although the normally dry channel of the Santa Cruz would not seem to form a natural obstruction to prehistoric transportation or settlement, a distinct lessening of site density east of the river suggests that the eastern limits of the survey parcel roughly coincide with the eastern edge of the prehistoric Los Robles Community. Indeed, this lack of sites is so striking that it has been suggested (P. Fish and S. Fish 1989: 120–121; P. Fish, S. Fish, and Madsen 1988: 233; see also Doelle and Wallace 1990: 245) that the area served as a sort of buffer zone, separating the settlement systems of the Tortolita and Picacho Mountains.

Within the area covered by the Los Robles survey, two major features, Los Robles Wash and the Samaniego Hills, dominate the natural setting and largely determine the environmental variability that structured settlement and land use. Los Robles Wash is a broad, sandy channel flanked by dense growths of mesquite and other desert riparian vegetation. It is a major tributary to the Santa Cruz River and serves as the main drainage for the northern end of the Avra Valley. The wash is formed by the confluence of Brawley and Blanco washes, both of which originate well to the south of the survey area in the mountains that form the eastern boundary of the Tohono O'odham Nation (formerly, Papago Indian Reservation). Brawley Wash, when it floods, is a particularly large and powerful desert drainage. It originates far to

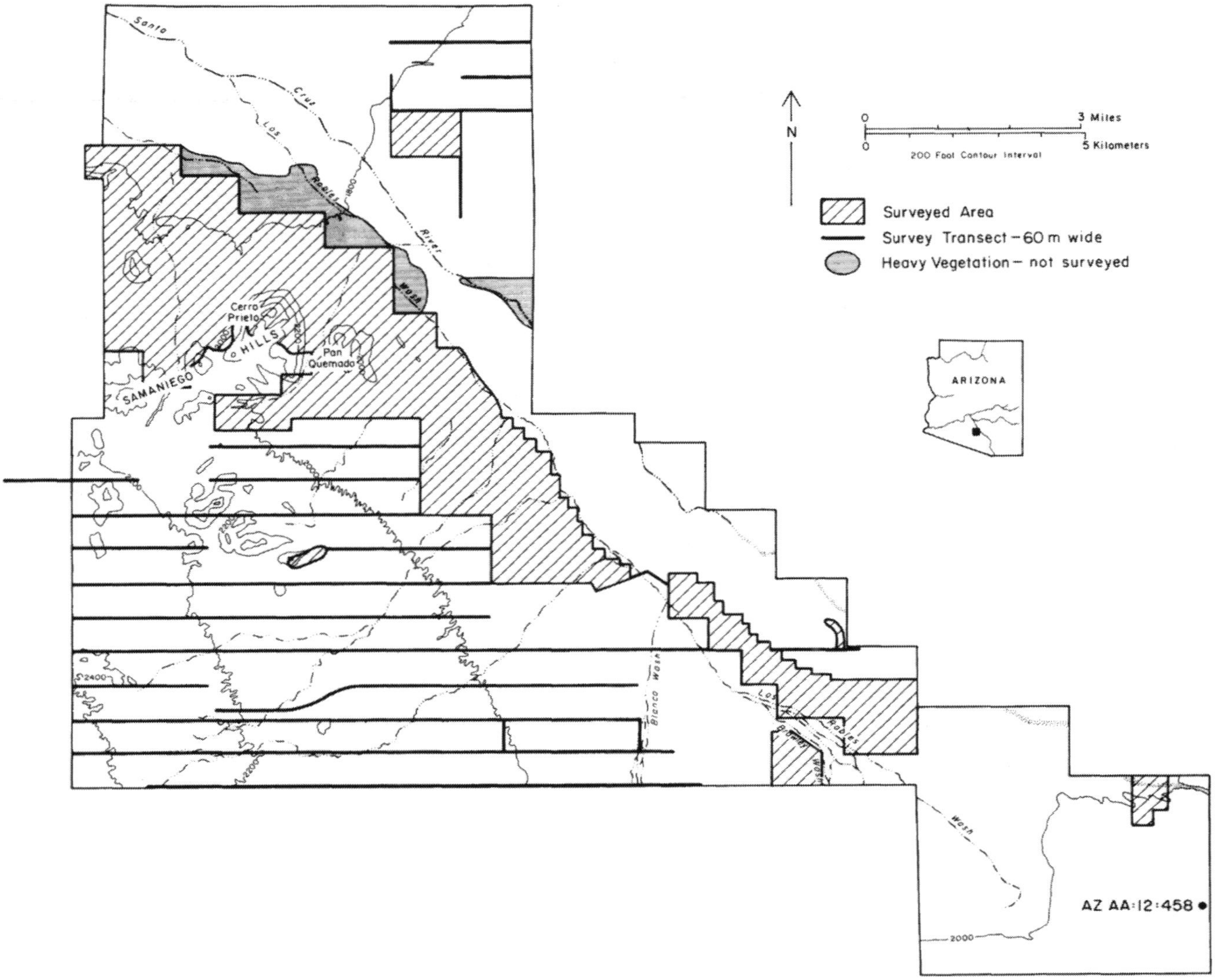

Figure 2.1. The Los Robles survey area, showing extent of block and transect survey coverage.

the south of the Los Robles survey area as Altar Wash, the trunk stream of the Altar Valley near the International Border. Around Three Points, Arizona, this valley becomes the Avra Valley, and the Altar Wash becomes Brawley Wash. Thus, for most of its length, Brawley Wash serves as the trunk stream for the Avra Valley, a broad, open basin between the Tucson Basin and the interior deserts of the Papaguería. Just south of the Pima-Pinal County line, Brawley and Blanco washes merge to form Los Robles Wash. From this point north, Los Robles is fed by a series of relatively small, northeast-flowing arroyos that originate from the northeast flanks of the Silverbell Mountains and the eastern and southern slopes of the Samaniego Hills.

The other major feature of the survey area is a chain of low igneous peaks and ridges named the Samaniego Hills, located just northeast of the Silverbell Mountains (Fig. 2.3). The hills, for the most part, are relatively small and widely scattered, but they do provide relief to the landscape and occasionally form extensive impediments to overland transportation. The general slope in this area is from southwest to northeast, so that drainages originating on the east side of the Samaniego Hills flow directly northeast toward Los Robles Wash. In places, the terrain is quite rugged, and the drainages flowing down from the hills have cut the bajada slopes into a series of finger ridges. Generally, the landscape becomes increasingly less dissected with distance from

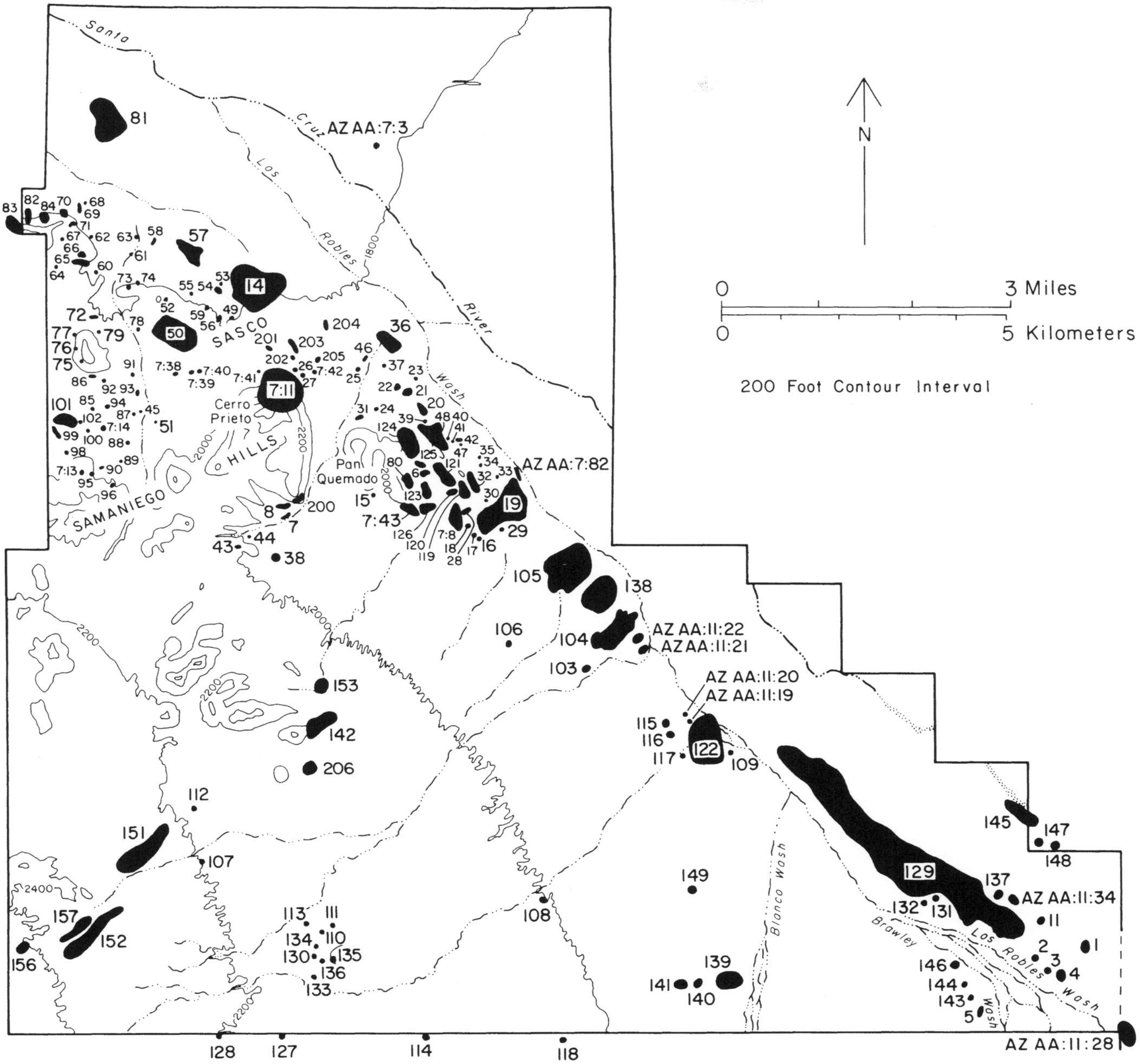

Figure 2.2. Archaeological sites within the Los Robles survey area. ASM site numbers are indicated in full (for example, AZ AA:7:82), or by quadrangle and site numbers ([AZ AA:] 7:11); other numbers are Robles Survey Site designations ([R–]129), see Chapter 3.

the hills, so that in the vicinity of Los Robles Wash the topography is dominated by a series of low, gently sloping alluvial fans, derived from the deposition of fine-grained sediments eroded from the Samaniego Hills. These fans were prime locations for prehistoric settlement, probably because of the opportunities they offered for floodwater farming and the protection they afforded from periodic flooding of Los Robles Wash.

CLIMATE

Climate of the survey area is typical of the Lower Sonoran desert. Summers are extremely hot, winters are mild, and precipitation is relatively scarce, falling mostly during a summer (mid-June to early September) season of intense thunderstorms and a winter season (November through late March) of more gentle rains. The nearest

Figure 2.3. View southwest across the northern end of the Samaniego Hills, toward Ragged Top Peak in the Silverbell Mountains. (ASM photograph 86821, by Christian E. Downum.)

weather reporting station is at Red Rock, Arizona, located about 11 km east of the confluence of Los Robles Wash and the Santa Cruz River. Here, average annual rainfall is 247 mm (9.63 inches) and the average number of frost-free days is 341 (Sellers and others 1985). The average daily temperature maximum in July is 40.2° C (104.4° F) and the average daily maximum in January is 18.0° C (64.4° F).

SPATIAL AND SEASONAL DISTRIBUTION OF SURFACE WATER

Extreme heat and low humidity combine to produce evapotranspiration rates that far exceed annual rainfall. At present, natural surface water is scarce or nonexistent in all parts of the survey area except during periods of heavy or prolonged precipitation. Even before modern environmental changes and a recent cycle of arroyo entrenchment, it is likely that all drainages, including the Los Robles Wash and the Santa Cruz River, would have been dry for most of the year. This certainly appears to have been the case in the 1690s when Father Eusebio Kino discovered the Piman village of Santa Catarina de Cuituabaga, believed to have been located along the Santa Cruz River somewhere west of Red Rock (Wilson 1980: 13). The area surrounding this village was characterized as "very dry and without water," and it was reported that residents were forced to obtain drinking water "from some little springs which are very far to the west" (Smith 1966a: 43; Bolton 1948; Burrus 1971; Ives 1973). It is possible that this water source was located at AZ AA: 7:43, Locus 4 (Site R-6), which features a small reservoir or catchment in a sand deposit near Pan Quemado.

The most likely time for local stream beds to carry water is during the summer thunderstorm season, when runoff from intense cloudbursts may induce a temporary flow. This runoff is usually quickly absorbed by alluvial deposits, or evaporates in a relatively short period of time. During intervals of heavy rainfall, however, the Santa Cruz River and its tributaries, particularly Los Robles Wash, can experience extreme flooding (Figs. 2.4, 2.5). Yjinio Aguirre (1983: 81), a pioneer rancher and

Figure 2.4. Aerial view of the Santa Cruz River at the Pima and Pinal County line during the dry season in 1985. Runways and aircraft of the Pinal Air Park are visible at upper right.

Figure 2.5. Aerial view of the Santa Cruz River, same location as Figure 2.4, during the height of flooding in early October, 1983. Nearly the entire area is covered with floodwaters. The standing waves in the main river channel at bottom indicate the magnitude of flow.

farmer in this area, describes the effects of a 1929 flood at Rancho Cerro Prieto, located in the north-central part of the survey area:

> the September rains of that year were exceptional in the Santa Cruz and Avra Valley basins. The Rillito River was flooded and overflowing, so was the Cañon del Oro wash. These channels and others flow their water into the Santa Cruz River. After the tributaries connected with the Santa Cruz overflowed, the river swelled to a point where it flooded all the lowlands along the river. When the flood of the Santa Cruz reached the Pima and Pinal county boundary line, it broke a new channel towards Cerro Prieto connecting its flood with the Avra [Brawley-Los Robles] wash, which was already rampaging.
>
> It took many days after the flood for the ground to dry up. This flood caused considerable erosion on the Santa Cruz River basin, burying four strand barb wire fences three feet deep with trash and river silt.

A slightly later flood was even more impressive:

> The next year, in October 1930, while my two brothers and myself were at the Rancho Cerro Prieto, we noticed some heavy storm developments to the south on to the Santa Cruz and Avra Valley basin. From the Cerro Prieto you can see south a hundred or more miles away.... It would take the water in the river twelve hours to reach Cerro Prieto from Tucson and more or less the same distance for the water in the Avra wash to reach the rancho.
>
> The next morning the flood water of the Avra wash started to move in, getting higher and higher, to the point that it was pretty close to the top of the dike. To our surprise, we could also hear the rampaging water of the flooded Santa Cruz River. It scared us. I told my brothers, 'Let's get the hell out of here!' We all agreed to leave.
>
> People who never have seen that area flooded like [that] would never believe that the Avra Valley Wash can carry that much water, especially when it joins the Santa Cruz river. We saw the two channels overflow and were surprised that when combined, they flooded an area about a mile and a half wide... (Aguirre 1983: 82–83).

Because more recent floods (for example, that of October 1983; Fig. 2.5) have probably been exacerbated by such factors as overgrazing, agricultural and residential development, and progressive stream entrenchment, the events witnessed by Aguirre may more closely approximate the potential effects of prehistoric floods. If so, it seems clear that even in premodern times, the Santa Cruz River and Los Robles Wash had considerable potential for short-term but severe flooding. Similar floods may have encouraged the location of prehistoric settlements in more upland settings, and may occasionally have had disastrous consequences for floodplain fields. It is noteworthy that the floods mentioned above (September of 1929, and October of 1930 and 1983) all came in the early fall, a particularly inopportune time for prehistoric farmers anticipating the harvest of summer crops.

ENVIRONMENT AND PREHISTORIC LAND USE

In terms of effective environment for prehistoric inhabitants, especially during the Hohokam period, the geomorphological and vegetational zones of the survey area offered three broadly defined zones of exploitation: (1) a floodplain or near-floodplain zone, composed of relatively flat, fine-grained alluvium deposited by the Santa Cruz River and its major tributaries, including Los Robles and Brawley Washes; (2) a bajada zone, consisting of more steeply sloping, dissected alluvial deposits eroded from the Samaniego Hills; and (3) a rocky upland zone, encompassing the slopes of the Samaniego Hills and isolated peaks and ridges in the southwestern portion of the survey area.

Throughout the prehistoric occupational sequence, and particularly during the Hohokam period, these zones would have provided a number of resources critical to human survival. The upland zone encompassing the Samaniego Hills offered a variety of wild plant and animal foods, including the fruit of saguaro, cholla, prickly pear, and barrel cacti, and such game animals as desert bighorn sheep, mule deer, and jackrabbits. Within the bajada zone, there would have been abundant wild plant and animal foods, including desert riparian resources, particularly mesquite beans. The bajada surface may also have provided opportunities for dry farming, especially in those areas with relatively gentle slopes where rockpiles, alignments, terraces, and other prehistoric agricultural features could be most effectively deployed. There is some evidence that such areas were farmed, as traces of prehistoric fields are still preserved in some localities, such as on the lower slopes of Cerro Prieto (AZ AA:7:116, 118, 135, 447–451, and 11:94). Based on analogy with rockpile fields from the Hohokam early Classic period Marana Community, located on the lower slopes of the Tortolita Mountains directly across the Santa Cruz River, it is presumed that crops were not necessarily confined to traditional domesticates, but included agave, amaranth, or other wild or only semi-domesticated plants (S. Fish 1984; S. Fish, P. Fish, Miksicek, and Madsen 1985; S. Fish and Nabhan 1991; S. Fish, P. Fish, and Madsen 1992).

The floodplain zone of the Santa Cruz River and Los Robles Wash could have supplied a number of resources in prehistoric times. In addition to seasonal drinking water, the floodplain would have supported dense stands of mesquite trees and other economically useful riparian plants. According to Charles Polzer (cited in Wilson 1980: 16), a descriptive term associated with the protohistoric Piman village of Santa Catarina, *Cuituabaga*, may be translated as "Mesquite Wells." As Wilson (1980: 16) has observed, this name may reflect an abundance of mesquite in the vicinity of Santa Catarina, which apparently was located on the Santa Cruz floodplain somewhere west of Red Rock, Arizona. As shown in Figure 2.1, this area today sports an exceptionally thick growth of mesquite and other riparian vegetation, so thick, in fact, that it was considered by archaeological survey crews to be impassable.

Perhaps the most important feature of the floodplain was the rich, alluvial soil, which would have been well-suited to cultivation. This zone's potential for prehistoric agriculture is reflected in the success of contemporary fields in the same area, now known as the Red Rock Farms. These fields today are irrigated by extensive canals carrying groundwater and effluent discharged into the Santa Cruz River, but historic accounts show that successful cultivation could also be achieved with agricultural efforts analogous to prehistoric techniques.

Yjinio Aguirre (1983: 61–62) recalls that exceptional yields from a variety of crops were often obtained by dry farming alone:

> dry farming operations located on the Avra Valley Wash and the Santa Cruz River basin produced fine crops in the rainy season.
>
> The dry farming operation would produce wheat, barley, corn, squash, watermelons, lentils, sorghum cane, milo and beans on years that the two above channels carried water.
>
> I remember one spring in the twenties when Mr. Ford [a local rancher who owned a threshing machine] harvested 7,700 sacks of wheat off my grandfather's field.

Fields on the Aguirre Ranch were also successfully watered with simple floodwater canals. These canals, dug by hand in the early 1900s by Yaqui labor crews, were about six feet wide and four feet deep, with masonry control gates set about one-quarter mile apart. According to Aguirre (1983: 61), the canals were designed by his father, Don Higinio, "to take the water out of the Avra Valley [Brawley and Los Robles] Wash and the Santa Cruz River to water his new cleared land where they planted considerable acreage in wheat and barley."

In addition to the masonry gates, historic canals were also supplemented with sets of brush dams or weirs, strategically designed to divert floodwaters away from buildings and into field areas. Aguirre (1983: 81) describes the plan of one such flood-control system:

> Since Don Higinio knew that his rancho headquarters was lower than the river, he tried to protect it. He also knew that the east side of the east bank was filling up with trash and young brush, and as this was the side where the river mostly overflowed when leaving its banks, he ordered his men to open the channels again. He also gave them instructions how he wanted various 'Estacados,' brush dams built in the river channel. These were built approximately on a forty-five degree angle, so when the water approached them, the water was pushed to the side you desired. In this case, Don Higinio wanted the overflow water of the Santa Cruz to stay on the east side of the river where it would not cause any damage. At the same time, the flooded area would sprout plenty of feed for the livestock.

Such floodgates were apparently quite effective. Aguirre (1983: 83) recalled that after the floods of 1929 and 1930, diversion dams along the Santa Cruz River made the fields "so well watered, that the wild sower-clover, that generally grew on an average season about six inches tall, this time grew to around five feet tall." Evidently, the floodplains of the Santa Cruz River and Los Robles Wash could be extremely productive zones for prehistoric dry and floodwater agriculture. No prehistoric canals of the type described above were observed during the Los Robles survey, but if they exist, they are probably covered by more recent alluvium.

In addition to plant and animal food resources and arable land, other important raw materials were also readily available in the survey area. The Samaniego Hills contain several kinds of rocks and minerals that are valuable for the production of chipped and ground stone tools, and numerous prehistoric quarry sites within the survey area are marked by evidence of such manufacturing activities (Chapter 3). A particularly noteworthy source of lithic raw material occurs at the summit of Cerro Prieto, where there is an outcrop of tabular andesite that can easily be fashioned into agave knives (Bernard-Shaw 1983: 432; Greenwald 1988: 155, 158; Madsen 1989). This source of raw material is surrounded by cleared areas, rock rings, hammerstones, lithic debitage, and broken or incomplete tabular knives, indicating the source was exploited prehistorically (Downum and others 1985: 550; Madsen 1989). Quantities of this material were also removed from the summit of Cerro Prieto and worked at nearby habitation sites. Robles Survey crews reported large quantities of tabular andesite debris at a number of sites along the west bank of Los Robles Wash, south of Cerro Prieto, particularly at the Los Robles Mound Site. During a 1981 powerline survey of the same area, John P. Wilson (1981: 60) also remarked on the abundance of debitage from tabular raw material, which he characterized as "metamorphosed slate." Some of these pieces are large, and it is possible that they were used not as tools, but perhaps as architectural elements such as roof hatch covers, steps, doorway lintels, or as slabs for lining roasting pits (see AZ AA:11:12, p. 27).

Along the Santa Cruz River and Los Robles Wash, alluvial deposits offer clays and tempering materials suitable for the manufacture of pottery. No detailed studies of ceramic production have yet been attempted, but Lombard (1986, 1987) has performed a preliminary analysis of the petrography of sherds from the site of Cerro Prieto (n = 14) and the Los Robles Mound Site (n = 13). Although the total sample is small, it revealed a high number of distinct temper sources. Some sources might be extralocal, but eight sherds (seven plain, and one decorated) were from vessels tempered with materials from the Samaniego petrofacies, an apparently local source. Thus, it would appear that local wash sands, and presumably native clays, were used prehistorically to produce both plain and decorated ceramic vessels. P. Fish, S. Fish, Whittlesey and others (1992) have also analyzed the sources of Los Robles area ceramics, but with only mixed success. Nine sherds of Tanque Verde Red-on-brown from three sites were assessed using neutron activation analysis techniques. Two of the sherds appeared to have been from imported vessels, perhaps manufactured in the Marana Community using clays obtained from the Santa Cruz River. The remaining sherds could not be linked precisely to a probable source area, beyond the inference that five of the represented vessels were likely manufactured from clays originating in the Tucson Basin.

MODERN DISTURBANCE

Human Activities

The two main sources of human-induced disturbance of archaeological sites and features are agricultural development and activities associated with the now-abandoned town of Sasco, located near the center of the survey area. Of the two, agriculture has been particularly destructive. Because of the excellent growing medium provided by fertile alluvial deposits, the floodplains and adjacent terraces of the Santa Cruz River and Brawley and Los Robles washes have been heavily modified by modern irrigation agriculture. These modifications include rerouting of wash channels, field leveling, construction of wells and irrigation canals, and raising of earthen levees. Unfortunately, no observations of archaeological remains were made prior to recent farming activities, and the extent of damage is unknown. Traces of prehistoric sites in plowed fields are notoriously elusive (S. Fish, P. Fish, and Madsen 1992: 27), so surface surveys provide little reliable information on the extent or magnitude of damage from agricultural activities. Many sites and agricultural features must have been destroyed by field leveling and repeated plowing. On the other hand, rapid rates of alluviation in the floodplain, perhaps accelerated by plowing and grazing, may have covered and protected some archaeological remains. These possibilities can be determined only through test excavations.

The direct impacts of the community of Sasco on prehistoric remains are evident in streets, railroad beds, buildings, cemeteries, and other built features. The name Sasco was derived from "Southern Arizona Smelting Company," an affiliate of the Imperial Copper Company (Wilson 1980: 17). The main activity at the town, and the reason for its existence, was a small smelting operation that received ore by railroad line from mines in the Silverbell Mountains. Construction of the smelter and town began in 1907, and occupation and activity reached a peak from about 1910 to 1920. Smelting continued only intermittently from about 1921 to 1930, and in 1934 the smelter was torn down and the railroad tracks removed, marking the end of the community (Wilson 1980: 17).

Any prehistoric remains within the limits of Sasco were severely damaged or destroyed when the town was built. No observations of archaeological sites or features were recorded before the town was created, so there is no way to gauge the extent of damage. Some features might survive in undeveloped areas, or beneath modern constructions, but only test excavations can reveal them. A subdivision of Sasco was planned in the area just northwest of Cerro Prieto. This subdivision was never built, but traces of roads, clearings, and fence lines are still visible on the ground, and particularly on aerial photographs. Such modifications are superficial, but they may have disarranged or destroyed prehistoric surface rock features and artifacts.

Peripheral impacts of Sasco must have been great, but again, they are difficult to judge. Traces of early twentieth-century activities, presumably by Sasco residents, have been noted at Cerro Prieto. These include hand-dug prospecting holes, modern petroglyphs (in the form of initials), isolated adobe or wooden structures, tent clearings, and scattered trash piles. Residents of Sasco may have engaged in some digging and artifact collection at nearby prehistoric sites, but the location and extent of such activities is unknown.

In one of the few documented impacts of modern settlement, Aguirre (1983: 91) notes that in removing building stones from the Samaniego Hills, large ceramic ollas (presumably associated with hillside talus pits; see Chapter 5) were sometimes found among the rocks. These would be transported back to Rancho Cerro Prieto, where they were recycled into water jars for use on the ranch. Aguirre also states that many stands of petroglyphs were "removed and destroyed by visitors from the cities," some through the use of dynamite. Unfortunately, the locations of such activities are unspecified, and it is unclear from Aguirre's account whether he himself observed such vandalism or whether such accounts were received secondhand. Considering the lack of evidence for dynamiting and large-scale destruction of rock at Cerro Prieto, Pan Quemado, and other petroglyph sites south of Sasco, it must be presumed that any such activities were confined to the heavily scarred hill slopes immediately around the town.

A recurrent form of modern disturbance, and one that may have a considerable history in the survey area, involves the damage or theft of petroglyphs. On the upper north slope of Cerro Prieto, and at AZ AA:7:446, boulders with petroglyphs had been rolled aside and holes had been dug nearby, evidently in the original location of the boulder. Whether these acts were accompanied by the recovery of artifacts or theft of petroglyphs is unknown. The evidence suggests that the diggers held the mistaken belief that the petroglyph boulders had marked the location of some buried artifact or feature.

It is often difficult to detect the theft of petroglyphs, many of which occur on small and easily carried boulders. In one case, the boulders were subsequently recovered from a Tucson residence by law enforcement officials, and prosecutions of the individuals allegedly involved in this theft are still pending (*Arizona Daily Star*, 7-27-91). Now protected by its designation as a future State Park, the Los Robles area may suffer less degradation. The area is now patrolled by rangers from nearby Picacho Peak State Park, and aerial surveillance is provided by military helicopter flights originating from Pinal Air Park.

Erosion and Alluviation

Effects of erosion and alluviation are highly variable across the survey area. Sites on the bedrock, pediment, and upper fan surfaces of the Samaniego Hills and Silverbell Mountains have been little affected by either process. Grazing may have accelerated erosion in some places, and some shallow deposition of alluvium may have occurred in certain localities, but overall the ground surface in upland settings appears to have changed little since prehistoric times.

Holocene fans adjacent to the floodplain have experienced differential degrees of erosion and deposition. In some areas, recent entrenchment of washes has resulted in considerable headcutting and destruction of prehistoric cultural deposits. Elsewhere, sheet flooding has deposited a very recent, thin veneer of fine sediments, partially covering and obscuring prehistoric artifacts and features. In such situations, there often can be a complex mixture of erosion and deposition across the surface of a single site. An excellent example occurs near the Los Robles mound, where young alluvial deposits have been eroded recently by sheet flooding or entrenchment of small streams. Figure 2.6 shows how a thin layer of such sediments, once completely obscuring prehistoric deposits, is now eroding once again to expose the prehistoric ground surface.

Slightly farther downslope on Holocene fan surfaces, the general trend is toward aggradation. On such surfaces, the results of site burial can be directly observed, with sharply defined features such as trash mounds protruding from fine-grained alluvium. This phenomenon makes it difficult to assess site characteristics and to define site boundaries. While surveying a narrow powerline corridor along the west bank of Los Robles Wash, Wilson (1981) defined several small and apparently isolated trash mounds as refuse from temporary settlements used during ak chin farming of small arroyo fans. He noted that these mounds "had sharply defined perimeters, with 100's or even 1000's of pottery sherds present," and suggested that they and perhaps other low rises without artifacts might have originated as the backdirt from prehistoric house pits.

From the wider perspective gained during the Los Robles Survey, however, it now appears that at least some of the mounds identified by Wilson as evidence of isolated, seasonal settlements are in fact components of extensive Hohokam villages that continue for several

Figure 2.6. Recent layer of fine-grained alluvium capping gravelly trash deposits (prehistoric ground surface) north of the Los Robles Mound Site (R-138). Recent erosion has removed fine-grained sediments to expose the older surface. The Los Robles Mound is visible in the background. (ASM photograph 69716, by Helga G. Teiwes.)

hundred meters west of the powerline corridor. Two of Wilson's "short term settlements," TEP 626 and 627 (AZ AA:11:23 and AA:11:24 in Wilson 1985: 130), are now considered to represent trash mounds within the boundaries of AA:11:23, a substantial late Colonial to early Classic period settlement. The sharply defined perimeters and isolated nature of these mounds, perceptively recognized by Wilson as distinctive traits, have evidently resulted from depositional processes. As fine-grained sediments have accumulated over broad areas adjacent to arroyo fans, the large trash mounds, built on low, probably natural gravel rises, have become ever smaller, more sharply defined, and isolated from surrounding site features. This has contributed to the impression that individual mounds on lower fan surfaces may represent individual sites. Only after inspecting unburied trash mounds upslope was it clear to Robles survey crew members that the apparently small and isolated mounds at AZ AA:11:23 and AA:11:24 were in fact components of a single large village.

Surfaces in and adjacent to the floodplains of major streams have experienced strikingly variable degrees of erosion and deposition. The active channels of the Santa Cruz River and Los Robles Wash are entrenched, and it is likely that any prehistoric remains there have been destroyed or severely damaged. Floodplains adjacent to major stream channels are zones of active deposition, and here prehistoric sites and features are probably buried. Evidence of former site burial in floodplain deposits was observed along Los Robles Wash at site AZ AA:7:82 (ASM). This site had been completely buried by recent sediments and was exposed during the severe flooding of early October, 1983. Floodwaters stripped approximately 1 m of overlying sediment and exposed a set of Classic period adobe structures and burials in an area that previously had shown only an intermittent, low density scatter of sherds and other artifacts (Farmer 1984). Other sites in this zone are still largely or completely entombed by recent, fine-grained alluvial deposits (Field and others 1989).

Note: Additional information on the environment of the Los Robles survey area is in the syntheses of Wilson (1980: 5–17), Dart (1984), and Rankin (1986). Vegetation of the survey area is described by Reichhardt (1989b). Lowe (1977), Hastings and Turner (1964), and Brown (1982) provide general descriptions of the plant communities of southern Arizona. Field and others (1989) discuss the specific geomorphology of the survey area; more general descriptions of Sonoran Desert geomorphology, hydrology, and soils can be found in publications by Bryan (1925) and Gelderman (1972). Excellent reviews of Hohokam environments, and the range of adaptive responses to them, are provided by McGuire (1982a) and S. Fish and Nabhan (1991).

CHAPTER THREE

Los Robles Survey Sites

A principal contribution made by the Los Robles Archaeological Survey was the discovery and recording of 145 archaeological sites. Additionally, 31 previously known sites were either revisited and re-recorded or were included in the study by examining the site files of the Arizona State Museum. Most of these sites belonged to a prehistoric settlement system consisting of villages, farmsteads, agricultural fields, and a variety of specialized activity areas. Based on ceramic evidence, this settlement system was established during the Snaketown phase of the Hohokam late Pioneer period (about A.D. 700–775; Fig. 1.2), and reached a peak during the early Classic Tanque Verde phase (about A.D. 1150–1300). No remains in the survey area have been dated to the late Classic period. A few protohistoric or early historic period activities (about A.D. 1539–1850) and some late nineteenth- or early twentieth-century Tohono O'odham locations were also identified.

A discussion of survey methods is presented below, with a consideration of how individual sites were dated with ceramic evidence to reveal overall temporal trends in the occupation and use of the Los Robles Wash area. Descriptions of the 176 Los Robles survey sites follow, using 14 formal and functional site categories. Most sites are briefly mentioned individually, but for certain site categories only selected examples are included. The importance of these sites with respect to a number of archaeological research issues is treated in the final chapter.

SURVEY METHODS

Within the 282 square kilometers (109 square miles) defined as the Los Robles survey area, approximately 57.5 square kilometers (22.2 square miles) were surveyed with block coverage, and 8.0 square kilometers (3.1 square miles) were inspected through survey transects (Fig. 2.1). A total of 5.3 square kilometers (2.0 square miles), mostly along the banks of Los Robles Wash, were not surveyed because of a thick growth of mesquite, catclaw, and other vegetation. Excluding this portion, approximately 23.7 percent of the survey area was covered with either block (20.8%) or transect (2.9%) survey.

Survey methods followed the general procedures outlined for the larger Arizona State Museum Bureau of Reclamation Mound Survey (Madsen and others 1989). For block survey coverage, crew members were spaced 20 m to 30 m (66 to 98 feet) apart, depending on vegetation and visibility conditions. The survey proceeded by 2.59-square-kilometer (1-square-mile) units, each of which was surveyed in quarter-section (160 acre) increments. All surface remains fitting site-level criteria (that is, 50 or more artifacts, or at least one cultural feature) were assigned a survey site number, and were usually mapped and collected as they were discovered. Mapping involved a compass-and-pace technique, but mapping instruments (alidade or transit) were occasionally used, especially for large sites. All sites were plotted on 1:12,000-scale aerial photographs; these plots were later transferred to USGS 7.5 or 15 minute quadrangle sheets to determine exact legal and UTM locations. For extremely large sites, the site boundary and major surface features were plotted directly onto the aerial photograph.

Collection procedures followed a number of strategies, including complete collections for those sites with a relatively small number of items (150 or less), and systematic transect or circle collection techniques when sampling was deemed necessary. All isolated artifacts were plotted on the 1:12,000-scale aerial photographs and were bagged by quarter-section provenience.

Transect coverage followed exactly the same recording, mapping, and collection procedures used for block surveys. Transects, averaging 60 m (197 feet) in width, were surveyed along section or half-section lines. Usually, transects were spaced at parallel, 800 m (0.5 mile) intervals.

Information contained on the Los Robles Survey site recording forms was standardized according to a selected set of variables. The coding for these variables and a complete listing of them for each site are on file in the Arizona State Museum Library, Tucson (Downum 1991).

Table 3.1. Temporal Periods and Ceramics Assigned to Los Robles Survey Sites

Number of sites	Period	Time range (A.D.)	Ceramics
2	Late Pioneer	700–775	Snaketown Red-on-buff
1	Late Pioneer-Early Colonial	700–900	Indeterminate: Either Snaketown Red-on-buff or Gila Butte Red-on-buff
1	Early Colonial	775–900	Gila Butte Red-on-buff, Cañada del Oro Red-on-brown
7	Late Colonial	900–1000	Santa Cruz Red-on-buff, Rillito Red-on-brown
7	Late Colonial-Sedentary	900–1150	Indeterminate: Either Santa Cruz Red-on-buff or Sacaton Red-on-buff, either Rillito Red-on-brown or Rincon Red-on-brown
20	Sedentary	1000–1150	Sacaton Red-on-buff, Sacaton Red, Rincon Red-on-brown, Rincon Red
23	Sedentary-Early Classic	1000–1300	Indeterminate: Either Rincon Red-on-brown or Tanque Verde Red-on-brown
34	Early Classic	1150–1300	Casa Grande Red-on-buff, Tanque Verde Red-on-brown, Gila Red, Salt Red, all in the absence of Salado polychromes or other late Classic period polychromes
8	Preclassic (phase unknown)	700–1150	Indeterminate Preclassic red-on-buff, indeterminate Preclassic red-on-brown
92	Unknown Hohokam	300–1450	Gila Plain, Wingfield Plain, other plain wares not classified as Papago Plain or Whetstone Plain(?)
15	Protohistoric-Early Historic	?1539–1860	Whetstone Plain(?), unidentified types with added neck coil (Chapter 5)
14	Late Historic	post-1860	Papago Plain, Papago Red, Mexican Green Glaze Ware, other historic crockery or trash

Note: Some sites are assigned to more than one time period.

SITE DATING

Methods

The issue of site dating is of critical importance to understanding the dynamics of prehistoric settlement. However, the ability to date Los Robles survey sites and to assess their intensity of occupation or use through time was hampered by a number of factors.

The surfaces of most sites with ceramics exhibited a low proportion of decorated sherds, and even those that were present were small or badly eroded, or both. Because of limited resources and the design of the survey, intensive surface collections were not made. The sample of reliably typed and temporally diagnostic sherds is small for individual sites and is relatively small for the survey area as a whole.

Several severe problems still plague Hohokam ceramic chronology: the serious effects that a few taxonomic ambiguities or errors may have on estimated site occupation spans, limitations imposed on dating precision by the Hohokam ceramic typology itself, and lingering controversies about the date ranges of particular ceramic types and cultural phases. In the case of the Los Robles sites, these difficulties may have been exacerbated by the uncertain origins, eroded nature, and small number of surface sherds retrieved during the survey.

Nonetheless, a primary goal of the Los Robles survey was to provide a first approximation of the history of settlement and land use along the lower Santa Cruz River, and this required some estimate of the potential occupation spans and growth histories of individual sites. Based on the range of ceramic types represented at Los Robles sites, 12 sherd-based temporal classifications were used to partition time according to the traditional Hohokam phase system and subsequent protohistoric and historic periods. The 12 categories, their date ranges (modified from Dean 1991), and the specific ceramic assignments used to define them are in Table 3.1.

Dating Results

A majority of sites (92 of 176) were designated only as "Unknown Hohokam" (Table 3.1), meaning that no specific phase or period of occupation could be ascertained. Most of these sites had sand- or micaceous-tempered pottery that could not be assigned to a specific Hohokam phase and did not resemble known protohistoric or historic ceramic types. Some of these sites may have diagnostic ceramics or other datable material beneath their surfaces, but many were surface scatters with no apparent depth of cultural deposits. Pending advances in dating techniques for plain ware ceramics, these sites are likely to remain poorly dated.

Among specifically dated sites, there is an apparent increase in dated components from the Snaketown phase onward, with site occupation or use reaching a peak during the early Classic period. Population densities throughout the northern Tucson Basin appear to be highest at this time (S. Fish, P. Fish, and Madsen 1992). The prehistoric occupation within the survey area evidently ended sometime before the early A.D. 1300s, for no Salado polychromes or other late Classic period ceramics were recovered or observed during the survey.

In addition to the sites assigned to the Hohokam period of occupation, 14 sites contained pottery resembling Whetstone Plain or had unidentified sherds showing an added rim coil. These ceramics are inferred to represent a post-Hohokam occupation or use of the area, but specific dates are difficult to estimate. In Chapter 5, Madsen provides a discussion of the problems associated with dating this pottery. The dates of 1539, marking the expedition of Fray Marcos de Niza into southern Arizona (McGuire and Villalpando 1989; Reff 1991), and 1860, marking the possible beginning date for carbon-core Papago pottery, have been provisionally and somewhat arbitrarily assigned to the Protohistoric–Early Historic period. In reality, the date range is probably more restrictive. Fourteen sites also produced reliably identified historic period ceramics or artifacts dating after 1860. These sites were evidently used or occupied during the late nineteenth and early twentieth centuries. Dating assigned to sites according to the categories listed in Table 3.1 is given at the end of each site description.

SITE DESCRIPTIONS

The Los Robles sites are grouped into 14 categories (with two subtypes) based on functional, formal, or temporal criteria (Table 3.2). Site Types 1 through 12 are based primarily on inferred function; Trincheras Feature Site (Type 6) and Artifact Scatter (Type 13) combine formal and temporal dimensions (all examples were presumed to be prehistoric or protohistoric); and Historic (Type 14) is based strictly on temporal criteria (all historic sites postdate A.D. 1850, although some indicate earlier use as well). This classification is believed to reflect the basic functional components of prehistoric Hohokam settlement systems in southern Arizona. Full documentation for each site is provided in Downum (1991) and in the site files of the Arizona State Museum.

Table 3.2. Categories of Los Robles Survey Sites

Category	Definition		Number
Site Type 1	Settlements exhibiting public architecture		2
Subtype 1a	Settlement with earthen mound	1	
Subtype 1b	Settlement with ballcourt	1	
Site Type 2	Compound settlement		2
Site Type 3	Noncompound settlement		14
Site Type 4	Farmstead		10
Site Type 5	Agricultural field		17
Site Type 6	Trincheras feature site		11
Site Type 7	Water diversion feature		1
Site Type 8	Petroglyph site		10
Site Type 9	Limited activity plant or animal food processing site		37
Site Type 10	Rock shelter		4
Site Type 11	Reservoir		1
Site Type 12	Quarry site		10
Site Type 13	Artifact scatter		51
Site Type 14	Historic camp or homestead		7

Note: Total number includes an unnumbered and unrecorded site on the Aguirre Ranch (Aguirre 1983: 127–133; see page 30).

Settlements Exhibiting Public Architecture
Site Type 1 (2 sites)

Settlement with Earthen Mound
Subtype 1a (1 site)

Definition: Prehistoric site with a large, rectangular, earthen mound, possibly representing a Classic period platform mound.

The one example of this site type in the survey area is the Los Robles Mound Site. It is presumed to have been a focal point of an early Classic period settlement system, referred to as the Los Robles Community, that arose in the Los Robles Wash–Cerro Prieto–Pan Quemado vicinity. The exact extent of this community has yet to be defined adequately, but it appears to extend northwest of the Los Robles mound, covering the west bank of Los Robles Wash and a portion of the north end of the Samaniego Hills. More surveys are needed, particularly of the east bank of Los Robles Wash and the Santa Cruz floodplain to the north, to explore the possibility that additional sites of the community extended into those areas as well.

The Los Robles Mound Site (AZ AA:11:25, R–138;) is on the west bank of Los Robles Wash, approximately 800 m south of the Pinal and Pima County line. Its principal feature is a rectangular, earthen mound, measuring approximately 35 m by 37 m and standing about 2 m above the surrounding ground level (Figs. 3.1, 3.2). The surface of the mound is marked by a high density of artifacts, consisting of plain ware and early Classic period sherds (Tanque Verde Red-on-brown, indeterminate red-on-brown, Casa Grande Red-on-buff, and Tularosa Black-on-white), chipped stone debitage, ground stone tool fragments, projectile points, obsidian, shell, and burned bone (Fig. 3.3). The mound has been slightly damaged by some small erosional channels, and there are a few small pothunter holes scattered across the top (Fig. 3.2).

Except for exposures provided by the pothunter holes and erosion, the contents of the Los Robles Mound are unknown, and no walls or other architectural features

Figure 3.1. The Los Robles Mound, view looking east. (ASM photograph 69709, by Helga G. Teiwes.)

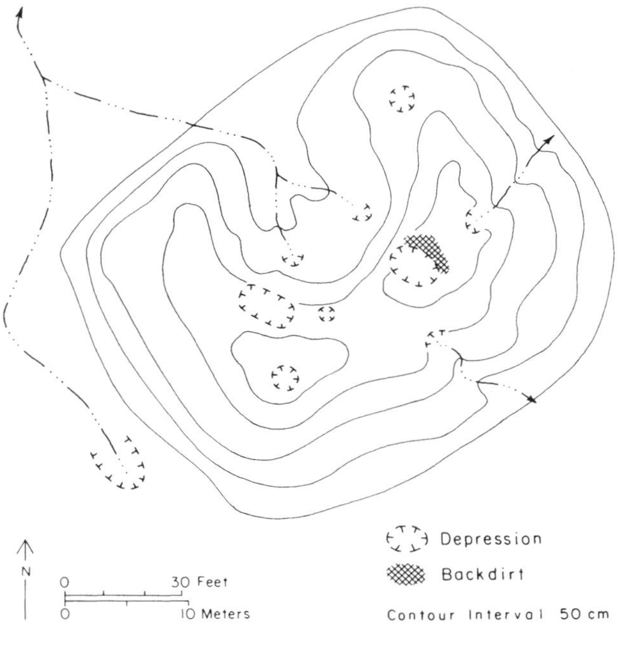

Figure 3.2. Plan of the Los Robles Mound Site.

are evident. There is a high proportion of gravel present at the surface of the mound, and in this respect it resembles the round or irregularly shaped gravel rises that exist at nearby sites along the west bank of Los Robles Wash (AZ AA:11:23 and 66). Many of these rises are covered with prehistoric artifacts and appear to have been used as trash mounds, but equally numerous are rises that may be of entirely natural origin. Wilson (1981: 60) suggests that "the rises are material from aboriginal excavations for pithouses. The occupants then added their refuse to the mounds. . . ."

Although the precise nature of the Los Robles Mound can be ascertained only through excavation, several observations strongly suggest that it represents a Hohokam platform mound (Haury 1987: 251; Downum and Madsen 1989) and not a culturally modified natural feature. First, although the mound has been dissected by small erosional channels, it maintains a distinctly rectangular outline. This shape is particularly apparent at the base of the mound, where gravelly sediments contrast sharply with the fine-grained alluvium that covers the surrounding area. Second, the mound exhibits an almost

Figure 3.3. Artifacts at the surface of the Los Robles Mound. (ASM photograph 69713, by Helga G. Teiwes.)

flat top, which drops off abruptly and more or less regularly along the sides. In this respect it is similar to several unexcavated but definite platform mounds, such as the Marana, McClellan Wash, and Adamsville mounds. Third, the mound is several magnitudes taller than surrounding ridges or gravel eminences, and its elevation equates with confirmed platform mounds. Fourth, as revealed by a 1-m-deep pothunter hole at the east end of the mound, the extraordinary density of artifacts at the top of the mound continues well below the surface. This observation is consistent with the proposition that the mound is an intentionally trash-filled adobe structure and not a natural gravel mound that is covered with artifacts. Fifth, the presence of a high density of surface gravel is not inconsistent with a platform mound interpretation. When platform mound "cells" at other sites (for example, Pueblo Grande, Las Colinas, Marana) were intentionally filled with trash, much of it came from nearby trash mounds or middens. Because trash disposal in the Los Robles area often took place on natural gravel ridges, a significant amount of gravel would have been gathered with the fill. Finally, the high density of gravel at the mound surface may have resulted from eroded retaining walls or structures made from adobe with a high gravel content.

No compound has been observed at the mound even though conditions of visibility are excellent and the surrounding ground surface has been repeatedly inspected since the mound was discovered. However, as noted in Chapter 2, this may be caused by alluvial deposition in the immediately surrounding area. The gravelly base of the mound contacts abruptly with a layer of extremely fine silt deposited by sheetwash and overflow from a few small drainages. Inspection of the channels of these drainages reveals artifacts buried at depths from 10 cm to 30 cm. Thus, although a surrounding adobe or rock compound wall would be an expected feature at a platform mound, in this case postoccupational sediments may make its observation impossible. By the same token, these sediments are probably covering and therefore protecting from erosion and vandalism a number of significant subsurface features such as adobe structures; cooking, storage, and adobe mixing pits; and trash mounds.

On the west, east, and south sides of the mound, dense concentrations of surface artifacts mark the apparent locations of partially buried trash mounds or middens and buried houses and other features (Fig. 3.4). Ten individual trash mounds or middens were observed. Two of these features are dominated by lithic debitage probably associated with the production of tabular agave knives. This debitage is visually identical to raw material occurring at the summit of Cerro Prieto and probably came from that source (Greenwald 1988: 155, 158). Some fragments too thick for tabular knives may have been used to line roasting pits or as architectural elements such as lintels, steps, roof hatches, or smokehole covers. (Dating: Early Classic.)

Settlement with Ballcourt
Subtype 1b (1 site)

Definition: Prehistoric site with an oval depression, surrounded by earthen embankments, interpreted as a ballcourt.

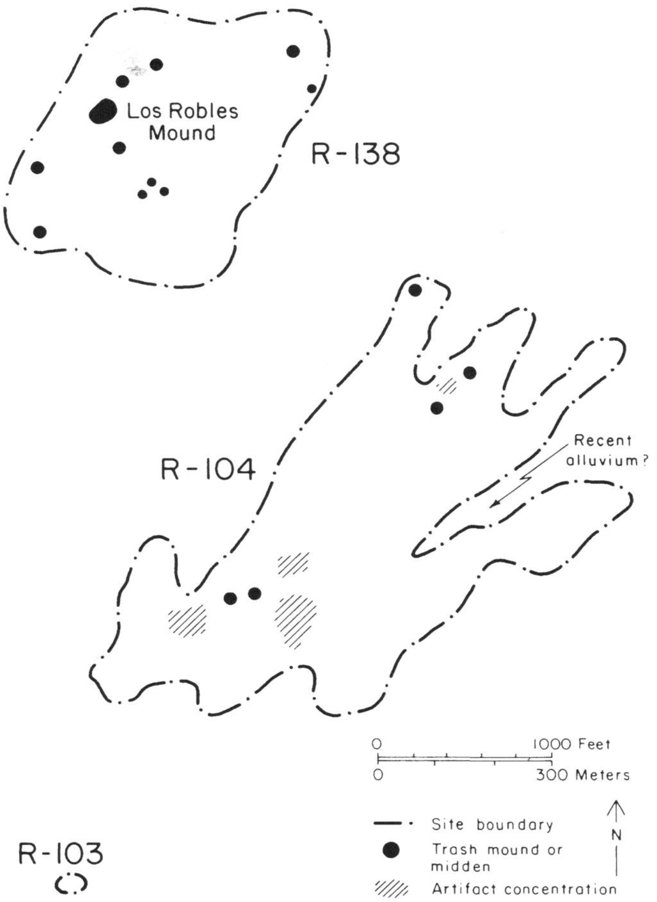

Figure 3.4. Area map of the Los Robles Mound and nearby sites, features, and artifact concentrations.

The only ballcourt settlement known in the Los Robles survey area is the Hog Farm Ballcourt Site, so named because it is located adjacent to a hog feedlot and exhibits a surface feature interpreted as a Hohokam ballcourt. It is presumed to have been an important and perhaps paramount village in a Preclassic settlement system that was centered slightly south of the Classic period Los Robles Community and on the opposite (east) bank of Los Robles Wash.

The Hog Farm Ballcourt Site (AZ AA:11:12, R-129) as currently defined is by far the largest settlement inspected during the Los Robles Archaeological Survey. It consists of a narrow band of trash mounds, eroding roasting pits, artifact scatters, and other items and features extending intermittently for several kilometers along the east bank of Los Robles Wash (Fig. 3.5). A ballcourt is in the far northwest end of the site.

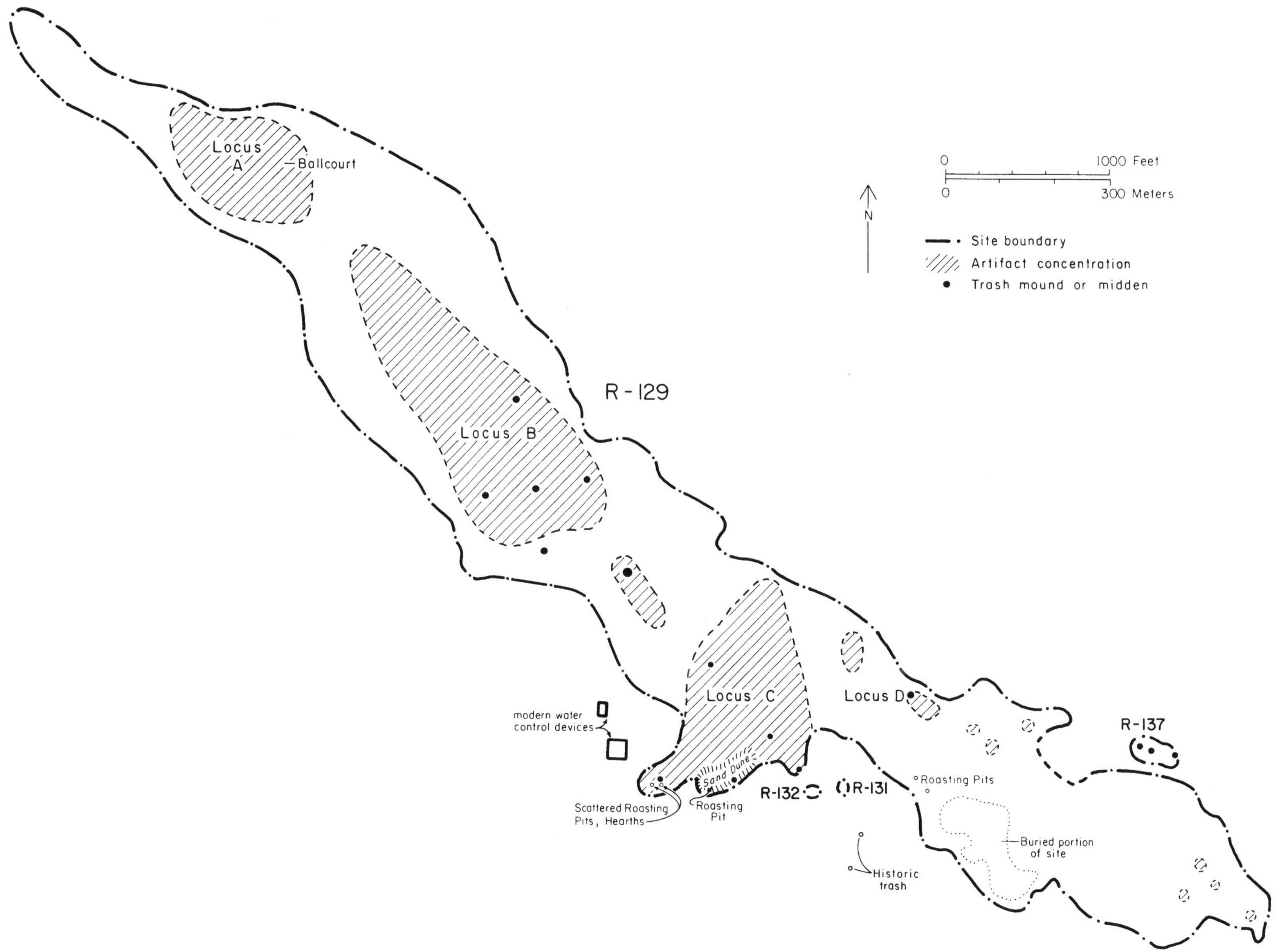

Figure 3.5. Plan of the Hog Farm Ballcourt Site (AZ AA:11:12 ASM, R-129).

Three small sites (AZ AA:11:54–56) are located just outside the boundary of AZ AA:11:12 (Site R–129). Although these sites might well have been considered components of AA:11:12, they were defined as separate sites because of distinct gaps in artifact distribution between them and the main concentration of features and artifacts that constitutes AA:11:12.

Information about the Hog Farm Ballcourt Site is still too sketchy to reliably discern temporally or functionally meaningful components. Five separate loci (A–D, and an unnamed locus near the site center) were identified by the Los Robles survey crew and were collected separately, but the sample of artifacts was too small to permit detailed analysis. The subsequent survey and mapping by Huntington and Holmlund (1986) provided more details from Loci A and B. Within a small portion of Locus A, eight features were defined, consisting of six small trash mounds and two areas of scattered, burned tabular andesite. The burned fragments of andesite were exposed in pothunter holes, and appeared to represent the remains of slab-lined roasting pits. Artifacts included pottery (sherds of plain ware, unidentified red-on-brown, Rillito Red-on-brown, Rincon Red-on-brown, and Tanque Verde Red-on-brown), lithic debitage, fragments of ground stone tools, cores, core-hammerstones, and a worked sherd disk. At the east end of Locus A, there was an oval depression surrounded by an earthen berm. This feature apparently represents a relatively small Hohokam ballcourt. The Los Robles survey crew did not make a detailed map of this court, but David Wilcox (1991b: 106–107) has presented some basic observations on its form. The court measures about 22.4 m long and is oriented at about 80 degrees east of north. Sherds around it indicate an early Colonial to early Classic period date.

Over a small area of Locus B, Huntington and Holmlund observed six features, consisting of three trash mounds, a scatter of tabular andesite and ground stone tool fragments (probably representing an eroding roasting pit), an ash stain identifying an eroding hearth or burned structure, and a concentration of ash and pieces of burned jacal in a rodent burrow indicating a burned structure. Locus B included lithic debitage, cobble cores, core-hammerstones, fragments of ground stone tools, tabular andesite, tabular knife fragments, pieces of shell debitage, worked sherd disks, and pottery (sherds of plain ware, red ware, Rillito Red-on-brown, Rincon Red-on-brown, Tanque Verde Red-on-brown, Gila Butte Red-on-buff, and Santa Cruz Red-on-buff). Collections made by ASM personnel at various loci included sherds of Rincon Red-on-brown, indeterminate Rincon Red-on-brown or Tanque Verde Red-on-brown, Tanque Verde Red-on-brown, Sacaton Red-on-buff, Salt Red, and Cibola White Ware.

From these remains it appears that the Hog Farm Ballcourt Site had an exceptionally long history of occupation, spanning at least the Colonial through early Classic periods. The presence of Sedentary and early Classic period sherds at Locus A, and the presence of Colonial through early Classic sherds at Locus B, indicate that there may be discrete temporal components in different areas of the site. Numerous trash mounds provide evidence of substantial population levels, though the precise nature of population growth and decline is not yet clear. (Dating: Early Colonial through Early Classic.)

Compound Settlements
(Site Type 2; 2 sites)

Definition: Prehistoric site with one or more residential compounds delineated or enclosed by an adobe wall.

The two compound settlements recorded by the survey may not represent the total number in this area. The geomorphic conditions at many large settlements limit our ability to perceive subsurface compounds through the usual signs of differential drying of surface sediments, slight mounding of melted adobe walls, or outlines of vegetation.

AZ AA:11:66 (Robles Survey Site R–105) is a large settlement located approximately 500 m northwest of the Los Robles Mound (Fig. 3.6). The west end of the site exhibits a number of linear ridges that appear to mark the locations of surface adobe compound walls. Major

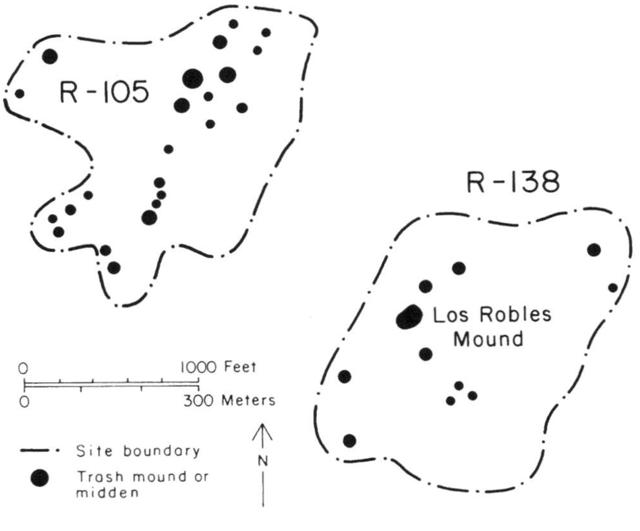

Figure 3.6. Area map of AZ AA:11:66 (R–105), showing site features and relationship to the Los Robles Mound Site.

surface features include more than 20 trash mounds, the largest of which measures at least 23 m in diameter and stands about 1.2 m above the surrounding ground surface. The abundant surface artifacts include pottery (sherds of plain ware, indeterminate red ware, Rillito Red-on-brown, Rincon Red-on-brown, Tanque Verde Red-on-brown, Santa Cruz Red-on-buff, and Sacaton Red-on-buff), chipped stone debitage, ground stone tools and tool fragments, shell jewelry, and tabular knives and knife fragments. Some fire-cracked rock and at least one roasting pit were also observed. The site has been only minimally damaged by erosion and many portions are partially buried by recent alluvium. (Dating: Late Colonial through Early Classic.)

Aguirre Ranch site, unnamed and unrecorded. As mentioned in Chapter 1, Aguirre (1983: 127–133) reports the excavation of several adobe rooms, cremations, and a 56.7-m (186-foot) segment of adobe wall foundation, evidently representing the remains of a compound wall that surrounded the rooms. The precise location of this site is unknown. Carl Halbirt of Northland Research indicated to me on 27 June 1989 that the site was probably located west of the Cake Ranch Site (AZ AA:7:3). Halbirt has recently surveyed this area in an attempt to relocate the site. He will report on the results of this investigation in a forthcoming report on the excavations by Northland Research, Inc. along a CAP distribution system right-of-way at the northern end of the Los Robles survey area. (Dating: Estimated as Early Classic based on photographs of the Aguirre vessels, see page 7.)

Noncompound Settlements
(Site Type 3; 14 sites)

Definition: Prehistoric site that lacks evidence of a compound, but exhibits other features indicating a habitation, such as formal mounds or refuse disposal areas with a diversity of artifact types, adobe or cobble-walled structures, pit house depressions, or other evidence of substantial structures.

Nine of the 14 noncompound settlements are strung out nearly evenly along the banks of Los Robles Wash; the remaining three (AZ AA:11:79, 11:80, 11:84) are clustered in the extreme southwest portion of the survey area. These sites represent a wide range of variability in size, form, artifacts, and features visible at the surface. Precisely what this variability means in terms of population levels, settlement structure, occupational histories, and intersettlement relationships is at present poorly understood and specific evaluations must await excavation data. However, there is little question that these sites provide evidence of a substantial and lengthy occupation in the Los Robles Wash drainage system. Ceramic evidence indicates that settlement in the area began at least as early as the late Pioneer and continued through the early Classic. Thick trash mounds and other features spread over a considerable area suggest that some sites achieved relatively high population levels, and that these populations in aggregate must have been an important presence on the regional cultural landscape. Many of these settlements in their last stages of occupation are inferred to have been part of an integrated early Classic period community.

AZ AA:11:43 (Robles Survey Site R-1) is located on the east bank of Los Robles Wash in the southeast portion of the survey area. Major features are two dense concentrations of artifacts that evidently represent eroding trash mounds or middens. Artifacts include pottery (sherds of plain ware, Rincon Red-on-brown, and Tanque Verde Red-on-brown), chipped stone debitage, and ground stone tool fragments. The two artifact concentrations, each of which covers about 1500 square meters, occur in the northeast and southeast portions of the site. Both appear to have been exposed by a combination of sheetwash erosion and gullying. According to the survey crew, it is likely that additional artifacts and features, perhaps including trash mounds or middens, are buried beneath surrounding alluvial deposits. The site, then, may be considerably larger than its evident dimensions of about 90 m by 170 m. (Dating: Sedentary through Early Classic.)

AZ AA:7:110 (Robles Survey Site R-14) covers an extensive area (680 m by 770 m) in the northwest portion of the survey area, about 1.2 km north of Cerro Prieto. The site was recorded as a series of "relatively dense" scatters of pottery (sherds of plain ware, Rincon Red, Rincon Red-on-brown, Tanque Verde Red-on-brown, and Sacaton Red-on-buff), chipped stone debitage, tabular knives and knife fragments, and ground stone tool fragments. A piece of shell jewelry and a sherd disk were also present. These items were spread over the entire site, but several areas, particularly near the center of the site, showed concentrations of artifacts that might reflect trash deposits. Numerous rockpiles, ranging from 1.0 m to 1.5 m in diameter, were in the south and northeast portions of the site. In the northeast location, the rockpiles had been eroded by steep, recently cut gullies, which had exposed several large plain ware sherds and knives fashioned from tabular schist. (Dating: Sedentary through Early Classic.)

AZ AA:7:9 (Robles Survey Site R-19) is located on the west side of Los Robles Wash, immediately east of the Inscription Hill petroglyph site (AZ AA:7:8). AZ

AA:7:9 contains at least 15 well-defined trash mounds, most of them in the southwest portion of the site. Two eroding roasting pits were also observed in the south section. According to the site's recorders, additional trash mounds and other features may be buried in the northeast portion, which is covered with recent, fine-grained alluvium deposited by overbank flooding of Los Robles Wash and its tributaries. Surface artifacts included pottery (sherds of plain ware, Rincon Red-on-brown, Tanque Verde Red-on-brown, Rincon Polychrome, Santa Cruz Red-on-buff, Sacaton Red-on-buff, Rincon Red, and Gila Red), ground stone debitage, and tabular knife fragments. (Dating: Late Colonial through Early Classic.)

AZ AA:7:126 (Robles Survey Site R-36) is located at the toe of a small, recent alluvial fan on the west bank of Los Robles Wash. It has at least two low, pebbly mounds with abundant pottery (sherds of plain ware, indeterminate red ware, Rincon red-on-brown, and indeterminate buff ware), chipped stone debitage, cores, and tabular knife fragments. One of the mounds also had a piece of shell jewelry. The mounds evidently represent trash deposits, perhaps formed on natural gravel rises. The east portion of the site slopes toward Los Robles Wash and may be covered with a thin mantle of recent alluvium. (Dating: Sedentary period.)

AZ AA:7:142 (Robles Survey Site R-54) is on a relatively flat, gravelly surface about 1.7 km northwest of Cerro Prieto, and a few hundred meters due west of AZ AA:7:110. The main surface features are a small (8 m by 20 m) trash mound, a dense artifact concentration about 10 m northeast of the mound, and a low density artifact scatter that extends for about 40 m north and west of the mound. The trash mound is low (about 40 cm high) and contains pottery (sherds of plain ware, indeterminate red-on-brown, and indeterminate Santa Cruz Red-on-buff or Sacaton Red-on-buff), chipped stone debitage, shell debitage, and some Whetstone Plain(?) sherds. (Dating: Late Colonial-Sedentary; Protohistoric-Early Historic.)

AZ AA:7:145 (Robles Survey Site R-57) is on a relatively flat alluvial fan surface about 2.5 km northwest of Cerro Prieto and approximately 500 m northwest of AZ AA:7:110. It consists of a scatter of pottery (sherds of plain ware, Rillito Red-on-brown, Tanque Verde Red-on-brown, and indeterminate Santa Cruz Red-on-buff or Sacaton Red-on-buff), lithic debitage, ground stone tool fragments, and a concentration of tabular andesite debitage. These items are occasionally clustered into denser concentrations that suggest eroding trash deposits. In the judgment of the survey crew, most of the site probably remains buried beneath a thin mantle of silt, sand, and gravel deposited by overbank flooding of a large wash immediately to the north. (Dating: Late Colonial; Late Colonial-Sedentary; Early Classic.)

AZ AA:11:23 (Robles Survey Site R-104) is just southeast of the Los Robles Mound on the west bank of Los Robles Wash. It is a large site with at least five trash mounds and extensive areas of dense sheet trash (Fig. 3.4). Artifacts observed at the surface include pottery (sherds of plain ware, indeterminate red ware, Rincon Red-on-brown, Tanque Verde Red-on-brown, Santa Cruz Red-on-buff, Sacaton Red-on-buff, and indeterminate Cibola White Ware), stone debitage, ground stone tools and tool fragments, shell jewelry, and tabular knives and knife fragments. Fire-cracked rock, roasting pits, and rockpiles were also observed. This site appears to have been a major settlement associated during its last period of occupation with the Los Robles Mound. Only minimal damage from erosion and pothunting has occurred, and large portions of the site appear to be buried beneath recent alluvium. (Dating: Late Colonial through Early Classic.)

AZ AA:11:13 (Robles Survey Site R-122) is on the west bank of Los Robles Wash, a few hundred meters northwest of the Hog Farm Ballcourt Site. The site consists of more than 15 obtrusive, well-defined trash mounds (Fig. 3.7) exhibiting pottery (sherds of plain

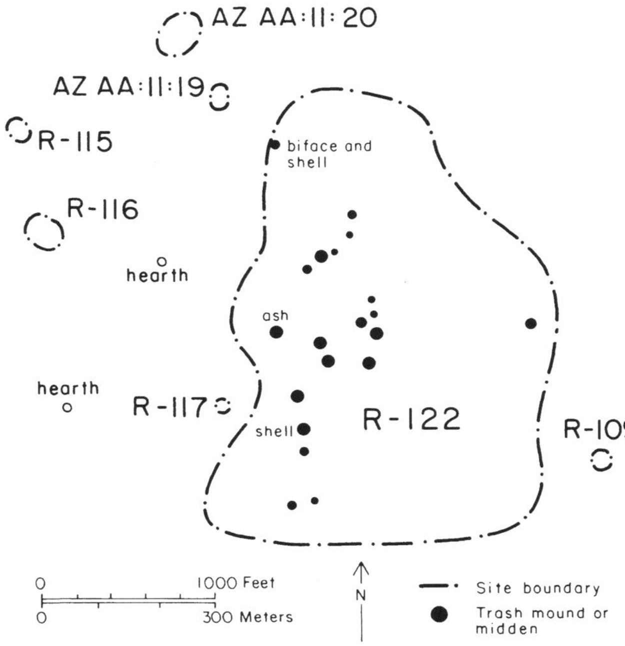

Figure 3.7. Area map of AZ AA:11:13 (Site R-122) and surrounding sites, features, and isolated artifacts.

ware, indeterminate red ware, Rillito Red-on-brown, Rincon Red-on-brown, Tanque Verde Red-on-brown, Santa Cruz Red-on-buff, and Sacaton Red-on-buff), chipped stone debitage, a biface, ground stone tools and tool fragments, cores, tabular knives, fire-cracked rock, and shell jewelry. One of the mounds was much higher than the surrounding ground surface. Areas between the mounds were mostly free of artifacts, perhaps because of recent deposition on the surface. The mounds themselves were gravelly and irregular in outline, suggesting that prehistoric trash was discarded on erosional remnants of natural gravel terraces. (Dating: Late Colonial through Early Classic.)

AZ AA:11:79 (Robles Survey Site R-151) is an extensive scatter of artifacts surrounding a central area of at least three distinct trash mounds and two large depressions that may represent prehistoric water catchments or sediment-filled reservoirs. Evidence of a pit house was recorded. Burned human(?) bone was observed in the backdirt of a rodent hole, and several cleared areas, perhaps representing small agricultural plots, were scattered across the southwest portion of the site. Artifacts include pottery (sherds of plain ware, indeterminate red ware, Snaketown Red-on-buff, indeterminate Snaketown Red-on-buff or Gila Butte Red-on-buff, and Papago Plain), and ground stone tool fragments. (Dating: Preclassic, phase unknown; Late Pioneer; Late Pioneer-Early Colonial; Late Historic.)

AZ AA:11:80 (Robles Survey Site R-152) is one of two, closely associated noncompound settlements identified in the southwest portion of the Los Robles survey area. The site rests on a rocky alluvial fan that has eroded from a set of low volcanic hills located immediately to the north and west. A large wash dissects this fan, forming the northern boundary of the site. Its main features are an extensive but low density scatter of artifacts surrounding a concentration of artifacts that appears to represent a trash midden. These artifacts include pottery (sherds of plain ware, indeterminate red ware, and indeterminate red-on-buff), and chipped stone and ground stone fragments. A rockpile and rock-outlined terrace are a few meters west of this concentration, and two rockpiles were recorded about 150 m northeast. (Dating: Preclassic, phase unknown.)

AZ AA:11:84 (Robles Survey Site R-157) is on a rocky alluvial fan surface immediately northwest of AA:11:80. It is composed of an extensive scatter of plain ware and indeterminate red ware sherds, chipped stone debitage, a mano, and ground stone tool fragments surrounding two low depressions that may represent pit houses. (Dating: Unknown Hohokam.)

AZ AA:7:3 (Cake Ranch), a site in the northern end of the survey area, is evidently a large, early Classic period settlement. Unfortunately, the only information currently available is a general description on an ASM site card, completed in February, 1951 (authors of the site card were Edward B. Danson, Rex Gerald, and Jim Hall). A rough sketch map on this card indicated that the site extended over an area approximately 1.6 km by 0.4 km west of a building labeled "Cake Ranch." However, beyond two notations of sherds near the center and south portions of the site, surface features were not specified. The description indicated that "floods have evidently deposited alluvium on the site," and recent erosion had exposed "sherds . . . several feet down," so the estimated site area may have been based on the distribution of eroding sherds.

The ASM site card records that the owner of Cake Ranch remembered that "[Byron] Cummings dug here in [the] 30s," but no records have been located to document these operations. Surface collections in 1951 from three localities at the south end of the site produced a number of potsherds, including indeterminate red ware, smudged and polished brown ware, Gila Plain(?), indeterminate buff(?) ware, and Tanque Verde Red-on-brown. "Stone hoes, trough metates, and manos" were either observed or collected.

Carl Halbirt of Northland Research has recently conducted a pedestrian survey around Cake Ranch to better define the limits of this site and document its features. In a preliminary assessment, Halbirt communicated to me on 27 June 1989 that the Cake Ranch site was once an early Classic period settlement of considerable magnitude, consisting of widely scattered residential localities (with compound walls?) and trash areas spread for several hundred meters along the east bank of the Santa Cruz River. A forthcoming report by Halbirt on the CAP Distribution System archaeological investigations by Northland Research, Inc., will document the Cake Ranch site survey in some detail. (Dating: Sedentary-Early Classic; Early Classic.)

AZ AA:7:82 was originally recorded as site C-AZ-1, "The Los Robles Wash Site," by T. Reid Farmer of the Gilbert-Commonwealth Company during a powerline survey for the Western States Microwave system (Farmer 1984). At the time of its discovery, the site had been eroded just days before by the severe flooding of early October, 1983. Floodwaters had exposed two burned, adobe-walled pit houses (House A was 3 m by 5 m, and House B was 2 m by 4 m); two burials (one an unidentified canid without offerings, and one the extended remains of a woman, aged 25 to 35, also without offerings); and two "smears" of fire-reddened clay and charcoal flecks, possibly the remains of badly eroded houses. Limited surface collections from the vicinity of the two houses and features produced pottery (sherds of plain ware, Gila Red, indeterminate red ware, and Tanque Verde Red-on-brown), cores, and chipped stone flakes. Only a small portion of AZ AA:7:82 was revealed by the 1983 flood. Scattered surface artifacts and dense concentrations of artifacts eroding from the sides of rills and washes indicate that the exposed features are a small portion of a much more extensive settlement that is now covered by recent sediments. Artifact distributions suggest that this settlement may cover an area in excess of 21,000 square meters. (Dating: Early Classic.)

AZ AA:11:22 was originally recorded as Site TEP 625 by John P. Wilson during a Tucson Electric Power Company utility corridor survey (Wilson 1981). The site is on the west bank of Los Robles Wash just southeast of AZ AA:11:23 and about 0.7 km southeast of the Los Robles Mound. Wilson (1981: 39–45) recorded five artifact localities (designated A–E), each of which exhibited a low, gravelly trash mound containing mostly plain ware sherds along with a few red ware, red-on-brown, and red-on-buff sherds and pieces of lithic debitage. These artifact localities, spread over an area of about 130 m by 150 m, ranged in size from 210 to 340 square meters. Decorated sherds were relatively abundant at Localities B, D, and E, and two pieces of a "copper mineral" were observed at Locality C. "Small fragments of metamorphosed slate" were present at all five localities. These fragments are probably pieces of tabular andesite from the summit of Cerro Prieto and may represent debitage produced during the manufacture of tabular knives.

The low gravelly mounds containing trash deposits were thought by Wilson to represent natural topographic rises that had been used for refuse disposal. Thus, the site was interpreted as representing one or more "short term settlement(s)," seasonally occupied by farmers engaged in ak chin cultivation of nearby arroyo fans. Based on the presence of late Rincon Red-on-brown and Tanque Verde Red-on-brown sherds, Wilson (1981: 39) assigned the site an occupation span of A.D. 1150–1215. (Dating: Sedentary-Early Classic; Early Classic.)

Farmsteads
(Site Type 4; 10 sites)

Definition: Prehistoric site with a small, dense, varied trash deposit or other evidence of a small-scale habitation, such as a pit house depression or adobe or cobble-walled structure, in association with agricultural features.

Seven farmsteads (AZ AA:7:40, 41, 76, 89, 121, 124, and 128) are concentrated in the Cerro Prieto–Pan Quemado vicinity. AZ AA:7:146 is in the northwest portion of the survey area on the lower slopes of the Samaniego Hills, AZ AA:11:68 occurs on a bajada surface in the southwest portion, and AZ AA:11:21 is near the floodplain of Los Robles Wash just southeast of the large settlement AZ AA:11:23 (R–104).

Farmsteads tend to be small, averaging slightly more than 2,300 square meters; seven cover less than 2,500 square meters, and none exceeds 10,000 square meters. Although seven sites cluster in the Cerro Prieto and Pan Quemado area, farmsteads occur in a diversity of geomorphic and vegetational settings. Only one, AZ AA:11:21, occurs in a floodplain environment. With one exception (AZ AA:7:89), farmsteads are located within a short distance (usually only a few hundred meters, but never more than 1.5 km) from a prehistoric settlement.

AZ AA:7:76 (Robles Survey Site R–22) exhibits a scatter of pottery (plain ware, indeterminate red ware, Rincon Red, Gila Red, Papago Plain, and sherds resembling Whetstone Plain), chipped stone debitage, ground stone tool fragments, and shell jewelry fragments. Features are a rockpile, a rock ring, and an eroding roasting pit. Some limited pothunting was observed. A light scatter of historic trash has been superimposed over prehistoric features and artifacts. (Dating: Sedentary; Early Classic; Protohistoric-Early Historic; Late Historic.)

AZ AA:7:121 (Robles Survey Site R–30) consists of two distinct scatters of pottery (sherds of plain ware, indeterminate red ware, and indeterminate red-on-brown), chipped stone debitage, ground stone manufacturing debris, a metate fragment, and tabular knife fragments. Additional artifacts and features may be buried beneath a thin mantle of alluvial deposits. (Dating: Unknown Hohokam.)

AZ AA:7:124 (Robles Survey Site R–34) has a concentration of plain ware sherds, surrounded by a scatter of plain ware sherds, chipped stone debitage, tabular knife fragments, a mano fragment, and a possible palette fragment. (Dating: Unknown Hohokam.)

AZ AA:7:89 (Robles Survey Site R–38) includes an area cleared of rock in the west portion, an extensive artifact scatter immediately east, and a rockpile in the far east portion. A rock alignment is about 20 m southwest of the site. The cleared area is surrounded by plain ware sherds (representing multiple vessels); other artifacts include chipped stone debitage and tools, and a polishing pebble. (Dating: Unknown Hohokam.)

AZ AA:7:128 (Robles Survey Site R-39) has a rectangular structure (2.0 m by 2.5 m) outlined by basalt cobbles. The structure is surrounded by at least two rockpiles and an artifact scatter that includes plain ware and Tanque Verde Red-on-brown sherds. Several large pieces of tabular andesite, clustered just east of the structure, may represent the remains of a constructed feature, such as a slab-lined roasting or storage pit. (Dating: Early Classic.)

AZ AA:7:146 (Robles Survey Site R-58) has two artifact concentrations that may represent trash middens, an eroding roasting pit adjacent to one of the concentrations, and a cluster of tabular knife fragments. There is a light artifact scatter across the site. Artifacts include pottery (sherds of plain ware, indeterminate Rincon Red-on-brown or Tanque Verde Red-on-brown, Tanque Verde Red-on-brown, Rincon Red, and Sacaton Red-on-buff), ground stone tool fragments, and a piece of marine shell. (Dating: Sedentary through Early Classic.)

AZ AA:11:68 (Robles Survey Site R-107) has a dense concentration of sherds surrounding a feature recorded as a "possible field house." Just to the east are two rock concentrations, perhaps representing rockpiles. A light artifact scatter extends across the site, including pottery (sherds of plain ware, indeterminate red ware, Rincon Red, Salt Red, indeterminate Rincon Red-on-brown or Tanque Verde Red-on-brown, and Tanque Verde Red-on-brown), a broken quartzite hammerstone, chipped stone debitage, and a unifacially flaked tool. (Dating: Preclassic, phase unknown; Sedentary-Early Classic; Early Classic.)

AZ AA:7:40 was originally recorded during a 1980 TEP survey by John P. Wilson (Site TEP 592). It was not rerecorded by the Los Robles survey crews. According to Wilson (1980: 45), the site consisted of a single rectangular room (1.9 m by 3.0 m), constructed of uncoursed basalt boulders. No other site features were present, and no artifacts were observed. Wilson concluded that the site probably represented a "brief occupation . . . associated with the *trincheras* community at nearby AA:7:11 [Cerro Prieto]." (Dating: Unknown Hohokam.)

AZ AA:7:41 was originally recorded by Wilson (1980: 48-50) as Site TEP 593; it was not rerecorded during the Los Robles survey. Three localities, designated A, B, and C, were noted by Wilson. Locality A consisted of two basalt boulder rooms, one measuring 3 m by 4 m, and one 3.5 m by 4.5 m. Plain ware sherds were scattered north (downslope) of the structures. Locality B exhibited a stone circle 4.5 m in diameter and a few plain ware sherds. Locality C consisted of another stone circle, approximately 7 m in diameter, and a few plain ware sherds. Like TEP 592, Wilson interpreted this site as a briefly occupied settlement associated with the larger community at nearby Cerro Prieto (AZ AA:7:11). (Dating: Unknown Hohokam.)

AZ AA:11:21 was recorded during a 1981 TEP survey by Wilson (Site TEP 624) and was not rerecorded during the Los Robles Survey. The site had five spatial components, designated by Wilson (1981: 34-35) as Localities A-E. Of these, Localities A-D were sherd scatters; Locality E was described by Wilson (1981: 34) as "a low, flat gravelly rise of probable natural origin, 16 m in diameter, used as a refuse area." Artifacts observed at Localities A-E included pottery (sherds of plain ware, indeterminate red ware, possibly Snaketown Red-on-buff, Rincon Red-on-brown, Tanque Verde Red-on-brown, indeterminate buff ware, and indeterminate red-on-brown), chipped stone debitage, a stone pestle, a one-hand mano, and debitage described as "small fragments of metamorphosed slate." The last items probably are fragments of tabular andesite originating from the summit of Cerro Prieto.

Considering the features and artifacts at the site and its position near small washes that empty onto alluvial fans on the west bank of Los Robles Wash, Wilson (1981: 34) concluded that the site probably had served as a "short term settlement(s) of seasonal agriculturalists with *ak chin* fields in [the] nearby alluvial fan." (Dating: Late Pioneer; Sedentary-Early Classic; Early Classic.)

Agricultural Fields
(Site Type 5; 17 sites)

Definition: Prehistoric site with rockpiles, rock alignments, check dams, and other features and artifacts such as hoes or tabular knives (suitable for harvesting and processing agave leaves) that indicate the site area was used principally for growing crops. These crops would have included traditional Native American domesticates such as corn, beans, squash, and cotton, but, in addition, it is likely other plants such as amaranth and agave were cultivated in some fields as well.

Probably because of the high visibility of rock features, all agricultural fields so far identified are located in or immediately adjacent to the Samaniego Hills where there is a stable ground surface and an abundance of cobbles and boulders. Certainly these were not the only agricultural fields used by the prehistoric inhabitants of the survey area, but the ephemeral nature of the fields themselves and site visibility problems hamper our ability to recognize prehistoric fields in other environmental zones. Additional methods of site discovery, for example aerial photography, subsurface testing, soil chemistry assays, and pollen analysis would be required to define field locations in these zones. Nine sites are concentrated on the rocky, dissected alluvial fan immediately north and northeast of Cerro Prieto (AZ AA:7:116, 118, 122, 135, 447-451); one site is located at the south end of Cerro Prieto (AA:7:109); one site is on the east slope of Pan Quemado (AA:7:125); and six sites are located on the west side of the Samaniego Hills (AZ AA:7:148, 154, 155, 174, 175, and 178).

AZ AA:7:109 (Robles Survey Site R-8) consists of a set of rock alignments, a large cleared area, and a scatter of chipped stone debitage on a low ridge just south of Cerro Prieto (Fig. 3.8). The rock alignments are arranged into a grid pattern that may represent a "waffle garden" used for the cultivation of crops. The large cleared area may also be an agricultural modification. (Dating: None assigned, presumed prehistoric.)

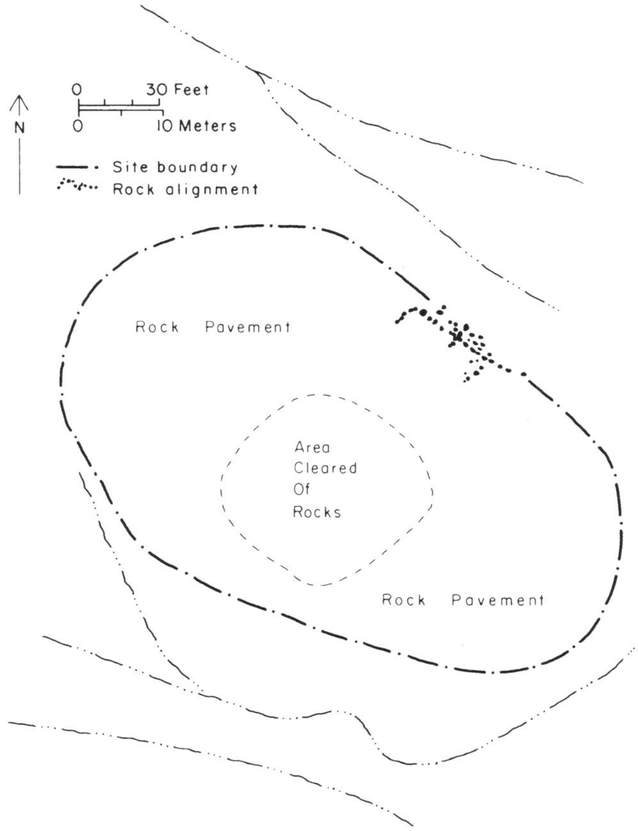

Figure 3.8. Plan of AZ AA:7:109 (Site R-8), an agricultural field site.

AZ AA:7:116 (Robles Survey Site R-25) includes three rockpiles, spread over an area of about 20 m by 40 m. The rockpiles consist of a small (1.5 m to 2.0 m in diameter) accumulation of cobbles, piled 15 cm to 20 cm high. There was no evidence that the rocks were fire cracked, and no stained soil was associated with them. A few plain ware sherds were scattered across the southeast portion of the site. (Dating: Unknown Hohokam.)

AZ AA:7:118 (Robles Survey Site R-27) exhibits eight rockpiles atop a low ridge between two small washes. The rockpiles, ranging in size from 1 m to 6 m in diameter, are arranged in a rough line that parallels the course of the washes. A few plain ware sherds were on the surface of the largest rockpile. (Dating: Unknown Hohokam.)

AZ AA:7:122 (Robles Survey Site R-31) has a number of rock features, including at least 4 rockpiles, 10 rock alignments, and 10 stone circles, all spread over an area about 75 m by 150 m on a rocky surface immediately north of Pan Quemado. A large wash forms the north boundary of the site. A few concentrations of artifacts were noted, and there was a light to moderate artifact scatter across the site area. Artifacts include pottery (plain ware, indeterminate red ware, Salt Red, and sherds resembling Whetstone Plain), chipped stone debitage, and ground stone tool fragments. (Dating: Early Classic; Protohistoric-Early Historic.)

AZ AA:7:125 (Robles Survey Site R-35) consists of a scatter of plain ware and Whetstone Plain(?) sherds, hammerstones, a mano fragment, one piece of debris from ground stone manufacture, and a single rockpile on a low, dissected ridge between the east slope of Pan Quemado and Los Robles Wash. (Dating: Unknown Hohokam; Protohistoric-Early Historic.)

AZ AA:7:135 (Robles Survey Site R-46) includes at least five rockpiles, a concentration of pottery (sherds of plain ware, indeterminate red ware, and indeterminate red-on-brown) and chipped stone debitage, and a prehistoric trail, formed by clearing a path through the desert pavement surface. Three of the rockpiles are associated with small, slight concentrations of artifacts. The site is on a flat, rocky, northeast-to-southwest trending ridge that is bounded by two large washes. (Dating: Unknown Hohokam.)

AZ AA:7:148 (Robles Survey Site R-60) consists of a small rockpile (85 cm in diameter) and a crude metate about 10 m west. (Dating: None assigned, presumed prehistoric.)

AZ AA:7:154 (Robles Survey Site R-66) includes nine rock concentrations, a concentration of chipped stone debitage, and a boulder with a bedrock mortar. The site is on a flat, dissected alluvial fan just south of a rock ridge and west of a large wash. Four of the rock concentrations appear to consist of fire-cracked stones and may represent eroding roasting pits. The remaining five, however, appear to be agricultural features, and two are in a small gully. A few plain ware sherds were scattered across the site. (Dating: Unknown Hohokam.)

AZ AA:7:155 (Robles Survey Site R-67) has a rock alignment that appears to represent a terrace, a concentration of pottery (sherds of plain ware, indeterminate red-on-brown, and indeterminate red-on-buff), chipped stone debitage, hammerstones, cores, and an isolated tabular knife. A few artifacts were scattered between and beyond these features. The site is on a silty alluvial fan just east of a talus slope eroded from a nearby volcanic hill, and north of a wash channel. The site recorders thought that the terrace may have been constructed to trap sheetflow runoff from the nearby hill. (Dating: Unknown Hohokam.)

AZ AA:7:174 (Robles Survey Site R-90) consists of at least 11 rockpiles, spread over an area of about 48 m by 125 m, surrounded by a scatter of chipped stone debitage. A single plain ware sherd was recovered. The site is on a dissected, rocky slope on the west side of the Samaniego Hills. (Dating: Unknown Hohokam.)

AZ AA:7:175 (Robles Survey Site R-91) has a rockpile approximately 1 m in diameter and a small rock ring with a 60-cm interior diameter. A single flake was the only artifact. The site is on a rocky surface between two small washes, about 100 m south of a low volcanic hill. (Dating: None assigned, presumed prehistoric.)

AZ AA:7:178 (Robles Survey Site R-94) has two small rockpiles approximately 1 m in diameter and 40 m apart. One of the rockpiles is surrounded by a light scatter of plain ware sherds and chipped stone debitage. The site is on a flat, gravelly surface between two small washes. (Dating: Unknown Hohokam.)

AZ AA:7:447 through 451 (Robles Survey Sites R-201 through R-205) are five similar and closely associated concentrations of rockpiles on the dissected, gravelly, alluvial fan surface just north of Cerro Prieto. The exact number of rockpiles at each of the sites was not ascertained. Rather, site boundaries were determined from a generalized plot of rockpiles on aerial photographs. No remains were reported from any of the sites, but the distributions of isolated artifacts around them suggest that a more detailed inspection would disclose more cultural evidence. (Dating: Unknown Hohokam.)

Trincheras Feature Sites
(Site Type 6; 11 sites)

Definition: Hillside site that exhibits prehistoric rock constructions, including terraces; circular, ovoid, and rectangular structure foundations; rock-lined pits ("talus pits"); boulder walls of unknown function; rock-walled compounds; trails; and petroglyphs (Stacy 1974: 1, 1977: 11). *Although exhibiting individual "trincheras" features, these sites are not necessarily* cerros de trincheras, *which are specialized sites confined to southern Arizona and northern Sonora that have substantial terraces on one or more slopes* (see Chapters 4 and 6).

Because these sites are defined on the basis of hillside rock features, they are always found on the slopes of volcanic hills, usually on the north or east sides. Four such sites are on the slopes of unnamed hills at the far northwest end of the survey area (AZ AA:7:158, 159, 187, 188). Sites AA:7:43, Loci 1 and 2 are on the slopes of Pan Quemado Ridge (Fig. 3.9), and AA:11:83 and 94 are on the sides of isolated volcanic hills near the center of the survey area. Site AZ AA:7:164 is on the west slope of a large volcanic hill in the west-central portion of the survey area, and AA:7:140 is about midway between Cerro Prieto and the group of sites in the northwest corner of the survey area. By far the largest and most complex trincheras site in the survey area is Cerro Prieto (AZ AA:7:11), a true *cerro de trincheras* located on the summit and north and east slopes of a volcanic mass named Cerro Prieto, at the northeast end of the Samaniego Hills. Chapter 4 describes the Cerro Prieto Site and Chapter 5 provides the results of field investigations at three additional trincheras feature sites consisting of open talus pits (AA:7:158, 187, and 188).

AZ AA:7:43, Locus 1 (Robles Survey Site R-48) consists primarily of a cluster of petroglyphs surrounded by at least nine talus pits on the northeast slope of a volcanic ridge just east of Pan Quemado, designated here as Pan Quemado Ridge (Fig. 3.9). Numerous pothunter holes were observed on the flat alluvial surface east and northeast of the Pan Quemado slope. It is presumed that these holes represent vandalized subterranean structures. (Dating: Sedentary-Early Classic.)

AZ AA:7:140 (Robles Survey Site R-52) is located on the northeast slope of a low volcanic hill just northwest of the abandoned town of Sasco. The main features are

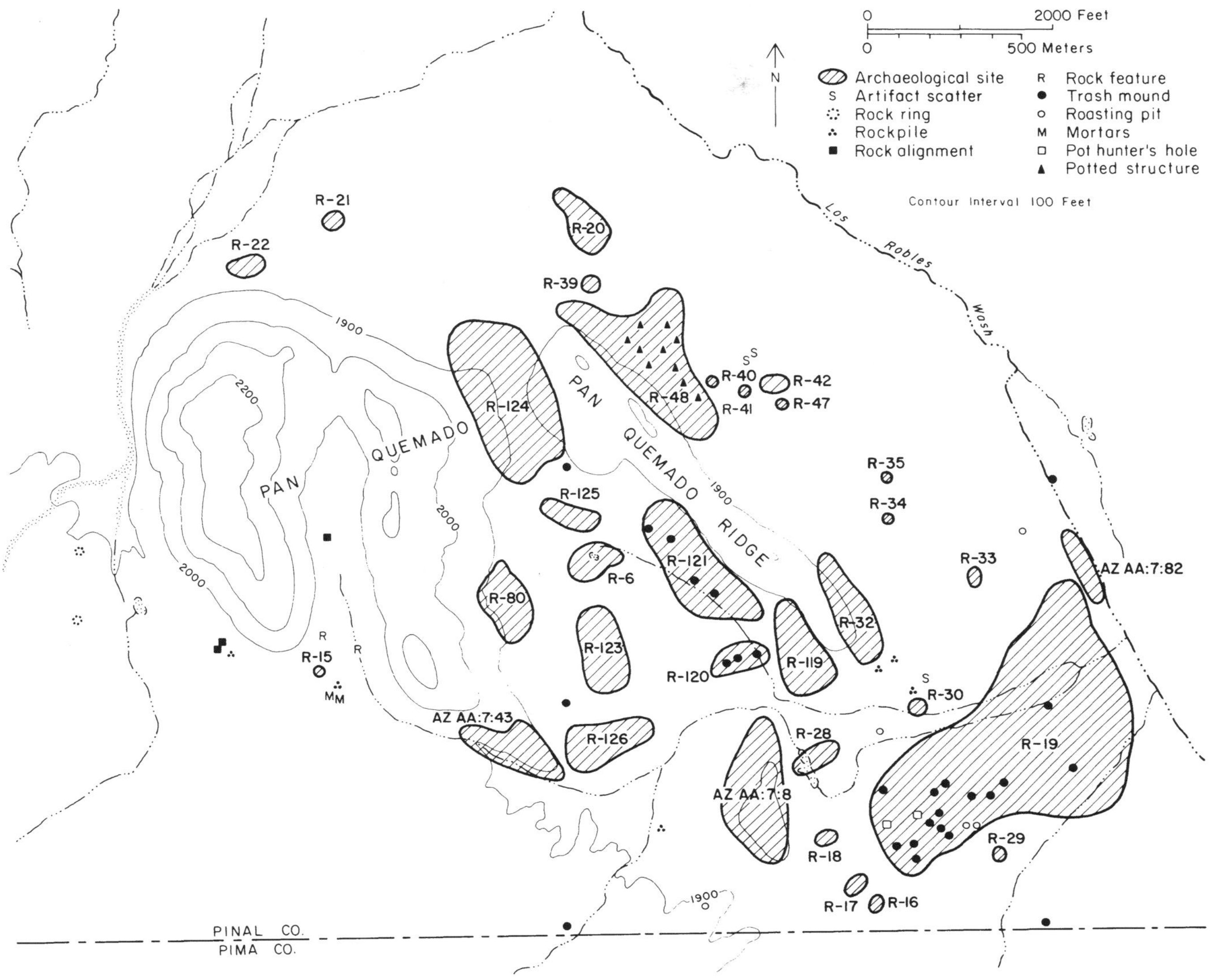

Figure 3.9. Area map of sites, features, and artifacts in the vicinity of Pan Quemado, including the Inscription Hill Site (AZ AA:7:8).

two stacked boulder retaining walls that enclose natural surfaces on the talus of the hill slope. The lower retaining wall is straight and about 40 m long; the upper one, 12 m west, is arc-shaped and encloses an area approximately 4 m by 9 m. A bedrock outcrop slightly farther upslope exhibits two petroglyphs: two concentric circles surrounding a dot, and an anthropomorph. Plain ware and Whetstone Plain(?) sherds were observed on the surfaces of the platforms and wedged between boulders. (Dating: Unknown Hohokam; Protohistoric-Early Historic.)

AZ AA:7:158 (Robles Survey Site R-70) consists of 38 open pits dug into steeply sloping talus deposits on the north side of a low volcanic hill in the northwest portion of the survey area. The pits, easily seen against a background of darkly patinated talus boulders, range in size from 1.5 m to 1.75 m in diameter and are approximately 1 m deep. Several of the pits contained sherds of an uncommon ceramic type, evidently of protohistoric or early historic period date. Madsen provides further information on this site's features and artifacts in Chapter 5. (Dating: Protohistoric-Early Historic.)

AZ AA:7:159 (Robles Survey Site R-71) is closely similar to AA:7:158. It consists of about six pits excavated into the steeply sloping talus of the northeast tip of a low volcanic hill in the northwest portion of the survey area. Approximately one-half of a ceramic vessel, of the same uncommon ceramic type found at AA:7:158, was discovered in one of the pits. (Dating: Protohistoric-Early Historic; Late Historic.)

AZ AA:7:164 (Robles Survey Site R-76), located on the west slope of a low volcanic hill in the northwest part of the survey area, was described by survey crew members as a large pile of cobbles and boulders heaped on the downslope side of two large (2 m to 3 m in height), adjacent boulders. The rockpile covered an area approximately 2 m by 3 m and stood about 75 cm high. Two small depressions had been excavated into the rockpile, one about 75 cm in diameter and 15 cm deep, the other about 1 m in diameter and 50 cm deep. No artifacts were found associated with this unusual feature. (Dating: None assigned.)

AZ AA:7:187 (Robles Survey Site R-83) consists of 56 open pits excavated into a talus slope on the north side of a hill in the northwest portion of the survey area. The pits were from 0.5 m to 2.0 m in diameter and 0.10 m to 1.97 m deep. At least six of the pits contained large sherds of apparently protohistoric or historic period pottery vessels. All the pits appeared to have been vandalized, probably a considerable time ago. Limited test excavations were conducted at the site and are described by Madsen in Chapter 5. (Dating: Protohistoric-Early Historic.)

AZ AA:7:188 (Robles Survey Site R-84) is similar in appearance to AA:7:187. It consists of 15 open pits dug into a steep talus slope on the north side of a hill in the northwest part of the survey area, only a few hundred meters east of AA:7:187. The pits ranged in size from 1.0 m to 3.0 m in diameter and were from 0.5 m to 1.0 m deep. All appeared to have been vandalized, and none contained artifacts. Additional information on this site is provided by Madsen in Chapter 5. (Dating: None assigned; based on similarity with AA:7:187, the site is presumed to be Protohistoric-Early Historic.)

AZ AA:7:43, Locus 2 (Robles Survey Site R-124) exhibits numerous stone features and petroglyphs surrounded by a scatter of sherds and chipped stone debitage. The site is in a saddle between Pan Quemado and Pan Quemado Ridge (Fig. 3.9). Features include at least four clusters of petroglyphs, three rock-outlined structure foundations, three talus pits, and a 10-m-diameter stone circle or spiral at the south end of the site. In the saddle between the east slope of Pan Quemado and Pan Quemado Ridge, there is a rock-outlined trail that begins midway through the saddle and continues for about 300 m to the northwest, toward Cerro Prieto. Two short trails branch from near the midpoint of the main trail and lead northeast for 100 m to 150 m. (Dating: None assigned, presumed Hohokam based on petroglyph designs.)

AZ AA:11:83 (Robles Survey Site R-142) consists of a series of pits excavated into a talus slope on the north side of an isolated hill at the south end of the Samaniego Hills. Three of the pits contained sherds that appear to be from protohistoric or early historic Pima ceramic vessels (Chapter 5). The east face of the hill exhibits numerous petroglyphs, and clusters of vesicular basalt debitage, probably from the manufacture of ground stone tools, were observed around the perimeter of the hill. (Dating: Protohistoric-Early Historic.)

AZ AA:11:94 (Robles Survey Site R-206) consists of a long boulder wall and other rock features on the east slopes of an isolated hill at the southeast end of the Samaniego Hills, near the center of the survey area. The main feature is a low, intermittent, meandering boulder wall that begins at the base of the east side of the hill and continues for several dozen meters upslope. The wall terminates at a walled terrace or built-up platform about two-thirds of the way to the hill summit. Just below the summit of the hill there is a small, circular foundation that may represent the remains of a rock-outlined structure. A few artifacts were observed, including plain ware sherds, ground stone debitage, and chipped stone debitage. (Dating: Unknown Hohokam.)

AZ AA:7:11, the Cerro Prieto Site, is a large, complex trincheras village (*cerro de trincheras*) with more than 250 masonry rooms and numerous stone compounds, terraces, walls, and other features. A detailed description of the site is in Chapter 4. (Dating: Early Classic.)

Water Diversion Feature
(Site Type 7; 1 site)

Definition: Prehistoric canal, canal-related feature, diversion ditch, or other evidence of devices constructed to divert water from streams, seasonal washes, hill slopes, or other drainages and watersheds.

Although other sites (for example, Cerro Prieto) exhibit stone walls and features that appear to have been used for the diversion of runoff, AZ AA:7:186 is the only site composed entirely of such features.

AZ AA:7:186 (Robles Survey Site R-82) is a set of stone walls that may have been constructed to divert slopewash from the lower portion of a small, volcanic hill onto the bajada slopes immediately below. If so, the purpose of these constructions may have been agricultural: to increase and direct the runoff from the hill slopes onto the bajada surface where crops could have been grown. (Dating: None assigned, presumed prehistoric.)

Petroglyph Sites
(Site Type 8; 10 sites)

Definition: Prehistoric site with pecked designs on rock outcrops or boulders as its preponderant feature. Such sites sometimes contain artifact scatters and other features.

The presence of petroglyphs is not a sufficient basis for assigning a site to this category. Some sites with numerous petroglyphs (for example, Cerro Prieto) are assigned to another site category based on other kinds of features that dominate the site surface.

There is a wide range of variation in the number and complexity of petroglyphs, ranging from only a handful of simple examples (AZ AA:7:13, 136, 139, 181), to several dozen elements (AZ AA:7:442), to hundreds of individual petroglyphs, some of which are quite complex (AZ AA:7:8, 43, 446). Sites AZ AA:7:43 and 136 are on or near the slopes of Pan Quemado; Site AZ AA:7:8 (Inscription Hill) is spread over the slopes of a small volcanic hill immediately south of Pan Quemado; Sites AZ AA:7:442 and 446 are at the south end of Cerro Prieto; Site AZ AA:11:81 is located near the center of the survey area; Site AZ AA:11:77 is on a rocky slope in the south central part of the survey area; and Sites AZ AA:7:13, 139, and 181 are scattered across the low volcanic hills at the western edge of the survey area.

AZ AA:7:442 (Robles Survey Site R-7) is a bedrock outcrop with an estimated 80 petroglyphs composed of a variety of zoomorphic and geometric figures, including lizard, sheep, dog(?), centipede, and scorpion forms. An artifact concentration extends northeast of the petroglyph area; it includes plain ware sherds, ground stone, and abundant chipped stone debitage. (Dating: Unknown Hohokam.)

AZ AA:7:136 (Robles Survey Site R-47) has only a single boulder containing four petroglyphs (reported as three spirals and a zoomorph, possibly a lizard), and an eroding, rock-filled hearth about 16 m west. A few isolated artifacts were noted in the general vicinity, but their association with site features is dubious. (Dating: None assigned, presumed prehistoric.)

AZ AA:7:139 (Robles Survey Site R-51) exhibits two anthropomorphic stick figures on a bedrock outcrop (approximately 20 m by 20 m) at the summit of a low hill about 2 km southeast of Cerro Prieto. No artifacts were observed. (Dating: None assigned, presumed prehistoric.)

AZ AA:7:181 (Robles Survey Site R-98) is located on the boulder-strewn slope of a hill in the west-central portion of the survey area. Major features are four boulders with petroglyphs and a set of parallel rock alignments, approximately 10 m long, that evidently represent a trail segment created by clearing boulders from the hill slope. Two of the petroglyph-bearing boulders are associated with the trail segment; one is located about 30 m northeast of the north end of the trail, and the remaining boulder is located about 15 m south of the trail's south end. The petroglyphs include a spiral; a single, straight line; a complicated set of meandering lines that form a "reticulate" pattern (Ferg 1979: 100, 103); and a sinuous line that terminates in a small oval, evidently representing a snake's head. Artifacts include chipped stone debitage and two crude ground stone tools, perhaps a mano and metate. (Dating: None assigned, presumed prehistoric.)

AZ AA:11:77 (Robles Survey Site R-135) consists of at least one hundred petroglyphs on a rocky knoll just southwest of "Red Hill," in the south-central portion of the survey area. The petroglyphs are pecked onto boulders on the upper south side of the knoll. No artifacts were observed. (Dating: None assigned, presumed prehistoric.)

AZ AA:11:81 (Robles Survey Site R-153) consists of an unspecified number of petroglyphs adjacent to a large wash near the center of the survey area. Petroglyphs are the only archaeological features recorded, and no artifacts are reported. (Dating: None assigned, presumed prehistoric.)

AZ AA:7:446 (Robles Survey Site R-200) is a substantial collection of petroglyphs (perhaps over 200 elements) pecked onto boulders and bedrock outcrops at the south tip of Cerro Prieto, where a large wash clips the end of the mountain. Petroglyphs include a wide range of zoomorphic and geometric forms, but no systematic inventory has yet been made. The site has experienced some vandalism, including a large pothunter hole dug beneath a large boulder at the hill base. A few plain ware sherds and chipped stone tools were observed on the ground surface below the petroglyphs. (Dating: Early Classic, based on petroglyph design elements.)

Figure 3.10. View looking west over a petroglyph cluster at the summit of the south end of the Inscription Hill Site (AZ AA:7:8 ASM). The Samaniego Hills are visible in the near background, with Ragged Top Peak and the Silverbell Mountains farther west. (ASM photograph 69726, by Helga G. Teiwes.)

AZ AA:7:8 (Inscription Hill) is the largest and most impressive concentration of petroglyphs in the survey area, and probably one of the densest groupings of petroglyphs in southern Arizona. Unfortunately, the site has never been adequately mapped or recorded. On the basis of a limited survey and recording effort, Wallace and Holmlund (1986: 211, and in personal conversation with me) have indicated the presence of at least 1,225 individual petroglyphs, as well as numerous bedrock metates, small trail segments, talus pits, and other trincheras features.

Inscription Hill is named for a low volcanic hill just south of Pan Quemado Ridge. It is strewn with large and small boulders covered with a black patina that provides an excellent medium for petroglyphs (Fig. 3.10). Most petroglyphs are concentrated on boulders at the summit and on the lower slopes near the south end of the hill. These petroglyphs are mostly prehistoric (Figs. 3.10,

Figure 3.11. Unusual petroglyph at the summit of the south end of the Inscription Hill Site. (ASM photograph 69729, by Helga G. Teiwes.)

Figure 3.12. Petroglyph, possibly historic (scratched cross), at the summit of the south end of the Inscription Hill Site. (ASM photograph 69730, by Helga G. Teiwes.)

Figure 3.13. Unusual zoomorphic petroglyph at the base of the north end of the Inscription Hill Site. (ASM photograph 69689, by Helga G. Teiwes.)

3.11), but a few possibly historic glyphs (some of which are scratched designs; Ferg 1979: 97-99) were also observed (Fig. 3.12). Other significant clusters of glyphs occur along the east slope and at the north end (Fig. 3.13), and isolated petroglyphs may be seen on boulders and small outcrops at various locations around the hill base. Along the west side of the hill, there are numerous check dams, rock alignments, and other features designed to slow and direct runoff from a small wash (Fig. 3.14). On the east side of the hill there is a wide, well-preserved trail that leads to the summit (Fig. 3.15). The trail was formed by clearing boulders and loose talus down to bedrock and caliche, then stacking the rocks on either side. The trail leads to a cleared area and several rock circles in the midst of the dense cluster of petroglyphs at the hill summit. Artifacts at the site include pottery (sherds of plain ware, indeterminate buff ware, and Tanque Verde Red-on-brown) and chipped stone debitage. (Dating: Preclassic, phase unknown; Early Classic; Protohistoric-Early Historic.)

AZ AA:7:13, recorded in April 1965 by author Stan Jones, is described on an ASM site card only as a petroglyph site covering an area 25 m by 25 m. Petroglyphs are reported as "mazes, scrolls, animal figures, and human figures." Two projectile points and an unspecified number of plain ware sherds were recovered. The site

Figure 3.14. Rock alignment, probably a check dam, across a small drainage on the west side of the Inscription Hill Site. (ASM photograph 69700, by Helga G. Teiwes.)

was not revisited by the Robles survey crew. (Dating: Unknown Hohokam.)

AA:7:43, Locus 12, is the second largest petroglyph locality in the survey area. According to Wallace and Holmlund, the site has a substantial number of petroglyphs (at least 600 elements in three loci) surrounded by numerous rock features, including talus pits, hillside terraces, and trails. One well-constructed trail passes through an area of talus at the southern tip of the east side of Pan Quemado. Another, located about 150 m northeast, leads upslope from a large wash to a set of hillside talus pits and terraces. A particularly intriguing aspect of this site is the presence of what may be Archaic-age petroglyphs, a number of geometric, heavily patinated elements (Fig. 3.16) that occur side-by-side with less patinated elements of more typical Hohokam form. (Dating: Unknown Hohokam.)

Limited Activity Plant or Animal Food Processing Sites
(Site Type 9; 37 sites)

Definition: Prehistoric site with a small artifact inventory, a lack of architectural remains, a lack of significant trash accumulations indicative of habitation, and the presence of roasting pits, rock rings, tabular knives, bedrock mortars or metates, portable ground stone tools, or other features or artifacts useful for food collecting or processing activities.

These sites show a wide range of variability in size, artifacts, and feature content. It is presumed, but by no means established, that most of the limited activity sites

Figure 3.15. Trail on the southeast slope of the Inscription Hill Site, leading to a cluster of petroglyphs at the hill summit, south end. (ASM photograph 86832, by Henry D. Wallace.)

identified by the Los Robles survey crew were affiliated with nearby settlements of Hohokam age. Some, however, may be Archaic, and some may represent places on the landscape repeatedly exploited over a long period of time, including the protohistoric and historic periods. Additional research is needed to sort temporal and functional variability for this site category, and to assess the role of such sites in the local subsistence system and economy. Fifteen of these sites, illustrative of the range of variability within the category, are described.

AZ AA:11:44 (Robles Survey Site R-2) consists of three areas of stained soil, exposed by three washes, and an associated concentration of chipped stone debitage, ground stone tool fragments, and plain ware sherds. The stained areas apparently represent recently eroded features, perhaps hearths. The site is on a gently sloping, sandy surface on the east bank of Los Robles Wash. (Dating: Unknown Hohokam.)

AZ AA:7:111 (Robles Survey Site R-15), at the south tip of the westernmost ridge of Pan Quemado, consists of a scatter of fire-cracked vesicular basalt cobbles and four nearby plain ware sherds. The cobbles may be the remains of an eroded roasting pit or hearth. (Dating: Unknown Hohokam.)

AZ AA:7:112 (Robles Survey Site R-16) is on a gravelly, dissected alluvial fan surface just southeast of the Inscription Hill petroglyph site. It consists of a scatter of dispersed fire-cracked rock and a concentration of plain ware sherds and chipped stone debitage. (Dating: Unknown Hohokam.)

Figure 3.16. Heavily patinated geometric petroglyphs, possibly Archaic in age, at Site AZ AA:7:43. (ASM photograph 86833, by Henry D. Wallace.)

AZ AA:7:113 (Robles Survey Site R-20) is located near the floodplain of Los Robles Wash, about 150 m northeast of Pan Quemado Ridge. An eastern boundary is provided by a dense mesquite thicket that grows in the floodplain of Los Robles Wash. Remaining site boundaries are difficult to define, but are based on the outlines of an extremely light scatter of artifacts, including pottery (sherds of plain ware and indeterminate red ware), chipped stone debitage, tabular knife fragments, and ground stone tool fragments. These items are occasionally clustered into small concentrations. (Dating: Unknown Hohokam.)

AZ AA:7:114 (Robles Survey Site R-23) is a light to moderately dense concentration of artifacts, with pottery (sherds of plain ware, indeterminate Preclassic red-on-buff, and Tanque Verde Red-on-brown), chipped stone debitage, and a hammerstone. A few fragments of fire-cracked rock were noted along the south boundary of the site. (Dating: Preclassic, phase unknown; Early Classic.)

AZ AA:7:119 (Robles Survey Site R-28), which is adjacent to the northeast end of Inscription Hill, is a concentration of plain ware and indeterminate red-on-buff sherds, surrounding an eroding, rock-filled roasting pit. One fragment of an unidentified ground stone tool was present. (Dating: Unknown Hohokam.)

AZ AA:7:120 (Robles Survey Site R-29) is a small artifact concentration along a small gully that drains into a larger wash to the south. Artifacts include plain ware, indeterminate red-on-buff sherds, and chipped stone debitage. A few pieces of fire-cracked rock were also observed. The site is just south of AZ AA:7:9, a large, noncompound settlement east of Inscription Hill. (Dating: Unknown Hohokam.)

AZ AA:7:43, Locus 10 (Robles Survey Site R-32) is located along the southeast end of Pan Quemado Ridge. It is composed of a concentration of pottery (sherds of plain ware, Gila Red, and Salt Red), chipped stone debitage, hammerstones, and ground stone tool fragments, surrounding a number of rock features, including a rock ring, three rock-filled roasting pits, and at least four rockpiles that may have served an agricultural function. There is a group of petroglyphs and at least three talus pits on a volcanic hill slope immediately west. (Dating: Early Classic.)

AZ AA:7:127 (Robles Survey Site R-37) is on a flat, sand- and gravel-covered alluvial fan surface several hundred meters west of Los Robles Wash, and about 1 km north of Pan Quemado. It consists of a scatter of fire-cracked rock, evidently an eroded roasting pit, and two small, plain ware sherds. (Dating: Unknown Hohokam.)

AZ AA:7:132 (Robles Survey Site R-43) includes a V-shaped rock alignment near the site center, and a small rock circle about 18 m to the west. These features are surrounded by a scatter of plain ware sherds. The site is on a rocky surface southwest of a small volcanic hill south of Cerro Prieto. (Dating: Unknown Hohokam.)

AZ AA:7:133 (Robles Survey Site R-44) is composed of a 2-m-diameter pile of fist-sized cobbles and a few plain ware sherds, located about 15 m southwest. Some of the rocks in the pile appeared to have been fire cracked, so the feature may represent an eroded hearth. The site is located a few meters northeast of AZ AA:7:132. (Dating: Unknown Hohokam.)

AZ AA:7:153 (Robles Survey Site R-65) is a roasting pit (Fig. 3.17) surrounded by two broadly spaced areas of pottery (sherds of plain ware and indeterminate red ware), ground stone tools and tool fragments, agave knives, chipped stone debitage, and hammerstones. Near the center of the site is a cluster of fire-cracked rock and plain ware sherds that represent the remains of a roasting pit and its associated artifacts. The site is on a low ridge formed by the intersection of two small washes. Three rockpiles, which may be either agricultural field features or eroding roasting pits, are at the east end of the site. (Dating: Unknown Hohokam.)

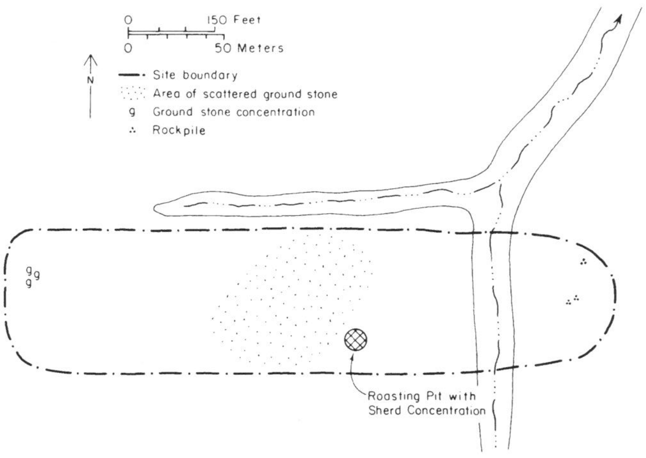

Figure 3.17. Plan of AZ AA:7:153, a resource processing site.

AZ AA:7:43, Locus 8 (Robles Survey Site R-120) consists of three eroding, rock-filled roasting pits and a 5-m-by-12-m cluster of basalt boulders surrounded by a scatter of plain ware sherds and chipped stone debitage. The possible function of the boulder cluster is unknown. (Dating: Unknown Hohokam.)

AZ AA:7:43, Locus 6 (Robles Survey Site R-121) includes four widely separated eroding, rock-filled roasting pits, surrounded by a light scatter of plain ware sherds, chipped stone debitage, ground stone tool fragments, and two hammerstones. (Dating: Unknown Hohokam.)

AZ AA:7:43, Locus 3 (Robles Survey Site R-125) has three eroding, rock-filled hearths surrounded by a light scatter of plain ware sherds, chipped stone debitage, and ground stone tool fragments. The hearths are about 1.0 m to 1.5 m in diameter and show dense clusters of fire-cracked rock eroding from a matrix of dark gray soil. (Dating: Unknown Hohokam.)

Rock Shelters

(Site Type 10; 4 sites)

Definition: Prehistoric site with artifacts, smoke-blackened ceilings, or other evidence of prehistoric use in a specific topographic location such as a cleft, opening, or other natural shelter on the side of a hill, canyon, or mesa.

Activities within rock shelters were probably highly variable, but it is likely the shelters were used for camping, short term habitation, and storage in association with seasonal agricultural or resource gathering expeditions. The four rock shelter sites were located on the sides of low volcanic hills in the west portion of the survey area.

AZ AA:7:134 (Robles Survey Site R-45) is a small rock shelter in the south face of a small volcanic hill about 2 km west of Cerro Prieto. The shelter is formed by a small retaining wall built along the southeast edge of a natural cliff opening (Fig. 3.18). Artifacts include pottery (plain ware, indeterminate red ware, Rincon Red,

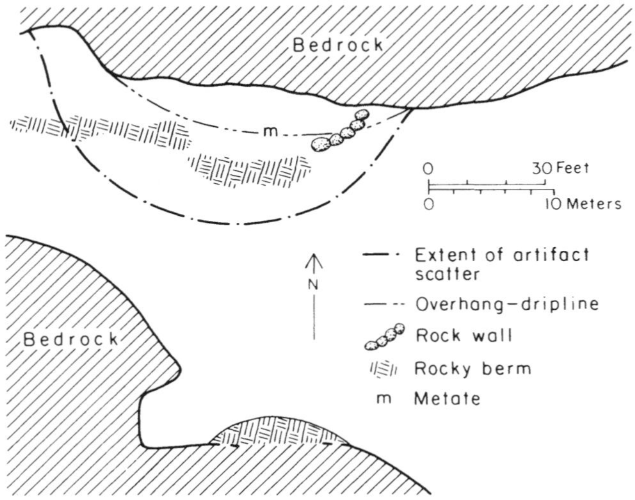

Figure 3.18. Plan (*top*) and profile of AZ AA:7:134 (Site R-45), a rock shelter in the Samaniego Hills.

and sherds resembling Whetstone Plain), chipped stone debitage, a biface, and a metate fragment. Part of the roof of the shelter has collapsed, sealing and protecting the deposits beneath. The shelter itself measures approximately 4 m by 10 m, with artifacts extending over an area of about 12 m by 26 m. (Dating: Sedentary; Protohistoric-Early Historic.)

AZ AA:7:163 (Robles Survey Site R-75) consists of a small (approximately 3 m by 15 m), south-facing rock overhang with a small scatter of plain ware sherds and a few large pieces of tabular andesite. The overhang is in a bedrock outcrop just above a steep talus slope on the southwest side of a volcanic hill. It is possible that slough from the top of the overhang is obscuring additional artifacts and features. (Dating: Unknown Hohokam.)

AZ AA:7:171 (Robles Survey Site R-87) is a small recess, approximately 6 m by 19 m, in the bedrock of a small hill about 2 km west of Cerro Prieto. The bottom of the shelter is flat; toward the back, there is a packrat nest of cholla cactus buds, and the floor of the shelter is covered by soft soil that appears to have been mounded by rodent activity. Some pottery (plain ware, indeterminate red-on-buff, sherds resembling Whetstone Plain, and Papago Plain) and a few pieces of chipped stone debitage were collected within the shelter and on the talus slope below. (Dating: Unknown Hohokam; Protohistoric-Early Historic.)

AZ AA:7:14, recorded by author Stan Jones in April, 1965, is described on an ASM site card as a "cave" site. It is located on the southwest side of a small hill just northwest of Cerro Prieto. Numerous artifact types are reported from the site, including Gila Plain and plain smudged sherds, a metate fragment, a mano, a chert scraper, "small waste flakes" (presumably, chipped stone debitage), and a "large stone chopping or digging tool," collected and assigned ASM catalog number A-24,942. The site was not visited by Robles survey crews. (Dating: Unknown Hohokam.)

Reservoir

(Site Type 11; 1 site)

Definition: Prehistoric site with a construction designed to capture and store seasonal rainfall for extended periods of time.

AZ AA:7:43, Locus 4 (Robles Survey Site R-6) is located near the center of a broad expanse of sandy sediments stretching between the east side of Pan Quemado and Pan Quemado Ridge (Fig. 3.9). A reservoir and surrounding berm were apparently constructed to contain the water captured within a natural topographic low point (Figs. 3.19, 3.20). The reservoir receives runoff from two small drainages that flow into it from the north. Some historic reinforcement of the berms may have occurred, but an abundance of prehistoric artifacts, including pottery (sherds of plain ware, Gila Red, indeterminate Sacaton Red-on-buff or Casa Grande Red-on-buff, and Sacaton Red-on-buff), chipped stone debitage, ground stone tool fragments, cores, hammerstones, and tabular knives indicate that it was initially a prehistoric

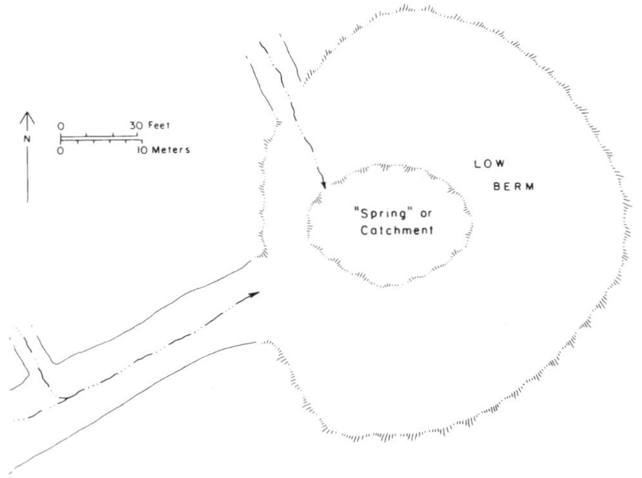

Figure 3.19. Plan of AZ AA:7:43, Locus 4, probably a prehistoric reservoir.

Figure 3.20. Reservoir, probably prehistoric, at AZ AA:7:43, Locus 4 (Site R-6), near Pan Quemado, holding water in October, 1988. (ASM photograph 69740, by Helga G. Teiwes.)

construction. Although no protohistoric sherds were recovered from surface collections, this feature may have been the water source for the protohistoric village of Santa Catarina, located on the floodplain of the Santa Cruz River a few kilometers east. The importance of this reservoir as a prehistoric water source is suggested by the presence of a trail that leads north from the north end of Pan Quemado toward the large trincheras village of Cerro Prieto (Chapter 4). Because the bed of the Santa Cruz River is generally dry in this vicinity, the reservoir may have been an important source of domestic water for a number of surrounding settlements, including the Los Robles Mound Site located a short distance to the south. (Dating: Sedentary through Early Classic.)

Quarry Sites
(Site Type 12; 10 sites)

Definition: Prehistoric quarrying location with hammerstones, cores, flakes, and other artifacts indicating that the primary site activity was lithic reduction.

Although most quarry sites were used to produce chipped stone artifacts, some apparently were used for the manufacture of manos, metates, and other ground stone tools. Nine sites are on the lower slopes of the low volcanic hills in the west and northwest portions of the survey area and one (AZ AA:7:43, Locus 9; Fig. 3.9) is at the south end of Pan Quemado. Dating of these sites is difficult. It is presumed that most, like the majority of Los Robles survey sites, belong to the Hohokam period, although Archaic and protohistoric use may have occurred.

AZ AA:7:138 (Robles Survey Site R-50) consists of a broad (120 m by 240 m) and relatively dense scatter of chipped stone debitage and cores spread over a low volcanic knoll about 1.5 km northwest of Cerro Prieto. Because all the artifacts are composed of locally available stone materials, the site probably represents a series of chipping stations, used during on-the-spot procurement of chipped stone raw material and tools such as flakes, blades, and perhaps bifaces. (Dating: None assigned, presumed prehistoric.)

AZ AA:7:150 (Robles Survey Site R-62) has a widely dispersed scatter of chipped stone debitage spread over the gently sloping east face of a rocky hillside. There is no outcrop of the chipped stone material at the site, but the survey crew speculated that the source might have been slightly upslope. A small rock ring was observed in the south-central portion of the site. (Dating: None assigned, presumed prehistoric.)

AZ AA:7:156 (Robles Survey Site R-68) is a small (approximately 3 m in diameter) concentration of crude flakes of vesicular basalt, evidently by-products from the manufacture of ground stone tools. A few plain ware sherds are scattered to the west of the cluster of flakes. (Dating: None assigned, presumed prehistoric.)

AZ AA:7:160 (Robles Survey Site R-72) contains at least five concentrations of chipped stone debitage representing two kinds of lithic material, andesite and basalt. These concentrations are spread over a surface of cobbles and desert pavement at the base of a large hill. Most of the flakes at the site appear to have resulted from the reduction of cobbles; many flakes exhibit cortex. The andesite flakes are heavily patinated, perhaps indicating they are considerably older than the basalt flakes. The survey crew speculated that these flakes were Archaic in age. One tabular knife fragment was observed at the site, but no other artifact categories were present. (Dating: Unknown Hohokam.)

AZ AA:7:166 (Robles Survey Site R-78) is a small (1.25 m in diameter) concentration of vesicular basalt flakes, some of which exhibit traces of cortex. From the size and amount of debitage present, the site recorder speculated that a single mano had been manufactured. (Dating: None assigned, presumed prehistoric.)

AZ AA:7:167 (Robles Survey Site R-79), located on the upper east slope of a small volcanic hill, consists of a large, mounded deposit of tabular andesite with two small depressions that may represent quarrying activity. No artifacts were observed. (Dating: None assigned, presumed prehistoric.)

AZ AA:7:177 (Robles Survey Site R-93) has several light concentrations of chipped stone debitage and two dense concentrations of debitage, approximately 10 m to 15 m in diameter, in the south and northwest portions. The site is on a cobble-strewn surface on the lower north slope of a small volcanic hill. The debitage appears to have come from the cobbles that occur naturally on this surface. A few plain ware sherds and a possible rock ring were the only other items or features observed. (Dating: Unknown Hohokam.)

AZ AA:7:180 (Robles Survey Site R-96) is on a small natural terrace, about 20 m wide, approximately half-way down the slope of the north side of a small, steep-sided wash cut between two small volcanic hills. The site consists of five scatters of chalcedony, rhyolite, and andesite debitage. No other artifacts or features were observed. (Dating: None assigned, presumed prehistoric.)

AZ AA:7:185 (Robles Survey Site R-102) is on a gently sloping alluvial fan surface covered with a desert pavement of andesite gravel and cobbles. Artifacts consist of approximately 75 flakes of basalt or andesite, concentrated into a cluster 1 m in diameter, and a few flakes of other lithic material types in scattered locations across the remainder of the site. (Dating: None assigned, presumed prehistoric.)

AZ AA:7:43, Locus 9 (Robles Survey Site R-119) exhibits an extensive concentration of ground stone manufacturing debris, mano and metate "preforms," and large, quartzite hammerstones. The debitage consists of vesicular basalt flakes, broken flakes, and debris detached from locally available boulders. Debitage is often large, and it sometimes occurs in dense clusters that evidently mark the places where ground stone tools were successfully manufactured (Fig. 3.21). Unsuccessful manufacturing attempts are also represented by flaked boulders and partially finished and sometimes broken tools in various stages of reduction from boulder to mano or metate. Plain ware sherds, tabular knives, and some chipped stone debitage are scattered across the site. A number of petroglyphs are near the center and in the southeast corner of the site (Figs. 3.22, 3.23), but these have not yet been systematically recorded. (Dating: Unknown Hohokam.)

Figure 3.21. Debris from the manufacture of ground stone tools, AZ AA:7:43, Locus 9. (ASM photograph 69697, by Helga G. Teiwes.)

Figure 3.22. Group of petroglyphs at AZ AA:7:43, Locus 9 (Site R-119), just east of ground stone tool manufacturing area. (ASM photograph 69706, by Helga G. Teiwes.)

Artifact Scatters
(Site Type 13; 51 sites)

Definition: Site with scatters of artifacts that cannot be interpreted as either a domestic refuse deposit, the remains of a plant or animal food processing event or episode, chipped or ground stone reduction, or any other functionally specific activity.

Artifact scatters are the most numerous and widely distributed sites in the Los Robles survey area. Most are relatively small and consist of a combination of sherds and lithic flakes. Additional research is needed to sort the temporal and functional variability that appears to be represented by this site category. It is presumed that the majority of these sites mark the locations of resource procurement or processing affiliated with the Hohokam

Figure 3.23. Petroglyph at AZ AA:7:43, Locus 9, just east of ground stone tool manufacturing area. The greatly exaggerated fingers and toes are a hallmark of petroglyphs in the Samaniego Hills area, according to Henry Wallace. (ASM photograph 69704, by Helga G. Teiwes.)

period occupation of this area, but this inference is by no means established and can be evaluated only through the careful study of individual sites. This category may subsume a variety of temporal affiliations, including the Archaic, Hohokam, and protohistoric, and sites assigned to it probably encompassed a number of functional types, including settlements, agricultural field sites, and resource procurement and processing localities. Five sites, illustrating the variability within the category, are described.

AZ AA:7:77 (Robles Survey Site R-21) has plain ware sherds, chipped stone and ground stone debitage, obsidian flakes, and a linear rock alignment of possible prehistoric origin. A twentieth-century artifact scatter has been superimposed over the prehistoric remains. Its contents include spent cartridges, cans, bricks, barrel hoops, and Tohono O'odham (Papago) pottery. A rock ring, eroding boulder alignment, and arrangement of mesquite posts are also of historic origin. Two rock terraces of probable historic origin are outside site boundaries to the southwest. (Dating: Unknown Hohokam; Late Historic.)

AZ AA:7:123 (Robles Survey Site R-33) is a scatter of pottery (sherds of plain ware and indeterminate red-on-brown), chipped stone debitage, a projectile point, and one piece of debris from the manufacture of a ground stone tool. The site has been severely damaged by excavation with mechanical equipment and the construction of a road. (Dating: Unknown Hohokam.)

AZ AA:7:130 (Robles Survey Site R-41) is a small (10-m-by-20-m) artifact scatter, consisting of plain ware and Tanque Verde red-on-brown sherds, chipped stone debitage, and tabular knife fragments. (Dating: Early Classic.)

AZ AA:11:49 (Robles Survey Site R-103) is a relatively small (20-m-by-30-m) concentration of artifacts distributed over a desert pavement surface a few hundred meters southwest of AZ AA:11:23 (Site R-104), a large, noncompound settlement. Artifacts consist of pottery (sherds of plain ware, indeterminate red ware, and indeterminate red-on-brown), chipped stone debitage, scrapers, and a bifacially flaked tabular rock. It is possible the site represents a small, specialized activity locus used by the residents of the nearby village at AZ AA:11:23. (Dating: Unknown Hohokam.)

AZ AA:11:19 was discovered in 1981 by John P. Wilson during a powerline survey along the west bank of Robles Wash. It was not revisited by Robles survey crews. Wilson (1981: 30-31) described the site as a scatter of sherds, including 7 Gila Plain, 42 unidentified plain ware, and 1 late Rincon Red-on-brown(?), with a trough metate fragment a few meters west. He speculated that this site was "probably a short-term, single component seasonal occupation, contemporary with nearby TEP 623" (now, AZ AA:11:20), which is another small artifact scatter just to the northwest. (Dating: Sedentary through Early Classic.)

Historic Camps or Homesteads
(Site Type 14; 7 sites)

Definition: Historic site with structures, features, trash, and historic Native American ceramics, indicating primary use as a late nineteenth- or early twentieth-century seasonal camp or residence.

The seven sites recorded do not reflect the total extent of historic remains in the survey area, only those also exhibiting historic Native American ceramics. Three sites previously recorded by John P. Wilson during a powerline right-of-way are included.

AZ AA:7:129 (Robles Survey Site R-40) consists of the remains of a historic structure surrounded by a large quantity of historic trash, including sheet metal, wood, broken glass, broken china, Tohono O'odham (Papago) pottery, chicken wire, bed springs, and barrel hoops. The structure is outlined by cobbles and wooden posts surrounding a cleared area. Immediately east of the structure is an excavated area surrounded by boards and sheet metal that may represent the remains of a privy. The range of items and the condition of features suggest a site date in the first half of the twentieth century. (Dating: Late Historic.)

AZ AA:7:131 (Robles Survey Site R-42) has heavy concentrations of historic trash, including lumber, glass, metal buckets, a stove, a bed frame, gas lamps, wash tubs, bicycle parts, bricks, sheet metal, and Tohono O'odham (Papago) pottery. At least two possible structures are indicated by fragments of upright posts, and several ash and charcoal piles were observed. The range and condition of items suggest a date somewhere between 1900 and 1950. Plain ware and protohistoric sherds were observed. (Dating: Unknown Hohokam; Protohistoric-Early Historic; Late Historic.)

AZ AA:7:144 (Robles Survey Site R-56) is a scatter of historic period trash, including tobacco tins, lard buckets, white china, purple glass fragments, barbed wire, meat cans, broken bricks, a barrel hoop, pieces of lumber, clear and amber glass, and Papago Plain and Papago Red sherds. Gila Plain sherds are also present. There was no unequivocal evidence of structures, although some piles of rock were noted. The recording crew speculated that this occupation dated to the Sasco era, around 1917 to the early 1930s. (Dating: Unknown Hohokam; Late Historic.)

AZ AA:11:57 (Robles Survey Site R-139) consists of several distinct areas of historic period trash, including concentrations of Papago Plain and Papago Red pottery, near a residential area along El Tiro Road in the southern portion of the survey area. One possible Tohono O'odham (Papago) house foundation is noted on the site map. Site recorders thought the site might have been occupied in the late nineteenth or early twentieth centuries, perhaps from about 1890 to 1915. Additionally, ground stone debitage and plain ware, indeterminate red ware, and indeterminate red-on-buff sherds were present. (Dating: Unknown Hohokam; Late Historic.)

AZ AA:7:38 was originally recorded as Site TEP 590 by John P. Wilson during a 1980 powerline survey for the Tucson Electric Power company (Wilson 1980). The site was not visited by Robles survey crews. Wilson describes the site as the "ruins of a 5-room adobe-walled structure on stone foundations; overall size 17 X 18.5 m," with several thousand items of modern trash. Wilson noted that the site was "not shown on a July 25, 1907 Sasco plat, but [was] probably [visible] in a 1914 Sasco photo." Additional information on this site is provided by Wilson (1980: 40-42). (Dating: Late Historic.)

AZ AA:7:39 was another site originally discovered by John P. Wilson during the 1980 TEP survey. The central feature was an area about 4 m by 4 m "outlined on three sides by cobbles and small boulders." A few broken beer bottles were seen north of this feature, but Wilson noted that the association was dubious since "artifacts over this part of the townsite would number in the 1000s." A more complete description of the site is given by Wilson (1980: 43-44). (Dating: Late Historic.)

AZ AA:7:42 was the third historic period site (TEP 594) recorded by Wilson during his 1980 powerline survey. Like the two described above, it was not visited by the Los Robles survey crew. The site is described as a "scatter of historical refuse only, primarily fragments of domestic discards (cans, bottles)," perhaps representing trash deposited during a "short-term campsite occupation" associated with "seasonal gathering activity." The site had several Papago Plain sherds, leading Wilson (1980: 51-53) to speculate that the site had been used or occupied by Tohono O'odham (Papago) people in the 1920s or 1930s. (Dating: Late Historic.)

CHAPTER FOUR

The Cerro Prieto Site

Christian E. Downum, John E. Douglas, and Douglas B. Craig

One of the most fascinating aspects of the prehistoric Los Robles settlement system is the presence of Cerro Prieto, a trincheras feature site now known to represent a terraced, hillside village of the early Classic period (Fig. 1.1). Although there are more extensive and elaborate trincheras sites in northern Sonora (for example, the Cerro de Las Trincheras site), Cerro Prieto is perhaps the largest such site in the U.S. Southwest. During the A.D. 1200s Cerro Prieto must have been one of the most heavily populated and visually striking settlements in the entire Santa Cruz River Basin.

Many aspects of this site mark it as an enigma and raise important questions regarding its functional role and overall significance. First, Cerro Prieto is less than 2 km from the Los Robles Mound and several other large Tanque Verde phase villages. The overall impression is that Cerro Prieto was an integral part of the community. Problematic issues exist, therefore, regarding the role of such a large trincheras village in the social, political, and economic network operating in the greater mound community. Was Cerro Prieto subordinate to the authority of the Los Robles mound settlement? Or were the two settlements noncompetitive, perhaps even complementary, centers within the larger community?

Although answers to these questions must await further investigation, Cerro Prieto has given us some hints that it indeed played a major role in the economic, ceremonial, and sociopolitical activities of the early Classic period Los Robles Community. The most direct evidence of Cerro Prieto's potential economic importance stems from its location just below a large outcrop of tabular andesite that is an excellent raw material for manufacturing tabular knives. Tabular knives, used for the processing of agave leaves, were an essential artifact for the agave cultivators during the early Classic period in southern Arizona. Control of such a relatively scarce and high quality source of raw material may have given the residents of Cerro Prieto the opportunity to develop a craft industry focused on the production and exchange of tabular knives.

Additional evidence of Cerro Prieto's productive capacity is provided by the abundant terraces and rock-outlined fields that extend within and around the site. If Cerro Prieto also controlled a zone of floodwater fields along Los Robles Wash, which seems likely, then these features might have provided a valuable food surplus in good agricultural years. In poor years, the terraces and rock-outlined fields might have been less subject to crop loss from drought, flooding, or frost. Thus, within the greater Los Robles Community, the residents of Cerro Prieto may have held a significant advantage over their neighbors who did not control hillside agricultural plots.

The location of Cerro Prieto and the form of many of its features indicate its probable role as a ceremonial and political center, probably for the Los Robles Community and perhaps for the lower Santa Cruz Basin as a whole. The site is strategically located to control access to travel routes along major drainages (Fig. 1.5). Massive masonry features made the village a commanding presence on the cultural landscape. Large terraces would have been visible for several kilometers to the northeast, and other features such as parallel boulder walls and walled compounds would have been visually imposing to all approaching visitors. These features suggest that Cerro Prieto had symbolic, ceremonial, and perhaps political functions not shared by other villages in the Los Robles Community.

Finally, Cerro Prieto shows intriguing similarities with contemporaneous hillside and hilltop sites of the Sonoran desert, particularly the site of Cerro de Las Trincheras in Sonora, the Fortified Hill Site near Gila Bend in Arizona, and a series of so-called "fortified" sites in the highlands of central Arizona. The large terraces on the northeast slopes of Cerro Prieto, although vastly smaller in number, are virtually identical in height and form to those on the north slopes of Cerro de Las Trin-

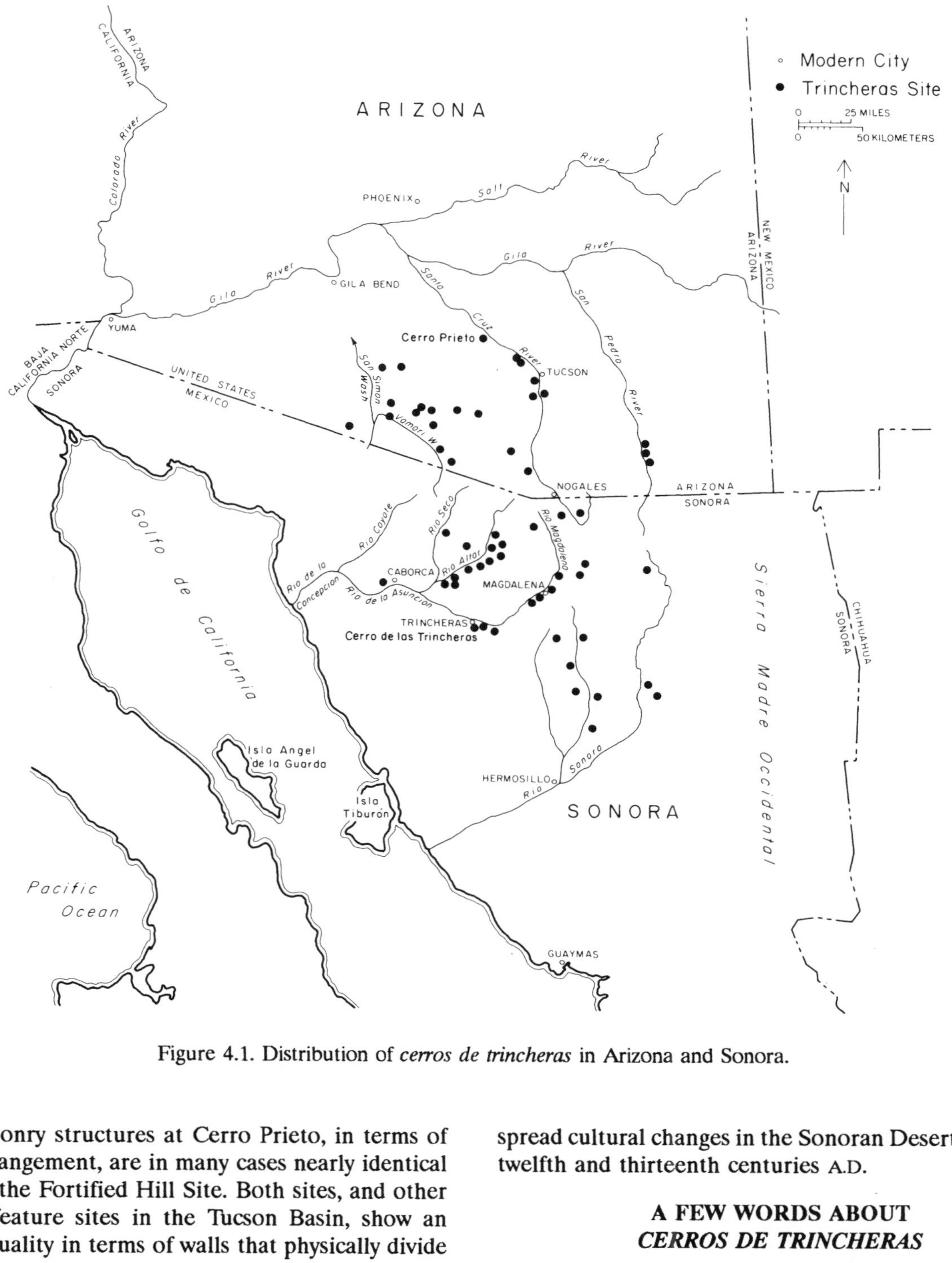

Figure 4.1. Distribution of *cerros de trincheras* in Arizona and Sonora.

cheras. Masonry structures at Cerro Prieto, in terms of size and arrangement, are in many cases nearly identical to those of the Fortified Hill Site. Both sites, and other trincheras feature sites in the Tucson Basin, show an intriguing duality in terms of walls that physically divide the sites into two precincts. Rooms, compounds, and other masonry features at sites along the New River and Agua Fria River are in many respects like those of Cerro Prieto. These similarities, spread across a vast regional scale, encourage a reevaluation of traditional interpretations of the "trincheras" phenomenon and a reconsideration of the role of Cerro Prieto in the context of widespread cultural changes in the Sonoran Desert during the twelfth and thirteenth centuries A.D.

A FEW WORDS ABOUT *CERROS DE TRINCHERAS*

The terms *trincheras* and *cerro de trincheras* have long been controversial in Southwestern archaeology. Several English translations of the Spanish term *trincheras* have been offered, including "entrenchments" (Sauer and Brand 1931: 67; Hoover 1941: 228), "trenches," "stockades," or "fences" (Stacy 1974: 20). Generally, the term refers to prehistoric rock walls, terraces, and other dry-

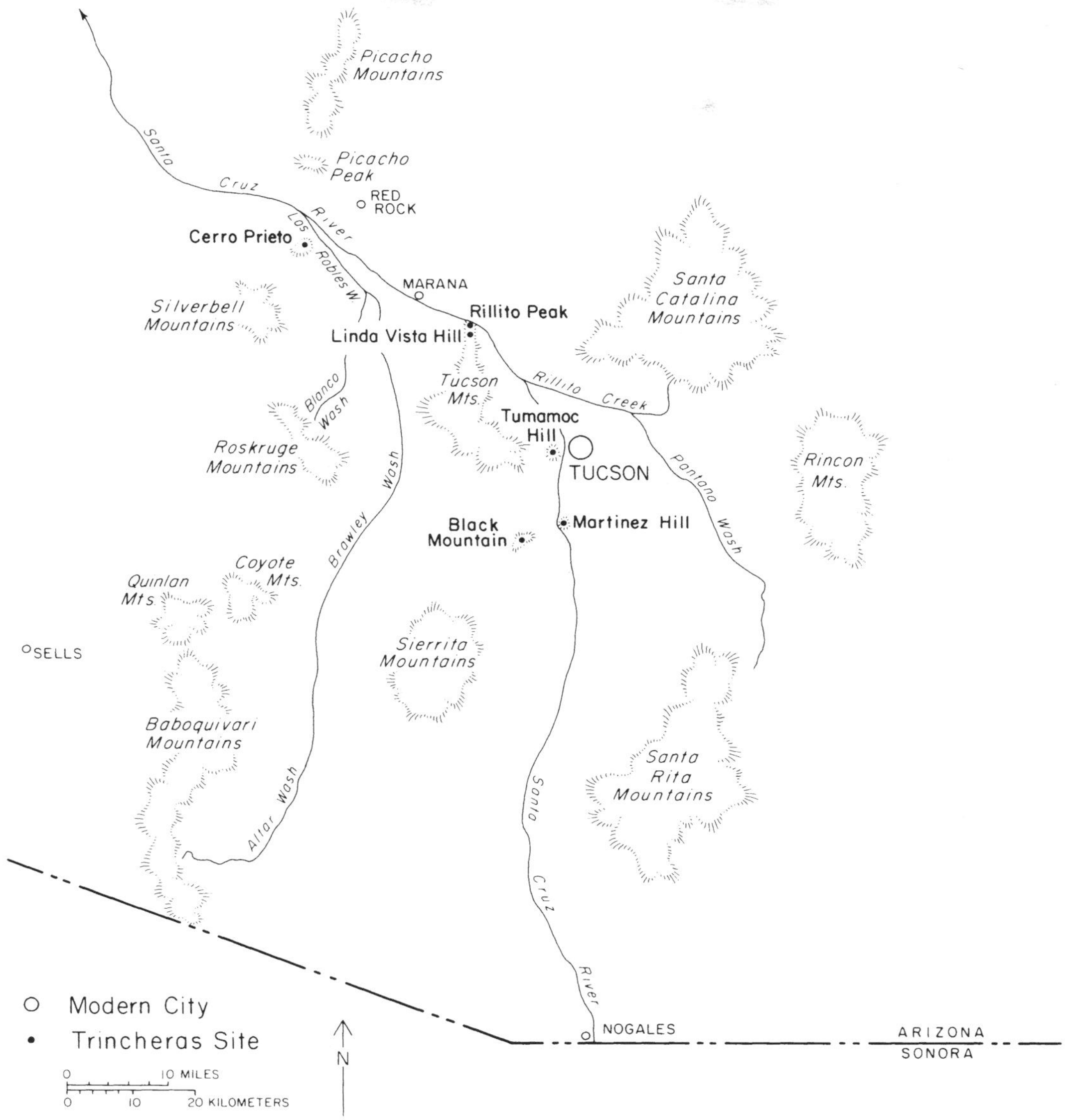

Figure 4.2. *Cerros de trincheras* in and around the Tucson Basin.

laid constructions that appear on volcanic hillsides in northern Sonora and southern Arizona (Figs. 4.1, 4.2). The word *trincheras* clearly has defensive implications, a legacy of early historic speculations relating trincheras features to indigenous Southwestern accounts of post-contact raids and warfare involving firearms, horses, and siege tactics (Stacy 1974: 4–19).

In the archaeology of Sonora, the term *Trincheras* (with a capital T) has been used to define both a prehistoric culture and a ceramic complex dating from the eighth through seventeenth centuries A.D. (Sauer and Brand 1931; Johnson 1960, 1963; Braniff 1990). Elsewhere, a wide variety of feature types has been characterized as *trincheras*. The term has been applied to such widely separated and different phenomena as modern terraced fields at Hopi villages (Hack 1942: 37); late prehistoric hilltop enclosures and rooms in the Prescott area (Fewkes 1912a: 218–219); hilltop compounds and rooms at sites along the New River and Agua Fria River (Spoerl 1984: 27); terraces, circular enclosures, masonry rooms, and walls at Classic period Hohokam hillside sites in the Tucson Basin and Papaguería (Stacy 1974, 1977; Wilcox 1979; Downum 1986; Downum and others 1985); massive hillside terraces at prehistoric sites in Sonora (Sauer and Brand 1931); and masonry check dams in Chihuahua associated with settlements of the prehistoric Casas Grandes regional system (Howard and Griffiths 1966).

Figure 4.3. The Cerro de Las Trincheras site in northern Sonora. Rectangular enclosure is visible on lower slope. (Photograph by Ellsworth Huntington, 1910; courtesy Yale University.)

In this report, the terms *trincheras* and *cerro de trincheras* have distinct meanings. *Trincheras* features are the individual, dry-laid masonry constructions that occur on volcanic hillsides in northern Sonora and southern Arizona. Most appear to date to the late prehistoric period, though many may also have been constructed in protohistoric or even in historic times. There is also a possibility that some stacked rock constructions date as early as the Archaic period (P. Fish, S. Fish, Long, and Miksicek 1986). Trincheras in this sense is a general term, flexible enough to include a wide variety of masonry features. As explained in Chapter 3, a trincheras feature site is any site exhibiting such constructions.

Our use of the term *cerro de trincheras*, however, has a more specific meaning. Following the usage of a number of authors (Sauer and Brand 1931; Hoover 1941; Schroeder 1985: 738; McGuire and others 1992), we believe that this term should be restricted to the terraced, late prehistoric hillside and hill summit sites of northern Sonora and southern Arizona. In order to be characterized as a true *cerro de trincheras*, a site must fit two criteria: first, it must exhibit hillside rock constructions that can be defined as terraces, and second, it must belong to the late prehistoric period. In this sense, *cerros de trincheras* are a phenomenon centered in northern Sonora, with the emphasis on terraces fading with distance north from the International Border. Most such sites belong to the period after about A.D. 1100, but as reported to us by Randall McGuire in 1992, some sites in Sonora may date as early as the ninth century A.D., and it has been claimed (Braniff 1990: 179) that some were used as late as the seventeenth century. The best-preserved and most spectacular of the *cerros de trincheras* is Cerro de Las Trincheras (Fig. 4.3), located just south of the town of Trincheras in northern Sonora (Huntington 1913; Sauer and Brand 1931). This site, recently

Figure 4.4. Cerro Prieto, view from the east, looking west toward concentration of archaeological features on the northeast hill slope. (ASM photograph 86822, by Glenn D. Stone.)

mapped under the supervision of Randall McGuire and Elisa Villalpando, consists of a hillside literally covered with massive stone terraces, which, from a distance, make the hill appear as a stepped pyramid.

By the above criteria, Cerro Prieto is both a site with *trincheras* features, and a true *cerro de trincheras*. In fact, Cerro Prieto appears to be the farthest north example of a trincheras site exhibiting massive terraces. A few sites to the north, such as the "Frog Tanks" site reported by Fewkes (1912a: 215–216, Plate 102) along the Agua Fria River and Site T:4:8 in the New River area (Ravesloot and Spoerl 1984), show some masonry walls that may or may not be considered as terraces. However, to our knowledge none of these sites or any others north of Cerro Prieto show the same sort of stepped terracing that characterizes the Cerro de Las Trincheras site and other *cerros de trincheras* in northern Sonora, the Papaguería, and the Tucson Basin. It is at present unclear what this distribution of terracing implies; this subject and general issues in the interpretation of *cerros de trincheras* are discussed in Chapter 6.

SITE DESCRIPTION

Natural Environment

Cerro Prieto ("Dark Hill") is the northernmost and highest extension of the Samaniego Hills, a low, igneous range that straddles the Pima-Pinal county line a few kilometers southwest of Red Rock, Arizona. The "hill" of Cerro Prieto is actually a massive, roughly horseshoe-shaped ridge, which covers an area approximately 2 km on a side and rises to a height of about 244 m (800 feet) above the surrounding alluvial fan (Fig. 4.4). The open end of the horseshoe is raggedly dissected by deep, boulder-strewn drainages that run in a southwesterly direction. The closed end is formed by an arc-shaped ridge, oriented about 20 degrees east of true north. Most archaeological features forming the site of Cerro Prieto

(AZ AA:7:11 ASM) are located in a broad band along the lower middle portion of this ridge. Unless noted otherwise, in the following discussion the term "Cerro Prieto" refers exclusively to that area.

The surface of Cerro Prieto is covered by varying densities of basaltic boulders and cobbles. Rock distributions are largely determined by gradient. The slope of the hill generally increases with elevation, and one-third of the way to the summit, there is a particularly sharp break in the degree of incline. On the hill's lower reaches, to about 650 m elevation, the grade averages around 23 percent; above this point the slope increases more than three-fold, to about 77 percent. Accordingly, there are marked changes in the composition of the hill surface. Lower areas have a mosaic of relatively open spaces, exhibiting various size classes of boulders and cobbles, interspersed occasionally with thick deposits of large boulders. Upper slopes are almost uniformly covered with thick talus deposits. Soils are thin or nonexistent across most of the hill, but there are some pockets of residual soil, particularly on the lower slopes where natural and cultural accumulations of boulders (for example, terraces; see description below) have created barriers to erosion.

Several clefts or drainages dissect the northern slopes of Cerro Prieto (Fig. 4.5). None has a clearly-defined channel that leads to a major wash on the surrounding alluvial fan, and many appear to be faults or other structural, rather than erosional, phenomena. The largest such cleft is located on the northeast tip of Cerro Prieto, near the east edge of the distribution of archaeological remains. This feature is several hundred meters long, at least 35 m wide, and perhaps 3 m to 4 m deep. Prehistoric trails lead across it, connecting houses and terraces on both sides, and numerous boulders along its margins are decorated with petroglyphs. Sides of the cleft, formed by bedrock and deposits of caliche-cemented boulders, have been undercut, creating many crevices and shelters. These hollows are presumably the outcome of natural erosional processes, but it is also possible that some are the result of prehistoric excavations into the caliche and decomposing bedrock. Similar features were observed by Greenleaf (1975: 219) at the Fortified Hill Site near Gila Bend. A few of the overhangs are partially enclosed by stone retaining walls, indicating use as shelters or dry storage facilities.

Elsewhere, hillside clefts and drainages are relatively shallow, marked by the stripping of surface rocks and soil and slight entrenchment into the caliche substrate. The largest of these features are sometimes flanked by parallel, linear arrangements of boulders that may represent the remains of relatively recent debris flows. This interpretation, by ASM geomorphologist James Lombard, is supported by the fact that some of the boulder lines terminate in distinctive, dark-colored lobes of sediment at the base of the hill. One set of parallel boulder lineaments, near the center of the site of Cerro Prieto, is particularly noteworthy because it has been prehistorically modified by straightening and augmenting the natural rock distribution. The walls thus created split the site into two roughly equivalent precincts, a fact that may have significant implications for early Classic period Hohokam social organization (see *Parallel Walls*, below).

At the top of Cerro Prieto there is a steep-sided bedrock outcrop formed of a lighter colored and less vesicular rock. This formation makes a plug-shaped cap that gives the hill a distinctive, flat-topped profile (Fig. 4.4). Portions of the outcrop have eroded into extensive deposits of thin, tabular plates of rock, which form an ideal raw material for tabular stone knives (Fig. 4.6).

Vegetation at Cerro Prieto varies considerably with gradient, elevation, and aspect. On the lowest margins, where local hill deposits merge with surrounding alluvium, vegetation is dominated by creosote bush, bursage, and jumping cholla cacti. The lower slopes of the hill, up to an elevation of about 650 m, are covered with a dense palo verde–saguaro association. Plant species include foothills palo verde; mesquite; ironwood; saguaro, jumping cholla, teddybear cholla, prickly pear, barrel, pincushion, and hedgehog cacti; creosote bush; bursage; brittlebush; and ocotillo. Among these, ironwood is relatively uncommon, and appears to be confined to a narrow band perhaps one-fourth to one-third of the way to the hill summit. On the upper slopes, across the boulder talus, the range and density of vegetation is greatly diminished, and many of the species observed below are completely lacking. A relatively abundant plant at higher elevations is the teddybear cholla, which seems well adapted to the steep, rocky conditions. The very top of Cerro Prieto supports a range of vegetation similar to that of the lower slopes.

Disturbance

In spite of its proximity to the historic town of Sasco (see Chapters 1 and 2), Cerro Prieto appears remarkably free of obvious modern disturbance and vandalism. Some archaeological features, however, particularly a set of large terraces on the eastern side of the site, have been disturbed by past digging. During the Cerro Prieto mapping project, pothunting within mapped structures was always recorded; 26 out of 232 masonry rooms on the lower slopes showed signs of vandalism, although only a few had been completely cleared of fill. As discussed in Chapter 2, some of the latter may have been excavated during a 1925 University of Arizona expedition led by

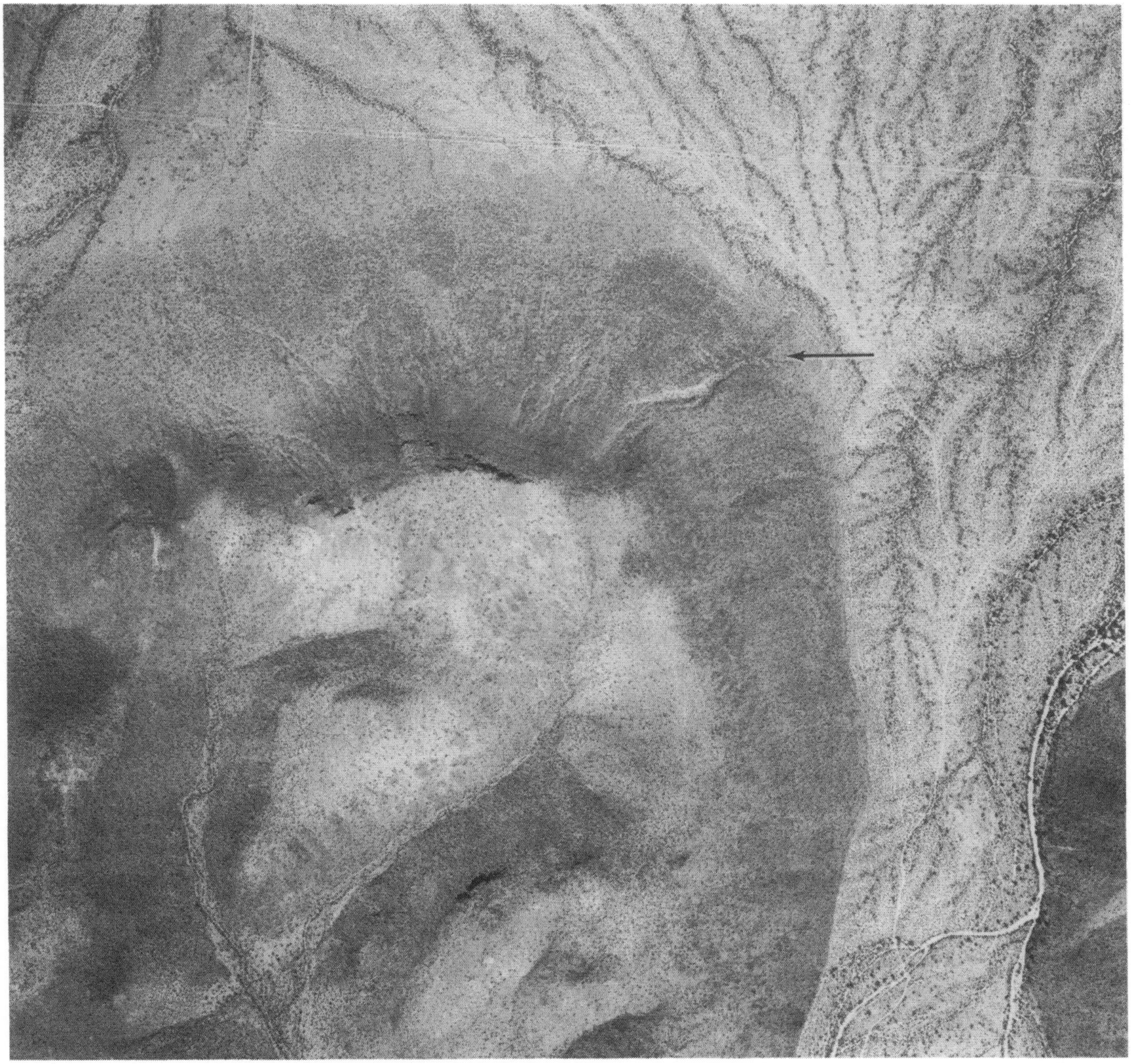

Figure 4.5. Aerial view of Cerro Prieto, with top of photograph oriented north. Large terraces in the northeast portion of the site appear as faint white streaks just north of the major fault and erosional feature (arrow, above *right center*). Outcrops of tabular andesite, used for manufacturing tabular knives, are visible as light patches near the hill summit.

Byron Cummings. Accompanying beer and soft drink cans suggest that a major portion of the pothunting was relatively recent, probably within the past 15 years.

There are also a few, small, hand-dug mining tests and scatters of historic trash on the lower slopes, and some initials were observed carved on a boulder near one of the larger prospect holes. An unknown quantity of boulders may have been removed for building material during the Sasco era. Some areas of the hill slope, particularly the lower portions on the east side, obviously have been

Figure 4.6. Outcrop of tabular andesite at east end of summit of Cerro Prieto. (ASM photograph 86823, by Christian E. Downum.)

modified by the rearrangement or removal of boulders (see Miscellaneous Features, below). Probably most of these features are prehistoric constructions built to manipulate hillside runoff for agricultural purposes, but it is also possible that some of the modifications are historic. Other potential sources of damage include removal of petroglyph-bearing boulders and the collection of surface artifacts. During mapping, piles of potsherds or ground stone tool fragments were sometimes observed in various areas of the site. Presumably, these represent the discards of artifact collectors who retained an unknown quantity of more desirable specimens.

The Cerro Prieto Mapping Project

Most of the archaeological data reported in this chapter were collected during a multi-year research effort referred to as the Cerro Prieto Mapping Project. In this project we investigated an area of about 300,000 square meters covering the approximate center of the site of Cerro Prieto. Data were collected on the locations and attributes of more than 200 stone structure foundations, 11 stone-outlined compounds, 6 major terraces and at least 30 smaller examples, and dozens of rockpiles, talus pits, petroglyphs, and other features (Figs. 4.7–4.9).

Mapping involved intensive inspection of the site surface for stone houses, terraces, and other constructions by making systematic sweeps across 100-m by 100-m grid squares, the boundaries of which had been previously marked with flagging tape, or across areas delineated by natural features. The survey was conducted by a crew of two or three persons spaced at 5-m intervals. Upon discovery, all features were temporarily marked with flagging tape for later recording and mapping.

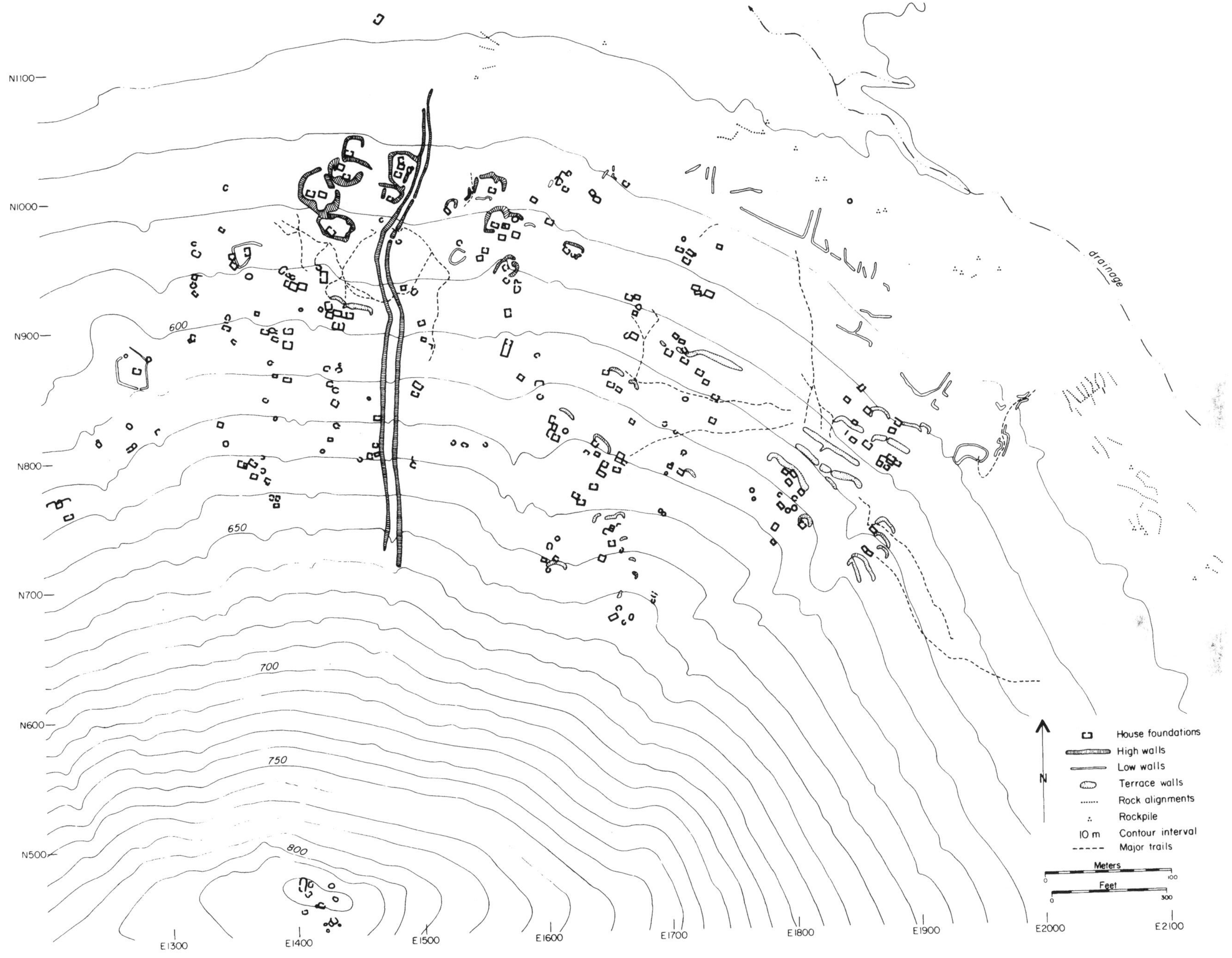

Figure 4.7. Plan of the Cerro Prieto Site.

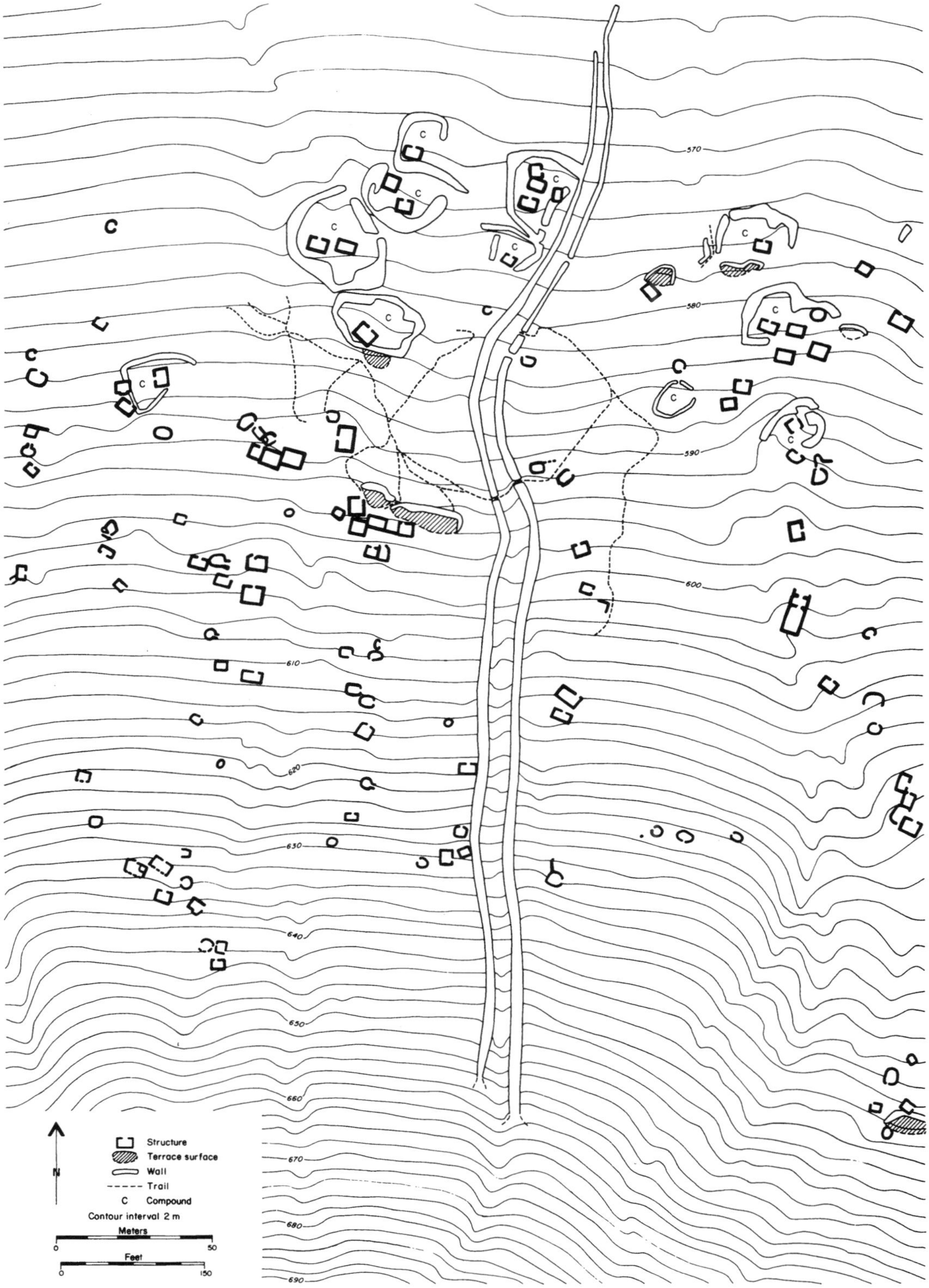

Figure 4.8. Structures, compounds, terraces, trails, and parallel boulder walls in the northwest portion of the Cerro Prieto Site.

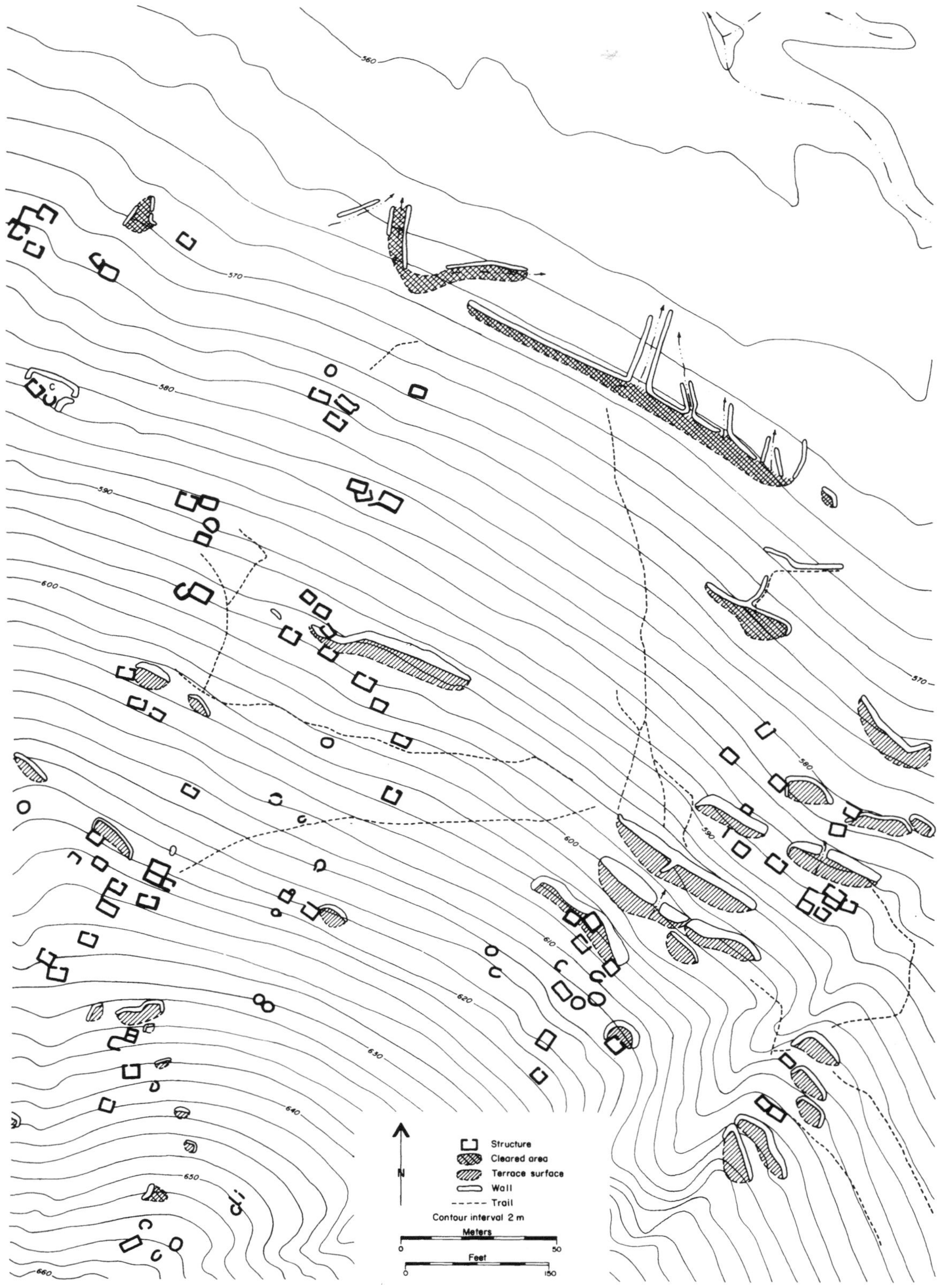

Figure 4.9. Structures, terraces, trails, and possible water diversion walls in the northeast portion of the Cerro Prieto Site.

Figure 4.10. Rectilinear structure (Feature 55) on the northeast slope of Cerro Prieto (see also Figs. 1.3, 1.4). View is west-northwest. (ASM photograph 69744, by Helga G. Teiwes.)

Features discovered during this initial survey were noted on field recording forms designed specifically for the project. Features judged to represent potential structures were first tagged with a small aluminum square, stamped with a feature number, and attached to a large nail driven into the ground somewhere within the feature. Next, features were recorded and mapped. A metric tape was stretched down the center of the structure along the long axis, and a Brunton compass was aligned with the tape to determine the azimuth orientation of that axis. The structure was then measured to determine interior length, width, doorway size, and wall height. A plan map of the structure was drawn to scale, showing orientation, length, width, doorway position and size, and any other salient attributes. Observations were made and recorded on the form regarding construction technique, coded as plane faced, simple stacked, and rubble core (see Structures, below). Finally, comments were recorded regarding any additional attributes of the structure, for example, the degree of vandalism or other disturbance, presence of nearby petroglyphs, relationship to other features such as terraces, or unusual aspects of wall construction. Other kinds of features, such as terraces, rockpiles, walls, and alignments, were noted, although less consistently. Usually these features were mapped using a Brunton compass and tape in much the same way that houses were mapped. Other features, most commonly terraces, were not assigned a number and no form was completed. Outlines of these features were mapped directly, using electronic distance measurement equip-

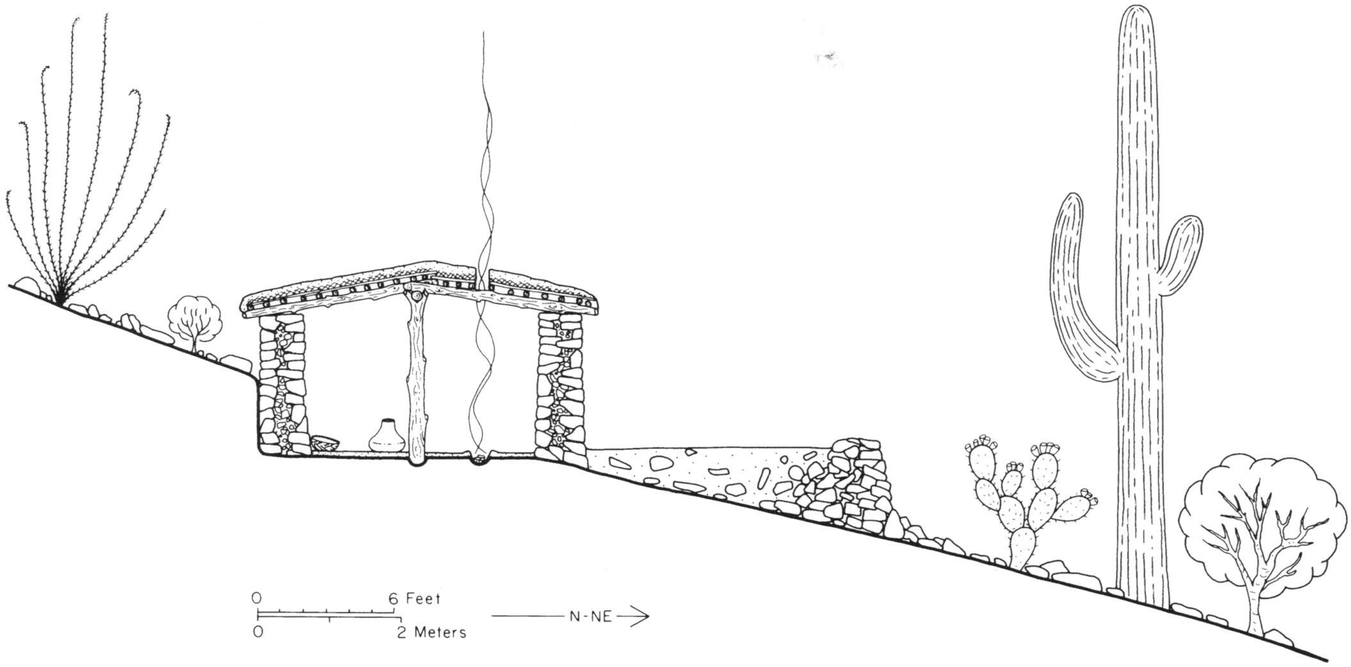

Figure 4.11. Hypothetical reconstruction of a masonry room at Cerro Prieto, based on architectural features visible at the surface of Feature 55 and its adjacent small terrace, Feature 367. Details of roof construction and structure height are conjectural, but are based on results of excavations at Cerro Prieto (Feature 4) and the Fortified Hill Site (Greenleaf 1975).

ment. Once features were tagged, mapped, and recorded onto forms, precise location coordinates were assigned using the electronic distance measurement equipment. During weekends of work, one day was usually spent locating, tagging, mapping, and recording individual features, and the next day was spent mapping the grid locations of previously recorded features so as to make maximum use of instrument time.

A final step in the mapping of Cerro Prieto involved production of a fine-grained contour map. Cooper Aerial Survey Company, Tucson, took a series of aerial photographs using ground control points established by the Cerro Prieto mapping crew and produced a 2-m contour interval map, referenced to the same grid system used to map the archaeological features. The contour map was transferred to the survey map of archaeological features.

Test Excavations

In the fall of 1981, a field class from the University of Arizona Department of Anthropology conducted limited test excavations in two features at Cerro Prieto. These operations were under the general supervision of Paul R. Fish of the Arizona State Museum, and the fieldwork was supervised by Henry D. Wallace of the Department of Anthropology, University of Arizona. The object of the excavations was to examine the fill and internal features of a rectilinear room and of a large terrace. Feature 4, a rectilinear room, and Feature 51, a large terrace located northwest of the main concentration of large terraces in the southeast portion of the site, were selected for testing. Results of test excavations are reported below in the extended descriptions of structure and terrace features.

Archaeological Features

There are several categories of archaeological features at Cerro Prieto: stone outlines or walls believed to represent structures (Figs. 4.10–4.15); compounds; terraces; cleared (and sometimes walled) trails; parallel boulder walls of unknown function; petroglyphs; concentrations of fire-cracked rock; and concentrations of debitage from the manufacture of tabular knives, vesicular basalt grinding tools, or chipped stone tools. Not all of these were given the same amount of attention by the Cerro Prieto mapping project. Structure foundations had the highest priority, and because the greatest amount of effort was

Figure 4.12. An unexcavated rectilinear structure (Feature 33) on the northeast slope of Cerro Prieto. Walls have collapsed, but sharp corners and plane-face masonry are visible near the ground surface at the interior of the structure. (ASM photograph 69745, by Helga G. Teiwes.)

devoted to locating and mapping them, the inventory of structures probably represents a complete or nearly complete list of all such features within the present boundaries of Cerro Prieto. Although of secondary mapping importance, we believe that all observable stone compounds within site boundaries were also located and mapped. Terraces were a lesser priority; the present inventory is partial, but all the larger terraces were mapped and those that might have been missed represent the smallest examples of this feature. Trails are much more difficult to assess; the best-preserved examples were mapped, but many indisputably prehistoric hillside trails remain to be mapped. Features such as alignments and rockpiles at the base of the hill; petroglyphs; roasting pits; and artifact concentrations were considered a low mapping priority and were only intermittently recorded. Without a doubt many more such features exist that could be systematically reported.

Structures

One of the most striking aspects of Cerro Prieto is the density of architectural features on the hillside, with enclosed stone foundations and walls the most abundant and widely distributed constructions. For several reasons, most of these features appear to represent ruined dwellings or other domestic structures.

Figure 4.13. Artist's reconstruction of rectilinear masonry rooms at Cerro Prieto. The drawing, based on a composite of the appearance of Feature 33 and Feature 55, is by Elena Campbell.

First, the size and form of most foundations and walls resemble similar structures at other trincheras feature sites that have been shown upon excavation to represent habitations. Specifically, the Cerro Prieto structures are similar to stone rooms or masonry-outlined pit houses that were excavated at the Linda Vista (S. Fish, P. Fish, and Downum 1984; Downum 1986) and Fortified Hill (Greenleaf 1975) trincheras sites. In fact, the Cerro Prieto and Fortified Hill sites show some exceptionally close similarities in the shapes, construction details, and arrangements of their structures (see Fig. 4.19). General similarities also exist between the rooms mapped at Cerro Prieto and those excavated at sites along the Agua Fria and New River drainages in central Arizona. Secondly, subsurface evidence from Feature 4 at Cerro Prieto provided good evidence that it had served as a dwelling. Test excavations in this feature established that it had a prepared floor, a doorway, and numerous artifacts consistent with use as a dwelling. Finally, the overall arrangement of stone structures at Cerro Prieto is consistent with what might be expected for a hillside village. The structures are arranged in definite clusters, often associated with one or more stone terraces, and many are on or near a well-defined trail connecting with other groups of structures.

There are 232 stone features on the lower slopes of Cerro Prieto that were field identified during mapping as probable domestic shelters. This classification does not

Figure 4.14. Unidentified feature in the northwest portion of Cerro Prieto. Plane-face masonry construction is visible on the interior walls, and a doorway is about midway along the east wall (lower *right center*). View is to the north across the Santa Cruz Flats. Picacho Peak is visible in the near background; Newman Peak in the Picacho Mountains is farther north. (ASM photograph 86829, by Christian E. Downum.)

incorporate all stone foundations and walls. There are perhaps 30 rock outlines at the hill summit, but for several reasons they do not appear likely to have served a habitation function. The summit features are less substantial and less well constructed, many lack clearly defined doorways, few show evidence of wall collapse or other fill, and there is little prehistoric trash on and around the hill summit. Additionally, various small rock circles and ovals on the lower hill slope, although technically representing structural foundations of some sort, also were rejected as possible rooms or pit houses because of their small size and insubstantial nature.

Distribution, Form, and Function of Cerro Prieto Structures

Those features considered likely to represent rooms and pit houses at Cerro Prieto are confined mostly to the lower one-fourth to one-third of the hill, between about 570 m and 650 m in elevation. A few are scattered across the alluvial fan surface at the base of the hill. There are two broad categories of structures, those with a rectilinear shape (Figs. 4.10–4.14), and those with an ovoid or circular plan (Figs. 4.15–4.17). Surface evidence alone provides no clear-cut functional division between the two. Both structural forms exhibit attributes commonly associated with a residential use, namely sufficient size of the floor area and gaps in walls that likely represent doorways. Both kinds of structures occur either in isolation or as members of well-defined clusters. Based on work at the Fortified Hill Site, Greenleaf (1975: 241–242) concluded that masonry rooms with curved corners were earlier than those with a rectangular plan. This proposition cannot yet be evaluated at Cerro Prieto, but the distribution and arrangement of structures suggest no obvious temporal sequence. Rather, rectangular and curvilinear structures alike occur across the hillside and appear to be integrated into coherent clusters.

Figure 4.15. Unidentified feature in the northwest portion of Cerro Prieto, showing typical form of a curvilinear structure foundation and rough-stacked masonry construction. (ASM photograph 86830, by Christian E. Downum.)

Detailed information was gathered by the Cerro Prieto mapping project for 232 probable residential structures. Roughly two-thirds of all masonry foundations could be classified as clearly rectilinear in shape, with the remainder curvilinear. The average maximum interior length of all structures was about 3.8 m, with a standard deviation of about 1 m. The average interior width was about 2.7 m, with a standard deviation of about 0.6 m. Average floor area for all structures was about 11.6 square meters, with a standard deviation of about 6 square meters. No strong central tendency could be determined for structure orientations. The average azimuth of the structures' long axes was about 98 degrees (standard deviation, 40 degrees), indicating a general east-west orientation. Much of the variability in orientations no doubt reflected a need to conform structures to the arc of the hill, and to accommodate variation in local topography and the placement of adjacent structures. About two thirds of the structures showed gaps in their walls or exhibited other features that could reasonably be interpreted as doorways. Most of the doorways faced east, with almost two-thirds oriented between 0 degrees and 90 degrees east of true north.

Two construction techniques were used for structure walls at Cerro Prieto: (1) simple stacked, using only large stones laid horizontally one atop the other (Fig. 4.12), and (2) rubble core, using pebbles and small cobbles to fill the space between two parallel courses of larger, carefully stacked stones (Figs. 4.10, 4.11). The former technique was used for about two-thirds of all Cerro Prieto structures, though the presence of rubble core walls might have been underestimated due to the obscuring effects of wall collapse. For both techniques, the builders usually arranged the stones so as to create a smooth, "plane" face on the interior wall (Fig. 4.11). The rubble core technique of wall construction seems to have been employed quite commonly for hill summit and hillside structure walls across a broad area of southern and central Arizona during the twelfth and thirteenth centuries A.D. Numerous examples have been recorded for

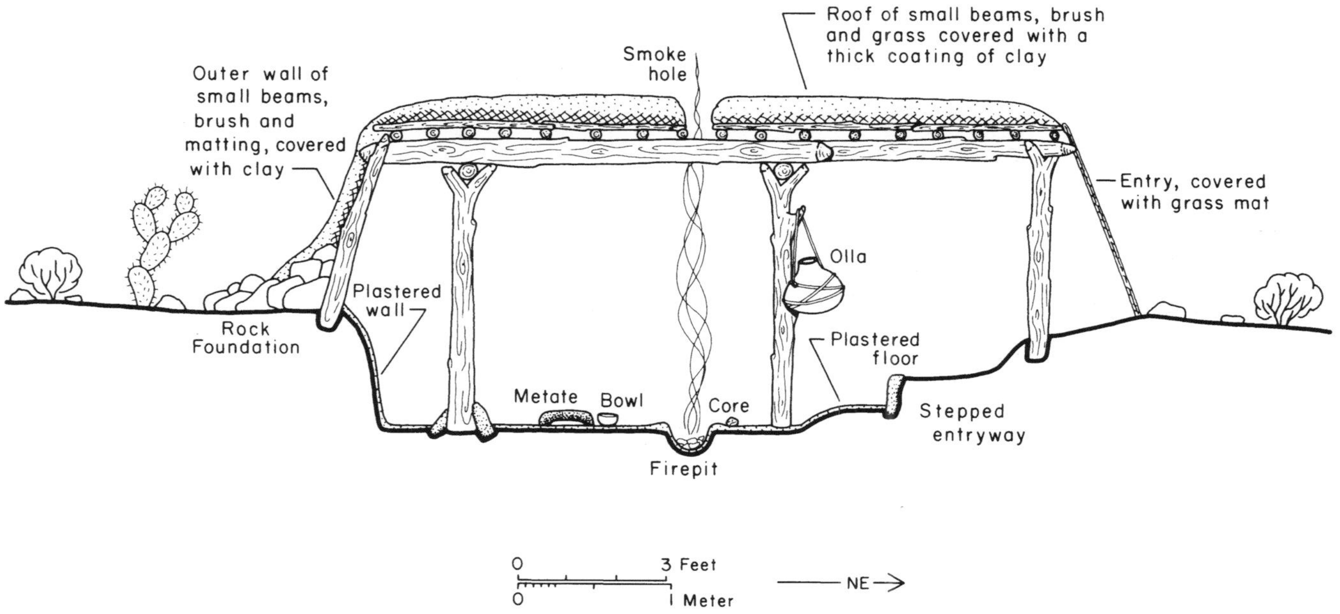

Figure 4.16. Hypothetical reconstruction of Feature 1987-1, a masonry-outlined, Tanque Verde phase pit house on the lower slopes of the northern Tucson Basin *cerro de trincheras* of Linda Vista Hill. The drawing is based on artifacts and other items recovered from the structure such as burned support posts, roof beams, roof closing material, and roof and wall clay. Many of the curvilinear masonry foundations at Cerro Prieto are believed to represent similar structures.

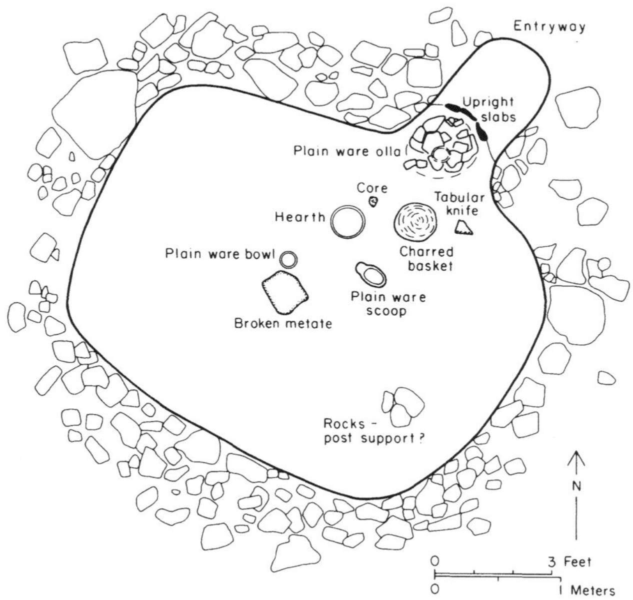

Figure 4.17. Plan of Feature 1987-1, a pit house at Linda Vista Hill. Prior to excavation, the surface appearance of this structure was identical to curvilinear masonry structure foundations at Cerro Prieto.

prehistoric structures in the Phoenix Basin (Schroeder 1940: 61-63), in the Gila Bend area (Greenleaf 1975: 236-237), along the New River (Ravesloot and Spoerl 1984: 68-69), and even as far north as the Walnut Creek drainage north of Prescott (Fewkes 1912a: 210-212). More is said of these regional similarities, and their possible implications, in Chapter 6.

Many details of structure interiors at Cerro Prieto are unclear, but excavated rooms and pit houses at other hillside and hilltop villages like the Fortified Hill and Linda Vista Hill sites provide appropriate analogies. At Linda Vista Hill, a *cerro de trincheras* at the northern end of the Tucson Mountains, excavations revealed that three circular rock outlines similar to those observed at Cerro Prieto represented stone walls erected around the perimeters of shallow pit houses (Figs. 4.16, 4.17). These walls evidently served to seal the house pits from slope wash during heavy rains. All three of the excavated houses showed a central, circular, clay-lined hearth, and all contained rich assemblages of floor artifacts, including intact or reconstructible pottery vessels, manos and metates, tabular knives, shell and argillite jewelry, projectile points, and other chipped stone tools. Two of the structures had burned, preserving numerous details of construction. Both were built over a vertical-sided, clay-

Figure 4.18. Excavated masonry room at the Fortified Hill Site. Numerous details of rooms at this site match those of rectilinear masonry structures at Cerro Prieto. (See Greenleaf 1975, Fig. 12; ASM photograph 9701, by William W. Wasley.)

plastered house pit, and both were evidently covered with a superstructure sealed with a thick coating of mud. One of the pit houses had a sloping earth entryway, and the other exhibited a stepped entry fashioned from vertical and horizontal stone slabs. Further information on two of the Linda Vista pit houses is provided by Downum (1986) and S. Fish, P. Fish, and Downum (1984). Although the circular stone foundations at Cerro Prieto remain unexcavated, their resemblance to the Linda Vista Hill pit house foundations strongly suggests a similar function.

For Cerro Prieto's rectangular masonry structures, comparisons may be made with the excavated rooms at Fortified Hill, a trincheras feature site near Gila Bend, Arizona (Greenleaf 1975). All rooms at Fortified Hill were rectangular or subrectangular, with mostly aboveground walls fashioned from masonry (Fig. 4.18) or, in a few cases, rock-reinforced adobe. (At least one structure at Cerro Prieto, Feature 82, appeared as if it might have been constructed of rock and adobe.) Structure floors at Fortified Hill were created by digging through decaying bedrock and caliche to form a level surface. Dips in the subfloor were leveled through the addition of dirt and pebbles, and the floor surface was coated with a thin layer of clay. A few houses showed evidence that the walls were plastered. No roof material was preserved intact, but it was surmised that roofs were probably flat and constructed of clay-covered thatch placed over longitudinal or transverse vigas. In most cases, only a single, central posthole was discovered, pecked into the caliche

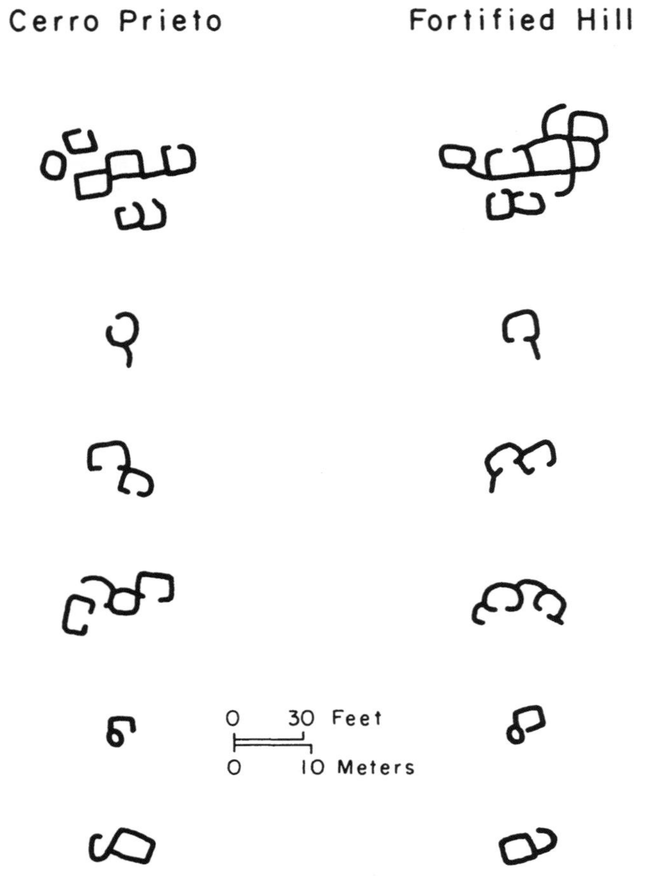

Figure 4.19. Comparison of shapes and arrangements of structures at the Cerro Prieto and Fortified Hill sites.

or bedrock substrate. The larger structures showed two postholes along the house midline. Few hearths had survived postoccupational erosion, but among these the general form was a shallow, clay-plastered basin located just within the entryway.

That these construction details might be extended to the rooms at Cerro Prieto is supported by a number of striking similarities in both the form and arrangement of rooms at the two sites (Figs. 4.18, 4.19). Room walls at Fortified Hill (Greenleaf 1975: 236–241) show a rubble-filled, plane-faced masonry construction technique that is identical to that used at Cerro Prieto. Although some of the room walls at Fortified Hill appear more massive than those at Cerro Prieto, the specific techniques of construction (for example, careful arrangement of undressed basalt boulders to present a plane face and use of small cobbles and pebbles to fill the masonry core) are indistinguishable between the two sites. Further, the use of large boulders as wall footings at Fortified Hill is a pattern repeated at Cerro Prieto. At Fortified Hill, the door jambs were occasionally strengthened by the addition of vertical slabs on both sides (Greenleaf 1975: 239–240, Fig. 17); at least nine of the rooms at Cerro Prieto showed an identical pattern. Doorway thresholds at Fortified Hill occasionally were marked by a rectangular slab; although most room interiors at Cerro Prieto were obscured by fill, in at least two instances a similar rectangular slab step was placed just inside the entry. Other formal similarities between individual rooms at the two sites include comparable shapes, attachment of slightly curved wing walls or wall stubs to exterior room corners, placement of entries along the long axis, and upward flaring of doorways (Greenleaf 1975: 228–230, 236–241).

Finally, some specific information about the nature of masonry rooms at Cerro Prieto was provided by the 1981 test excavations in one hillside room, Feature 4. This feature was excavated initially with a 1-square-meter test unit placed near the center of the room (Fig. 4.20). A 30-cm-square unit was later added to the southeast corner of the original test to explore the junction of the room floor with its south wall. Level 1 extended from surface to 15 cm below, and Level 2, from 15 cm to 30 cm. A surface collection of artifacts was made prior to excavation. All excavated sediments were screened through ¼-inch mesh screen.

Feature 4 was a burned room that had undergone a considerable amount of postoccupational erosion and other disturbance. The general stratigraphic sequence consisted of an upper level of silt, gravel, and small cobbles that represented natural wash deposits. Below

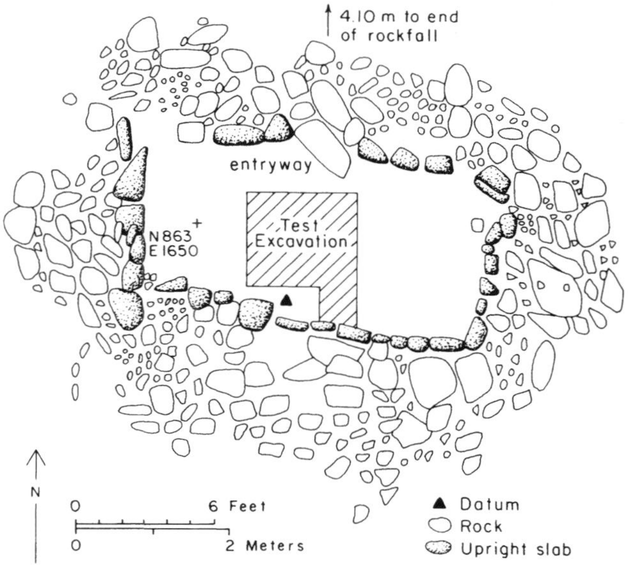

Figure 4.20. Plan of Feature 4 at Cerro Prieto, showing location of test excavation unit.

Figure 4.21. Nonceramic objects from excavated features at Cerro Prieto: *a*, fire-hardened clay with stick impressions, evidently a fragment of burned roofing material; *b*, fragment of burned shell bracelet (*Laevicardium elatum*), probably a cremation offering; *c*, bone awl fashioned from a deer metapodial (*Odocoileus* sp.); *d*, *e*, flakes of fine-grained basalt, made from cobbles widely distributed across the slopes and summit of Cerro Prieto; *f*, *g*, tabular knife fragments, manufactured from tabular andesite found at the summit of Cerro Prieto; *h*, *i*, cores of fine-grained basalt; *j*, discoidal chopper of fine-grained basalt; *k*, broken vesicular basalt mano, probably made from local raw material; *l*, battered cobble (hammerstone). Maximum dimension of *f* is 10.8 cm. (*a*, *c*, *j*, and *l* are from the masonry room, Feature 4; remainder are from the terrace, Feature 51.)

this, but still within Level 1, were small fragments of burned clay, at least one of which had stick impressions (Fig. 4.21*a*). On this evidence it is inferred that the room had burned, but either the burning had been incomplete or much of the evidence for burning had been lost to erosion. Throughout Level 1 there was a high density of artifacts, including plain ware, Tanque Verde Red-on-brown, Rincon Red(?), and unidentified red-on-brown sherds, chipped stone tools and debitage, hammerstones, a pestle, fragments of malachite, and a bone awl fashioned from a deer metapodial (Figs. 4.21, 4.22, Table 4.1). (Downum reexamined the Rincon Red sherd reported from this provenience, and its identification as that type is equivocal. Considering the preponderance of Tanque

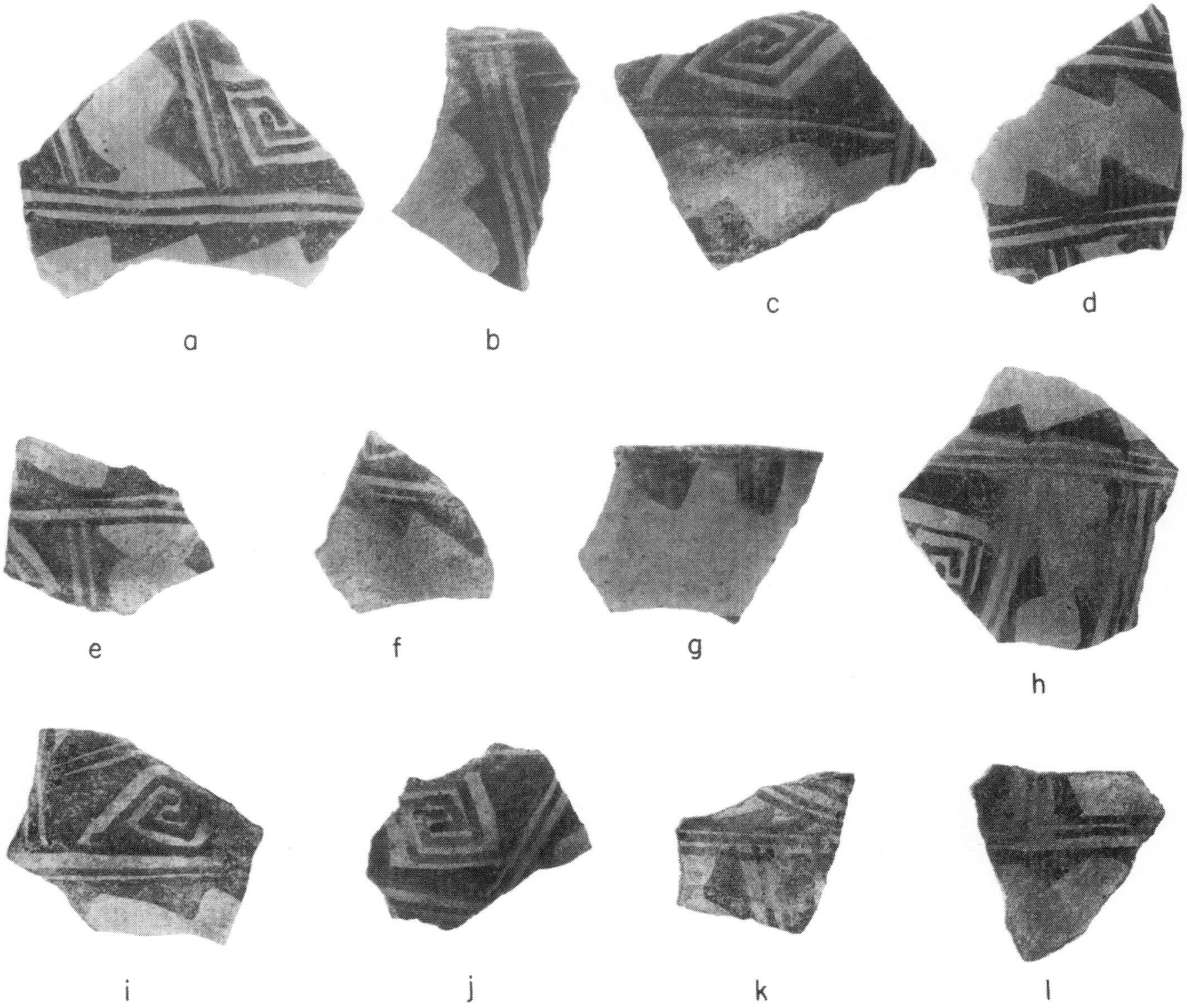

Figure 4.22. Tanque Verde Red-on-brown pottery from excavated features at Cerro Prieto. These sherds are from jars, except *g*, which is a rim sherd from a large bowl. Maximum dimension of *a* is 11.5 cm. (*a–c* are from the test pit excavated into the terrace, Feature 51; *d–l* are from the test unit in the masonry room, Feature 4.)

Verde Red-on-brown sherds throughout the excavation, and the complete absence of Sedentary period sherds elsewhere on the site, no chronological weight is given to its presence.) Some of these items had apparently washed into the room after it burned, but most are presumed to represent items left or discarded as trash in the room before it burned.

No identifiable floor remained in Feature 4. Instead, an uneven caliche surface was encountered within a few centimeters of the top of Level 2. There was no trace of a plastered surface, and no floor features were uncovered. A few sherds and a fragment of malachite were the only items recovered from Level 2; it is presumed that they represent artifacts present when the room burned.

Compounds

Other major constructions at Cerro Prieto, occurring mostly in the central and western portions of the site, are massive stone enclosures that are best characterized

Table 4.1. Artifacts Recovered from Test Excavations at Cerro Prieto (AZ AA:7:11 ASM)

	FEATURE 4 (structure)			FEATURE 51 (terrace)					
		Level 1	Level 2		Level 1	Level 2	Level 3	Level 4	Level 5
Artifacts *Depth in cm*	*Surface*	*0–15*	*15–30*	*Surface*	*0–30*	*30–45*	*45–60*	*60–75*	*Below 75*
Tanque Verde Red-on-brown sherds	1	44							12
Rincon Red(?) sherd		1							
Indeterminate red-on-brown sherds		5	1	6	1				
Indeterminate red ware sherds				2		1			
Micaceous plain sherds		144		93	4	3	5	8	1
Nonmicaceous plain sherds		85	9	90	52	47	28	6	
Flakes or flake fragments		7		64	9	11	7	1	
Discoidal chopper		1							
Hammerstones		2		1					
Cores				2			1		
Vesicular basalt mano fragment (one-half complete)				1					
Vesicular basalt metate fragment				1					
Vesicular basalt ground stone tool fragments, unidentified				2					
Abrading stone or small metate						1			
Pestle		1							
Malachite fragments		3	1						
Burned clay fragments, one with stick impressions (burned structural material)		2							
Burned shell bracelet fragment, *Laevicardium elatum*								1	
Burned shell fragment, species indeterminate						1			
Animal bone awl, distal portion of metapodial, *Odocoileus* sp.		1							
Burned animal bone fragments:									
Lepus sp., proximal portion of right tibia						1			
Odocoileus sp., shaft portion of left tibia							1*		
Odocoileus sp., anterior portion of ascending ramus								1	
Mammalia, unidentified							8*	3	
Burned human bone fragment:									
Shaft portion of fibula						1			
Anterior portion of parietal								1	

* From Levels 3 and 4.

as compounds. These features consist of large, often irregularly shaped boulder walls that enclose a level interior surface containing one or more stone structures (Figs. 4.23, 4.24). They are distinguishable from terraces because they have much wider, built-up walls that enclose one or more sides and the back of the flat surface. A few are completely enclosed.

Some compounds cover extensive areas (up to 28 m by 32 m) and evidently involved a considerable effort to construct, particularly in leveling the compound interior. In one case, the back wall of a compound could be seen resting on a shelf of solid caliche hewn from the hillside. This indicated that its floor had been leveled by the removal of at least 1 m of rock and solid caliche. Elsewhere, level interiors were achieved by building up the natural slope of the hillside. Considering the degree of slope and the overall profile of the compounds, this would have required the addition of at minimum a meter of boulders, cobbles, and dirt fill.

Although most compound walls are now badly collapsed, surviving footings and intact lower courses reveal impressive workmanship. Some compounds were built similar to the largest and best-constructed stone houses, with plane-faced, rubble core walls supported by boulder footings. Again, this construction technique can be compared with that used to build similarly massive enclosing walls on hill slopes and summits across southern and central Arizona during the early Classic period. The volume of collapsed stones at Cerro Prieto indicates that compound walls were sometimes quite massive; several walls stood more than 2 m high, and most were between 1 m and 2 m. Upslope walls are generally higher and thicker than those on the downslope side, and sometimes contain small cobbles and fragments of caliche

Figure 4.23. View looking west across stone compound, northwest portion of the Cerro Prieto Site. Collapsed rubble-core compound wall is visible in the left center of photograph, level compound interior near the center. A structure foundation, toward the rear of the compound, is just left of center. (ASM photograph 86825, by Glenn D. Stone.)

presumably excavated from the upslope or back side of the compound interior.

A few compounds display irregularities in their outlines that appear as indentations or niches. None of these niches show evidence of a structure, but it is possible they were once enclosed or roofed by a brush shade or other feature that has since perished. Most compound walls contain gaps or other openings that provide clear access to the interior. Such openings usually occur on the downslope (north), or east sides. A few walls have clearly defined entryways marked by upright slabs or a narrow break in the wall rock. One compound appears to be completely enclosed, but its doorway could be obscured by collapsed rubble.

All but one of the compounds contain from one to four stone structures; the exception has none. The majority of compound rooms are rectangular, relatively large and narrow, and were built in a simple stacked fashion. Only two circular rock foundations were observed within the limits of a compound. Otherwise, the structures appear similar to noncompound structures, and no unusual features or objects were seen in or near them. One rectilinear room exhibits an internal subdivision in its west end, and one has built into the exterior compound wall an expansion or alcovelike feature along its back wall. Such features also were observed in rooms elsewhere, so no special significance is attached to them.

Functions of Compounds

Functions of compounds and the activities that took place within them are unknown and puzzling. Based on the low number of houses in the compounds, it appears they probably did not function simply as enclosed residential areas. Three of the most extensive compounds at Cerro Prieto contain only a single visible structure, and

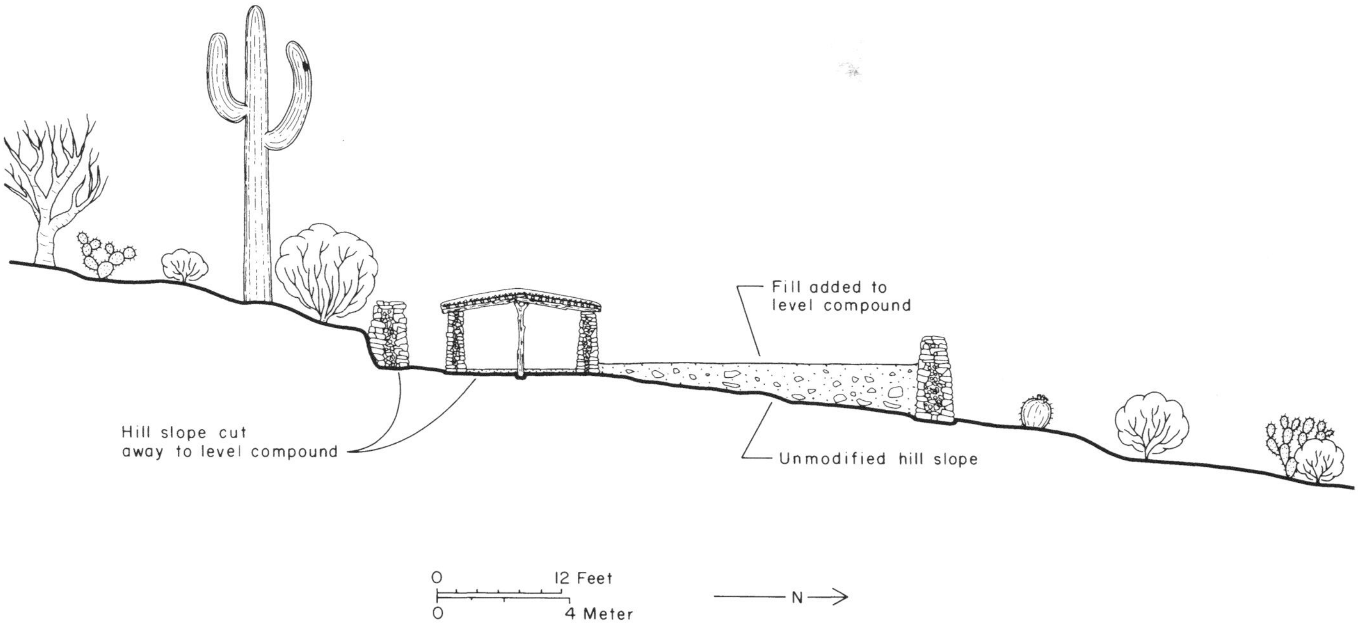

Figure 4.24. Hypothetical reconstruction of a compound at Cerro Prieto. The drawing is based largely on a detailed plan map by Allen Dart of Feature 140, a compound, and an associated masonry room, Feature 199. The reconstruction of the room has been aided by excavation data from Feature 4 at Cerro Prieto, and various rooms of similar form at the Fortified Hill Site.

the largest compound contains only two structures. This small number of structures seems unusual when we consider the presence of many large, multiroom clusters of structures outside the compounds. If the structure arrangements within compounds are interpreted as households, it is unclear why the smallest domestic groups at Cerro Prieto would require such massive enclosures.

A second perplexing aspect of the compounds is their clustering. Although many areas of the lower slopes appear suitable (and perhaps even preferable) for the construction of compounds, all twelve are located within an area of about 100 m by 300 m. Five compounds are on the east side of a set of boulder walls that bisects the site (description below), and seven are on the west. Thus, it appears that a certain portion or precinct of the village was devoted to the construction of large compounds, and that there is a certain symmetry in the distribution of these compounds with respect to an east-west division of the settlement.

What, then, was the function of Cerro Prieto's compounds? In the absence of excavation data, we hesitate to offer any definitive conclusions. However, we do make the following observations. First, none of the compounds appear to have been well suited for community defense. All are located on the lower slopes of Cerro Prieto, where the gradient is not particularly steep and attackers could have moved fairly easily between and within the compounds. In addition, walls of the compounds are usually breached by downslope entrances that would have provided relatively easy access to interiors. Furthermore, the clustering of these features argues against a defensive use. If the compounds were built for protection from attackers, why were they placed in a restricted area of the settlement, and why were they removed by several hundred meters from significant clusters of residential structures? It would seem far more logical for defensive compounds to have been evenly distributed across the hill slopes and to have contained the majority of hillside residences rather than the small number of structures that were actually enclosed.

In the absence of convincing evidence that the compounds served as either residential enclosures or defensive fortifications, we offer that they served a community function, perhaps ceremonial in nature, that involved the periodic accommodation of a number of people. It may be significant that *cerros de trincheras* in Sonora and Arizona, and other hillside or hilltop sites with trincheras features in southern and central Arizona, often exhibit similar large, masonry enclosures. For example, the site of Cerro de Las Trincheras has two extraordinarily large masonry enclosures, one on its summit and

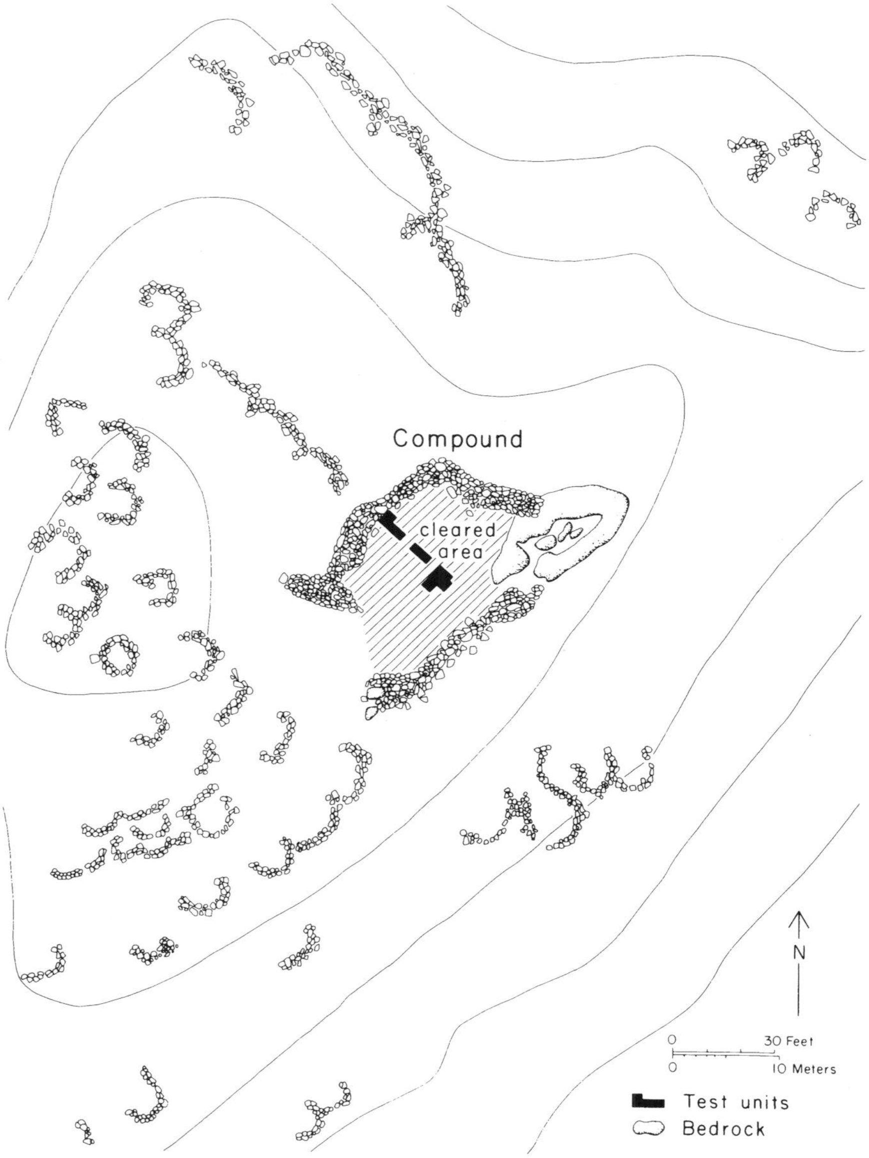

Figure 4.25. Walled compound at the summit of Linda Vista Hill. The compound is surrounded by various trincheras features, including terraces and rock circles.

one on its lower slopes that Huntington (1913: Plate 3; see also Fig. 4.3 herein) speculated was some form of religious structure. The Linda Vista Hill Site, a *cerro de trincheras* near the northern end of the Tucson Mountains (Fig. 4.2; Downum 1986; S. Fish, P. Fish, and Madsen 1992: 34-36), has a large, walled compound at its summit (Fig. 4.25). Test excavations of this feature disclosed the remains of post-reinforced adobe structures. Large masonry enclosures or compounds have also been reported from the Tucson Basin *cerros de trincheras* of Martinez Hill (Gabel 1931: 38; Hartmann and Hartmann 1979: 60-62) and Black Mountain (Martynec 1987: 30-33). Hilltop sites along the New River, exhibiting a variety of masonry rooms, walls, and other trincheras features, also show large, walled compounds (Spoerl 1984; Ravesloot and Spoerl 1984). Massive walls constructed in a rubble core masonry technique enclose the summits of several hills in the Walnut Creek area north of Prescott (Fewkes 1912a: 206-213, Plates 96-97, 99; Wilcox and Samples 1992).

Although we cannot presume that all late prehistoric hilltop or hillside masonry enclosures in the Sonoran

Desert served a common function, excavation data from two support our tentative hypothesis of ceremonial use. Limited test excavations within the hilltop compound at Linda Vista Hill produced only a few artifacts, but among those recovered were a neatly cylindrical schist pestle, carved into the shape of a human phallus, accompanied by a small, carved stone bowl. These items do not suggest a defensive or residential function for the compound, but can reasonably be interpreted as artifacts used in rituals or ceremonies. At AZ T:4:8 (ASM), a hilltop village along the New River, excavation of a large room adjacent to a stone-walled compound or plaza produced an intact shell (*Strombus galeatus*) trumpet (Ravesloot and Spoerl 1984: 90–92). In Classic period Hohokam contexts such trumpets are usually found only at platform mound sites, often from within or near the platform mound itself (Nelson 1991: 68–70, 81). Discovery of such an artifact at AZ T:4:8 suggests that in some areas at least, hilltop compounds might have had ceremonial functions roughly analogous to those of platform mounds.

Thus, although the true functions of Cerro Prieto compounds remain to be discovered, we propose the hypothesis that they served as community meeting places, used for ceremonies and perhaps other activities involving a relatively large number of people. We return to this hypothesis and its implications in Chapter 6.

Terraces

Also abundant at Cerro Prieto are terraces, consisting of masonry walls that retain a quantity of sediment on their upslope sides. There is a surprising range in the size, shape, and location of terraces. The most impressive examples are in the east portion of the site, on the north side of the large channel or fault that cleaves the hill slope there. In this area, five of the largest terraces at Cerro Prieto rise evenly up the hill slope, one above the other, in steplike fashion (see Figs. 4.27, 4.28). They are massive rock constructions, up to 4 m high and 60 m long, with level surfaces that often support structure foundations or other features. Erosional cuts and test excavations (see below) show that terrace fill is a combination of boulders, cobbles, gravel, and gray, ashy cultural deposits. Surfaces are covered with an exceptionally high density of artifacts, dominated by plain ware sherds, but also including Tanque Verde Red-on-brown and indeterminate red ware sherds, chipped stone debitage, shell jewelry and debitage, and burned bone. A sixth massive terrace is isolated about 60 m northeast of the main group, and at least five less-massive terraces are on the south side of the channel. These features are connected by a system of well-defined trails that lead west to other portions of the village, or north and southeast to the bottom of the hill.

Smaller terraces are scattered across the hill slope. Although the Cerro Prieto mapping project did not make an exhaustive inventory of small terraces, the majority probably have been recorded, resulting in a total of 30 such features. They are highly variable in length, shape, and orientation, but most are relatively shallow and hold less than 1.5 m of sediment. Half of the terraces are immediately downslope from a house cluster or isolated room, and most of these are oriented so that one or more room doorways open directly onto the flat terrace surface. The remaining 15 terraces, some of which are quite small, are sufficiently removed from the nearest room to make an association doubtful.

To assess the contents of terrace fill and determine the techniques of terrace construction, Feature 51, a large terrace, was tested with a 0.5-m by 1.0-m trench placed against the wall near the south end of the feature (Fig. 4.26). Excavations proceeded by five levels: from surface to 30 cm below, and the remaining four by 15 cm increments. All excavated sediments were screened through ¼-inch mesh screen, and a collection was taken from the surface of the terrace prior to its excavation.

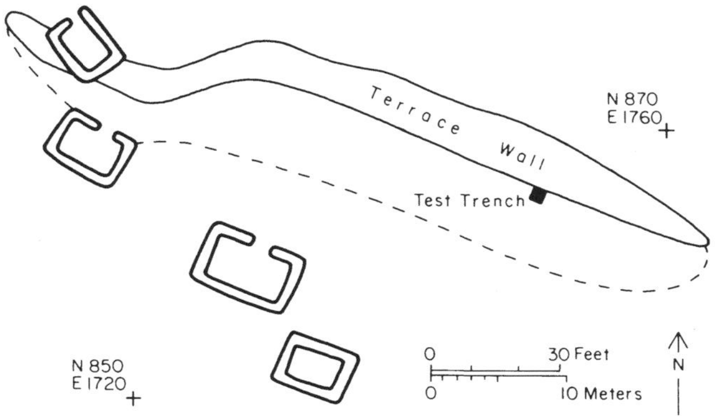

Figure 4.26. Plan of large terrace on the northeast slope of Cerro Prieto, showing the location of the test excavation trench and surrounding features.

The terrace fill was of loose, rocky sediment, and it contained a high density of artifacts throughout (Table 4.1). This density was so high, in fact, that it is likely a substantial portion of the terrace fill consisted of secondary refuse intentionally deposited within the rock retaining walls. The presence in the fill of burned human bone and a burned fragment of marine shell (Fig. 4.21*b*) is intriguing and suggests that the terrace was used at one time for the disposal of cremations. Large Tanque Verde

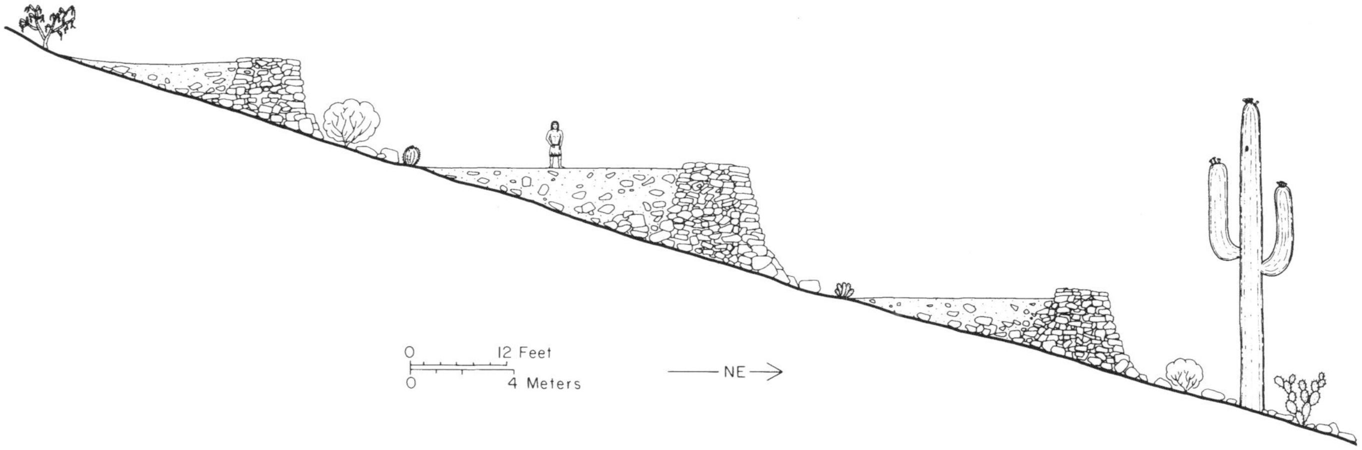

Figure 4.27. Hypothetical reconstruction of large, stepped terraces on the northeast slopes of Cerro Prieto. Terrace retaining walls and the nature of terrace fill are based on surface appearances and cross sections visible in erosional cuts. The hill slope and overall terrace heights have been calculated from 2-m interval contour maps. The drawing has also been aided by data gathered from test excavation of a large terrace, Feature 51. The terraces today appear much less vertical in cross section, because of the downslope collapse of retaining walls and subsequent erosion of fill.

Figure 4.28. Large terraces on the northeast slope of Cerro Prieto. Saguaro cactus provides rough scale of magnitude of terrace construction; height of largest terrace is approximately 4 m. (ASM photograph 86827, by Christian E. Downum.)

Red-on-brown jar sherds (Fig. 4.22*a-c*) were in the vicinity of the burned human bone, indicating that originally the bones might have been interred within one or more ceramic vessels. (The area within which the test trench was excavated had been churned by previous pothunting and rodent activity, so it was impossible to determine whether the vessel had been part of a disturbed cremation urn.) Alternatively, the burned human bone and shell may have been part of an earlier trash mound or midden deposit elsewhere on the hill that had been redeposited as terrace fill.

Function of Terraces

Like the compounds at Cerro Prieto, functions of terraces have not been definitively established. One traditionally popular idea is that features such as the Cerro Prieto terraces could have functioned as defensive platforms or revetments, providing an advantage to defenders engaged in hand-to-hand combat with attackers from below (Wilcox 1979). However, this does not seem a particularly plausible interpretation for the terraces at Cerro Prieto for the following reasons.

First, terraces seem too few to have been useful for village-wide defense, and they are not distributed in a way that would suggest a defensive function. As noted by Katzer below, the largest terraces are concentrated on the east slopes of the hill, a curious location if they were used as fortifications, but perhaps a reasonable expectation if they were used for agricultural or residential purposes. Conversely, the absence of large terraces in the densely populated western portion of the village precludes a defensive interpretation.

Second, many of the terraces are connected with the lower hill slopes by cleared trails or corridors that provide easy access. It seems unlikely that defensive features would have been built that provided attackers with such an easy approach. In particular, some of the largest terraces on the east slopes are connected directly to the hill base through a series of interconnected trails. This same area also has a broad, cleared corridor that passes along the north side of the large cleft or drainage on the east slope of Cerro Prieto (see Miscellaneous Features, below), providing easy access to the terraces. Thus it is difficult to interpret the terraces as defensive ramparts unless perhaps the combat was of a stylized and ritual form.

Third, from our perspective it would seem more sensible to build defensive platforms higher upslope, in the thick talus deposits where the footing for an attacker would be especially precarious. Terraces are entirely lacking there, however, and their absence is not because of differential feature preservation. Talus pits and rooms built in talus on the east slopes of Pan Quemado, just east of Cerro Prieto, demonstrate that such features should remain visible today, if they were originally present.

Finally, if terraces were intended to serve the defensive needs of the larger Los Robles Community, other hillsides offer a more logical choice than Cerro Prieto for a defensive refuge. The volcanic hills and ridges of Pan Quemado, for example, are suitable for the construction of terraces and are about two miles closer to the Los Robles mound settlement and several other large Tanque Verde phase villages that apparently formed the heart of the Los Robles Community. Furthermore, Pan Quemado and the adjacent Pan Quemado Ridge enclose a reservoir, apparently prehistoric, at AZ AA:7:43, Locus 4, an asset that would have given the defenders of Pan Quemado a distinct advantage over attackers. However, no large terraces have been identified at Pan Quemado, leading one to wonder why, if such features served a defensive function, they would have been concentrated on the slopes of Cerro Prieto.

Considering the wide variety of sizes, shapes, and locations, terraces may actually have been used for several different purposes. Previously (Downum and others 1985: 548–549) we have suggested that some of the terraces at Cerro Prieto served as agricultural plots. This argument is based on several factors, including formal similarity of Cerro Prieto terraces with a world-wide sample of known agricultural terraces (Donkin 1979); the evident moisture retaining properties of terrace fill; the probability that hillside terraces would have offered an extended growing season because of nighttime temperature inversions and reradiation of heat at night from dark hillside rock; and analogy with prehistoric hillside terraces at the nearby Linda Vista Hill Site, which produced pollen from corn, yucca or sotol, and other possible cultigens, as well as disturbance plants whose growth would have been encouraged by cultivation (S. Fish, P. Fish, and Downum 1984). It can also be argued that the extremely high density of artifacts and the presence of dark, ashy soil in some of the Cerro Prieto terraces indicate intentional filling with household garbage in an attempt to enhance soil fertility. Finally, the aspects, orientations, and potential watersheds of terraces support the idea that they were used as garden plots (see Katzer, below).

It is also possible that some Cerro Prieto terraces were used primarily as exterior courtyards for individual dwellings or clusters of rooms (for example, the terrace shown in Fig. 4.11). The gradient of the hill slope is often considerable (averaging over 20 percent in most areas with archaeological features), and terraces would have provided an indispensable flat surface on which to cook, prepare food for storage, manufacture household or craft items, and otherwise carry on daily activities.

Some terraces, particularly the largest examples, might have been constructed to serve ritual purposes, including use as cremation areas or cemeteries. The presence of a badly disturbed secondary cremation in Feature 51, and bits of burned bone, apparently human, at the surfaces of others, suggest this possibility.

Finally, it is possible that the large terraces at Cerro Prieto, and similar features at other *cerros de trincheras*, also served a largely symbolic function. This idea is not new. Some authors (Fontana and others 1959: 51; Haury 1976) have observed that terraces often give the hillside a stepped appearance reminiscent of Mesoamerican pyramids. According to Haury (1976: 348):

> Without attempting to argue for or against the many ideas that have been expressed explaining the existence of *trincheras*, whether for agriculture, domestic home sites, defensive measures, and others, it seems worth considering the possibility that they represent a northern modification of the terraced pyramid, using a natural hill as a substitute for a totally artificial structure.

This proposition may have some merit, particularly when one considers the form and distribution of terraced sites along the northern Mesoamerican frontier. Haury (1976: 348) notes that the Schroeder Site in Durango "exemplifies the terracing of a natural hill for sacred uses." Kelley's (1971: 788) description of the site recalls features of several Southwestern *cerros de trincheras*, including Cerro de Las Trincheras and Cerro Prieto:

> the entire northern or occupational face of the higher western hill was terraced with such regularity that it must have resembled a tremendous pyramid. Scattered over hilltops, saddle, natural terraces, and nearby flats are the ruins of many masonry structures. Former roadways connecting them can be traced. On the lowland at the northeast edge of the site are large natural boulders.... One has a petroglyph-a stick figure of a man with one arm up and one down-and others have mortar holes and grinding areas. Mortar holes occur elsewhere in the site on boulders and bedrock ledges.

Additional examples of terraced hillsides, sometimes supporting pyramids or other sacred constructions at their summits, occur across a broad area of the northern Mesoamerican frontier. Included are sites such as Loma San Gabriel near the Durango-Chihuahua border (Kelley 1953, 1971: 799). Given the massiveness and stepped nature of terraces at some *cerros de trincheras* in Sonora and Arizona (including Cerro Prieto), it does not seem totally implausible that these sites were, in fact, the northernmost extension of a widespread, longstanding phenomenon involving the construction of terraces for symbolic purposes.

Certainly this is a difficult proposition to test with current archaeological data. However, one important point in its favor lies in the geographic distribution of terraced hillsides in the Southwest. As we have noted, an emphasis on terraces seems to be centered in northern Sonora, with terraces diminishing in size and number north of the International Border. To the north of Cerro Prieto, many contemporaneous sites exhibit masonry features such as rooms and hillside or hilltop compounds, but terracing apparently drops out from the architectural repertoire. It is difficult to explain why this would be the case if all terraces were constructed in response to common regional stimuli such as agricultural intensification or warfare. However, if large and highly visible terraces are considered as symbolic phenomena, then their seemingly clinal distribution might be better explained by a model of ideological diffusion, rather than ecological imperative.

The apparent northward orientation of most terrace locations complicates the picture somewhat (see Katzer, below), but this trend might simply reflect local, environmentally conditioned decisions about where to situate the majority of village features once a particular hillside was selected as a *cerro de trincheras*. Choosing for environmental reasons to locate houses and small residential or agricultural terraces on the north slopes might have determined that larger, symbolic terraces would be located on these slopes as well. Further research on both sides of the border, including excavation of terrace fill, an accurate inventory of *cerros de trincheras*, and detailed information on the magnitude and orientation of terraces at individual sites, would contribute greatly toward testing this and other hypotheses regarding terrace functions.

Trails

The numerous trails at Cerro Prieto form a network that connects houses, compounds, terraces, and other features (4.7-4.9). The best-defined trails consist of linear, narrow, cleared surfaces, usually no more than 50 cm to 75 cm wide, which continue for several dozen meters. The longest individual segments that can be traced with any certainty are between 100 m and 150 m long; these trails originally may have been longer and connected to adjacent paths no longer visible.

Trail surfaces are usually devoid of rock down to the level of caliche or caliche-cemented bedrock. Often the loose surface rocks that were removed to construct the trail were cast aside haphazardly, but some trails are lined on one or both sides by stacked boulders and cobbles (Hartmann and Hartmann 1979). Many of the trails extend in a straight line for most of their length, but those that angle up a steep slope often exhibit sharp bends or switchbacks (see Fig. 3.15, Inscription Hill trail). The inclined paths occasionally have boulders in them that served as steps. In most cases, trails can be easily followed from one feature to another, but short segments may be blocked by vegetation or obscured by erosion.

The overall pattern of the trails suggests links between the far west side of Cerro Prieto and the farthest east portions of the village. Although there are significant gaps in the network as mapped, field observations indicate that there probably existed a continuous or near-continuous distribution of trails extending across the village. It is noteworthy that the mapped trail system extends through the massive parallel boulder walls that bisect the site, and that two trails pass across the large cleft or fault in the far eastern part of the site. On the assumption that trails would have connected only contemporaneous features, these observations indicate that the village at Cerro Prieto was indeed extensive at the peak of its occupation.

No trail has yet been found connecting the lower features of Cerro Prieto to the hill summit. The upper portions of the hill are extremely steep and rocky, and a trail in the talus there would have been difficult to construct and maintain. Through trial and error, we discovered two viable routes from the lower slopes to the top. One route leads directly up the major cleft in the east portion of the site, until the cleft plays out, then goes south to a ridge top that connects from the east-southeast with the summit. The second (and more hazardous) route follows the set of parallel boulder walls near the center of the site until that feature merges with thick talus, then proceeds directly up the talus slope. Neither of these routes would have sustained a lasting trail, so we could not determine if they had been used prehistorically.

Parallel Walls

Perhaps the largest and most unusual single feature at Cerro Prieto is the set of parallel boulder walls that extends more or less vertically up the hill slope in the western part of the site (Figs. 4.7, 4.8, 4.29). The walls stretch from near the base of the hill to a thick talus deposit, approximately 135 m above. The horizontal distance between the two walls ranges from about 2 m to 8 m. The walls are separated by a channel or fault containing exposures of caliche, occasional boulders and cobbles, slight accumulations of soil, sand, or gravel, and some vegetation. There is a definite size gradient in the rocks in the wall, from large boulders at the upper elevations, to fist-size or smaller stones in the lower reaches. In the upper portions, the walls rise to a height of 1.5 m to 2.0 m above the channel that separates them. Toward the bottom of the hill, the walls are only a few centimeters high. The walls are lowered in several places, apparently where they are entered by trails. One well-preserved trail segment crosses the walls directly.

According to University of Arizona geomorphologist James Lombard in 1985, the walls may have originated as parallel ribbons of stones left behind during a prehistoric debris flow of unknown but perhaps considerable antiquity. If so, the walls would have accumulated along the margins of the channel as a mass of sediment became saturated with rainfall and slumped to the bottom of the hill. There is supporting evidence for Lombard's interpretation, including the size sorting of the stones along the sides of the channel and the fact that on aerial photographs the parallel walls terminate in a dark colored lobe that probably represents the sediment that flowed down the channel.

There is no doubt, however, that even though the feature may trace its origins to natural processes, it also has undergone cultural modification. Some of the boulders at the top of the walls are covered with a crust of caliche, whereas those near the bottom do not show such a crust. Hence, it would appear that the top-most boulders of the walls were uprooted and overturned when stacked atop the natural boulder accumulations along the channel sides. In doing so, perhaps the inhabitants of Cerro Prieto were attempting to augment and straighten the natural lines of boulders and cobbles along the margins of the channel. Evidently, boulders and cobbles were taken from around the margins of the debris flow and stacked to form double rock walls somewhat higher than the natural deposits. A scarcity of boulders and cobbles within the channel indicates that some of the stones may have come from there. Additionally, prehistoric use is indicated by plain ware potsherds wedged between the wall stones at various locations. Where prehistoric trails intersect the walls, boulders and cobbles have been removed and rearranged to allow passage through, rather than over, the accumulations of boulders.

At first we thought the parallel walls might represent an attempt to harvest water from the hill slope by clearing the channel between them, thus concentrating runoff and directing it onto fields at the hill base. However, further observation showed such was not the case. At the base of the hill, the channel between the two walls becomes shallow and indistinct, and it eventually is lost in a jumble of boulders that are strewn about on the dark

Figure 4.29. View downslope (to north) of west side of parallel boulder walls that divide the Cerro Prieto Site. (ASM photograph 86826, by Christian E. Downum.)

lobe of sediment believed to be the terminal end of the debris flow discussed above. There are few rockpiles, terraces, or other agricultural modifications near the termination of the walls. No clear drainage leads from the lower end of the walls to more distant agricultural features and, indeed, the local topography seems to prohibit the possibility that runoff could have been directed from the channel to surrounding plots.

Perhaps the walls are the outcome of an attempt to provide a vertical trail up the hill slope. Inhabitants of Cerro Prieto may have taken advantage of the natural corridor created by the debris flow by clearing the boulders and cobbles that had accumulated in the channel since the flow took place. The parallel walls, then, might be an incidental outcome of trail building and not an intentional construction.

Related to the proposition that the walls represent some sort of trail, Emil Haury in 1986 suggested to us that the path might be a prehistoric "race track," used for organized foot races up the hill slope. His suggestion was based in part on observations of ethnographer Frank Russell, who interpreted cleared corridors at several southern Arizona sites as the prehistoric equivalent of historically documented race tracks (Russell 1908: 173):

> At various points in Arizona the writer has found what appear to have been ancient race tracks situated near the ruins of buildings. One of these was seen on the south bank of the Babacomari, 3 miles above the site of old Fort Wallen. It is 5 m wide and 275 m long. It is leveled by cutting down in places and the rather numerous bowlders [*sic*] of the mesa are cleared away. In the Sonoita valley, 2 miles east of Patagonia, there is a small ruin with what may have been a race track. It is 6 m wide and 180 m long. At the northern end stands a square stone 37 cm above the surface. These will serve as examples of the tracks used by the Sobaipuris, a tribe belonging to the Piman stock. The dimensions are about the same as those of the tracks that the writer has seen the Jicarilla Apaches using in New Mexico. The tracks prepared by the Pimas opposite Sacaton Flats and at Casa Blanca are much longer.

Although the features mentioned by Russell evidently did not extend vertically up a hill slope, the fact that they are roughly similar in size to the Cerro Prieto corridor is intriguing, as is the reference to the clearing away of "rather numerous bowlders." Whether or not such clearings did serve as prehistoric race tracks, their existence at several widely separated sites in southern Arizona is worth noting, and additional investigation and comparison should be pursued to assess the similarities or differences of such features.

A final consideration is that the walls might be an attempt to divide the community into two zones or precincts. The walls separate the structures at Cerro Prieto into two roughly equivalent groups and may have been constructed to formalize a social division of residents. As discussed below (Organization of Cerro Prieto), the Tanque Verde phase trincheras sites of Tumamoc Hill, Linda Vista Hill, and Fortified Hill exhibit similar divisions.

Alignments and Rockpiles

On the lower slopes of Cerro Prieto there are concentrations of rockpiles, cleared areas associated with rockpiles, and rock alignments that evidently represent contour terraces and waffle gardens (Fig. 4.30). Many of these features were located and plotted during the Cerro Prieto mapping project, but time did not allow an exhaustive inventory. The features mapped (Fig. 4.7) are only a partial representation of the total number now visible.

In spite of the incomplete mapping of agricultural features, it is apparent that rockpiles, alignments, and other features of presumed agricultural function are clustered in particular locations. One is on the lower slopes at the far east portion of the Cerro Prieto Site. Interestingly, a trail in the southeast quadrant of the site turns downhill and heads toward this concentration of features. Other sets of features, particularly rockpiles and cleared areas, are clumped on the lower slopes in the east part of the site. This pattern, along with the presence of terraces just upslope from the two areas previously mentioned, suggests that the northeast slopes of Cerro Prieto were devoted to agricultural production, whereas the northwest slopes, occupied by the large compounds and the parallel boulder walls, were used for a different purpose.

Although a thorough search of the area beyond the lower slopes was not attempted, several reconnaissance inspections indicated that the density of agricultural features declines considerably just beyond the limits of the Cerro Prieto Site. The alignments, rockpiles, cleared areas, and other presumed agricultural features at the base of the hill, therefore, were probably tended by the occupants of Cerro Prieto, and they had selected only a limited area for agricultural modifications. It is likely this area offered optimum environmental and geomorphic conditions for cultivation. The lower slopes of the hill provide a gently sloping deposit of sand, silt, and gravel that appears ideal for runoff floodwater farming, and the hill itself represents a substantial watershed that might

Figure 4.30. View south-southwest across rock alignments (terrace gardens), lower northeast slope of Cerro Prieto. (ASM photograph 69741, by Helga G. Teiwes.)

have meant the difference between agricultural success and failure in dry years. Many of the alignments and waffle-gardens are exceedingly well preserved, and small swales and gullies leading to them show the micro-environmental conditions that the plots were intended to exploit. The general location of such features also may have been significant, because the northeast slope of the hill would have provided somewhat cooler and wetter conditions than other aspects. Proximity to the Cerro Prieto village was in itself an advantage, as fields could be easily watched by nearby residents and defended from predators. Nearness would have minimized transport costs and promoted mulching or fertilization of fields with household garbage. Clearly, the fields along the northeast base of Cerro Prieto would have been particularly productive when compared to alternative locations nearby.

Petroglyphs

Petroglyphs are relatively abundant at Cerro Prieto. Frequently they occur in isolation, but they are also in clusters of up to several dozen elements on bedrock outcrops or large boulders. Occasionally they are found on

Figure 4.31. Petroglyph with rectilinear interlocking scroll design, upper slope of Cerro Prieto. (ASM photograph 86828, by Christian E. Downum.)

Figure 4.32. Petroglyph with barbed, rectilinear scrolls similar to designs found on Tanque Verde Red-on-brown pottery, upper slope of Cerro Prieto. (ASM photograph 86831, by Christian E. Downum.)

boulders or bedrock outcrops that form room foundations and walls. A few petroglyphs were observed on small boulders at the hill summit, in association with the tabular andesite quarries. There is a wide range in the quality and complexity of designs, from small and poorly made single elements (for example, a spiral) to the elaborate and well-executed panels depicted in Figures 4.31 and 4.32.

Petroglyphs were not systematically recorded and studied by the Cerro Prieto mapping project, but the abundance and distribution of glyphs indicates great potential for future research. Of particular interest is the distribution of petroglyphs in and around house clusters, where design elements are associated with aggregates of structures presumed to represent significant social units. Additional study of these designs may indicate important facts about the use of petroglyph designs as markers of social identity.

Miscellaneous Features

Of the miscellaneous features observed at several locations, one of the largest and most interesting is a horizontal, cleared, T-shaped corridor that is at the base of the northeast hill slope. This feature, easily visible both on aerial photographs and on the ground, consists of a linear area 5 m to 10 m wide and about 120 m long that has been almost entirely cleared of bedrock and soil down to the level of caliche. This cleared area is oriented parallel to the hill slope, and a rock wall, consisting of one or two courses of large boulders, extends along the downslope side. In the approximate center of the corridor, there is a break in the downslope wall, and another cleared and walled corridor, about 3 m to 4 m wide and 25 m long, opens perpendicular to the main clearing and runs directly downslope. South of this are three smaller, rather evenly spaced openings in the long corridor; these, too, are demarcated by boulders on one or both sides, and they also lead downslope from the long corridor. The whole arrangement is thus configured like a misshapen T, with the base of the T formed by the short corridor leading downslope and the much longer top of the T formed by the corridor oriented parallel with the hill slope (Figs. 4.7, 4.9).

The function of this feature is unknown. There is some possibility that it represents a historic period modification, perhaps the result of removing boulders to construct buildings at Sasco. The feature also resembles in some respects the race tracks described by Russell (1908: 173; see above). However, two observations suggest this feature might represent a prehistoric attempt to harvest water from the east slope of Cerro Prieto and direct it onto agricultural features farther downslope.

First, the feature today funnels a considerable amount of runoff from the east slope into the short corridor that forms the base of the T. Only a few of the small gullies surrounding the base of Cerro Prieto are entrenched or eroded to any degree, but at the bottom of the T there is a distinct, entrenched drainage. The feature today is singularly effective at capturing hillside runoff and concentrating it into a specific channel. Second, the main gully that leads from the entrenched area at the bottom of the feature flows directly into a concentration of alignments and rockpiles a few meters below and to the northeast. If the T did serve to deflect slope wash, this concentration of prehistoric agricultural features at the hill base can be identified as the area intended to receive the runoff. Short cleared and walled segments northwest of the T (Figs. 4.7, 4.9) also may have served as water harvesting devices. Their capability to channel and concentrate runoff could have been enhanced by the construction of brush weirs or fences, similar to those currently used by Tohono O'odham ak chin farmers (Nabhan 1983, 1986; Gasser 1990).

On the north side of the large fault or drainage in the far southeast portion of the site there is a wide trail that angles upslope from the bottom of the hill to the first of the concentrations of large terraces north of the fault. It has been cleared of boulders and is flanked on either side by a rough wall of boulders one or two courses high. The feature is of interest not only as a particularly wide and well-made trail, but also because it leads directly to the large terraces and may have been associated with some special function of those features. Unfortunately, the mapping project did not attempt an accurate plot of this corridor, so it is not featured on site maps.

Artifacts

Although surface artifacts at Cerro Prieto were not systematically collected or inventoried, a few general comments can be made about them. The density of artifacts at Cerro Prieto is greater than appears on first examination. The rocky surface of the hill is not a particularly good substrate for observing artifacts, but close inspection of many areas between definable features reveals a light to moderate scatter of sherds and chipped stone debitage, often wedged between cobbles and boulders. This trash accumulated during the Tanque Verde phase occupation of Cerro Prieto. Much of it has been rearranged slightly by gravity and slope wash, but its widespread distribution suggests that a common method of trash disposal was simply to broadcast it downslope from houses and activity areas. Greenleaf (1975: 222) observed that trash disposal at the Fortified Hill Site was similarly informal, with "the bulk of debris . . . tossed over the steep sides of the site."

Other areas of Cerro Prieto show definite accumulations of trash, particularly the large terraces in the east portion. Here terrace surfaces exhibit an impressive density and diversity of items, including plain and decorated sherds, chipped stone debitage, hammerstones, cores, ground stone tool fragments, shell jewelry and shell debitage, and burned bone. Terrace fill often appears as a dark, ashy matrix, containing an extremely high density of artifacts. This fill has been badly churned by past pothunting and rodent burrowing, so the exact mode of deposition is unclear. It was certainly intentionally dumped behind terrace walls, but whether this was to fill the terraces during their construction, or whether the fill later accumulated during use of terrace surfaces, is unknown.

Plain ware sherds are the most abundant surface artifacts, but chipped stone debitage, usually a fine-grained gray to black basalt or andesite, is also frequently observed. Many of the plain ware sherds are heavily tempered with crushed mica and are exceedingly thin. Most seem to be from jars, and many of these have a sharply angled shoulder near the pot base that is a characteristic of Tanque Verde phase plain ware vessels. Decorated sherds are relatively infrequent (possibly because they have been collected by souvenir hunters), but the vast majority appear to be in the Tucson Basin red-on-brown series. All that could be given an unambiguous type assignment were Tanque Verde Red-on-brown. A few of the Tanque Verde sherds exhibit a black painted design applied to a thick, chalky white slip. No polychrome or black-on-white sherds have yet been observed at the site, and only a single, highly eroded buff ware sherd was recorded. Although the erosion of surface sherds may be a contributing factor, only a few possible red ware specimens were observed, and these could not be placed into established types. Other artifact categories include shell jewelry (mostly *Conus* tinklers, *Olivella* beads, and *Glycymeris* bracelets), vesicular basalt mano and metate fragments, tabular knife fragments, a vesicular basalt "stone doughnut" fragment (near a set of agricultural alignments at the northeast portion of the hill base), and debitage from the manufacture of ground stone tools.

ORGANIZATION OF CERRO PRIETO

The high visibility of Cerro Prieto's masonry structures, terraces, and other features provides an excellent opportunity to assess the spatial organization of the village. Two of us (Craig and Douglas) have made a detailed analysis of Cerro Prieto, focusing on architectural variability between individual structures, between clusters of structures, and between the eastern and western halves of the village. The complete results of this analysis, now on file at the Arizona State Museum, (Craig and Douglas, in Downum 1991; see also Craig and Douglas 1984) cannot be repeated here. We present the following summary.

Based on an inspection of the arrangement of Cerro Prieto structures, and considering local topographic variability, we were able to discern 46 clusters of structures (Fig. 4.33). This did not count the compounds near the base of the hill that contained only a single structure. Precisely what social units might be reflected in these clusters has not been established. However, following Wilcox and others (1981) and other Hohokam researchers (Sires 1984; Howard 1985; Elson 1986; Henderson 1986; Huntington 1986), we presume that such clustering does provide a material reflection of significant social relationships. At Cerro Prieto, the arrangement and number of structures within the clusters suggests that they were made up of households and perhaps small groups of households.

Roughly three-fourths of all structures at Cerro Prieto belong to one of the 46 clusters. The remainder occur as widely scattered isolates that could not confidently be assigned cluster membership. Houses within clusters were larger and better constructed, as measured by the overall floor area and the frequency of plane-faced walls, than isolated structures. Furthermore, cross-tabulation of individual attributes demonstrates at a statistically significant level (chi square = 12.70, d.f. = 1, p = < .001) that the larger and better-made structures were more commonly found in the larger clusters (6 to 9 structures), whereas smaller, more poorly built structures tended to be isolates or components of the smaller clusters (2 to 5 structures). On this basis, we might conclude that some social groups at Cerro Prieto were wealthier and perhaps enjoyed greater power and prestige than others, but in the absence of supporting data from excavations, such interpretations remain tentative.

At the site-wide level of analysis, we note that Cerro Prieto is split into two roughly equivalent halves or precincts by the double row of boulders that has previously been described and discussed. Approximately 60 percent of all structures are located east of this feature, with the other 40 percent to the west. The purpose of the boulder walls is unknown, but one possible function may have been to split the village into two distinct social groups. Dividing walls are known from several large prehistoric pueblos, and are thought by some (for example, Rohn 1965) to reflect the organizational division of the site into moieties. Perhaps the Cerro Prieto wall served a similar purpose. Although this idea is admittedly speculative, it is not without some ethnographic basis. The O'odham, thought by many to be the descendants of the Hohokam, are divided into patrilineal moieties (Bahr 1983: 187; Underhill 1939: 31–32). Although these moieties serve only a ceremonial function in modern O'odham society, there are indications that they were more important in the past (Russell 1908: 197; Underhill 1939: 31).

Interestingly, Cerro Prieto is not the only hillside or hilltop village where this type of dual division can be observed. Some form of dividing feature is documented for the *cerros de trincheras* of Tumamoc Hill and Linda Vista Hill in the Tucson Basin, and at the Tanque Verde phase hilltop village of Fortified Hill, near Gila Bend. At Tumamoc Hill, the dividing feature is a wide, cleared strip flanked on both sides by lines of closely spaced structures (Larson 1979: 75–76). For the Linda Vista Hill Site, the split is accomplished by a linear bedrock outcrop on the upper slopes, supplanted by a boulder wall at the hill base. Excluding features at the top of the hill, Linda Vista has 36 dwellings southeast of the split and 41 dwellings to the northwest (Downum 1986: 222). The dual division of the Fortified Hill Site is especially pronounced. The village is split by a high, massive wall into two precincts designated by Greenleaf (1975: 228) as the "upper" and "lower" villages; the upper village has 34 rooms, the lower has 15 rooms. This wall runs across most of the site's width, forming a formidable barrier between upper and lower residential components.

Specific arrangements of structures at Fortified Hill and Cerro Prieto show further intriguing similarities that may reflect additional social organizational equivalencies. Both show a combination of closely-grouped or contiguous rooms, surrounded by isolated structures. In the two major village segments at Fortified Hill, Greenleaf (1975: 223–235) identified 11 units, incorporating 39 rooms, with 11 structures counted as isolates. These clusters ranged in size from two to eight rooms. For Cerro Prieto, the 46 clusters that we have identified were composed of 169 masonry rooms (out of 232) arranged into clusters of two to nine rooms each. In the percentage of rooms belonging to clusters (78% vs. 73%; z = –.75; p = .45), average cluster size (3.5 rooms vs. 3.7; t = –.16; p = .88) and the overall range of cluster sizes (2 to 8, vs. 2 to 9), the Fortified Hill and Cerro Prieto sites appear comparable if not statistically indistinguishable. As previously mentioned, specific room arrangements at Cerro Prieto are intuitively reminiscent of Fortified Hill, and particular details sometimes closely match (Fig. 4.19). It may also be significant that the largest rooms at the two sites, both of which are unusually large, are roughly similar in interior dimensions: Room 24 at Fortified Hill measured 4.75 m by 7.00 m; Room 138 at Cerro Prieto was 4.70 m by 7.40 m.

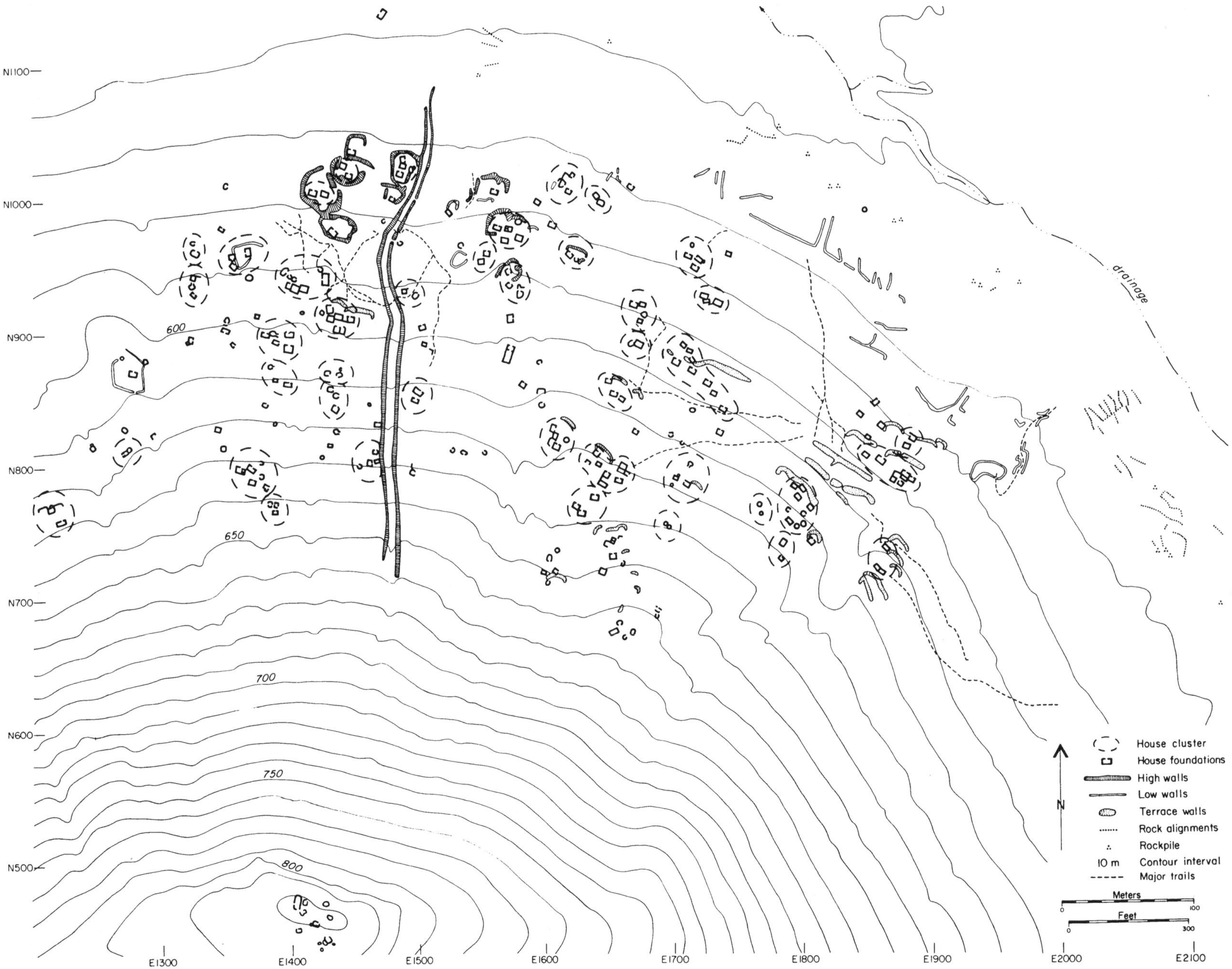

Figure 4.33. House clusters at Cerro Prieto.

SUMMARY AND CONCLUSION

Information from mapping and test excavations at Cerro Prieto indicates a prehistoric hillside village of considerable size and complexity. The most abundant features are circular and rectangular masonry foundations that evidently represent the remains of habitation structures. These structures and their arrangements show strong similarities to the excavated early Classic hilltop site of Fortified Hill, located about 125 km northwest of Cerro Prieto near Gila Bend, and exhibit general similarities to other hilltop or hillside structures across a broad area of southern and central Arizona. Other important features at Cerro Prieto are massive stone compounds, terraces, trails, agricultural field systems, and miscellaneous features that include long, linear boulder arrangements, apparent water-control alignments, and petroglyphs. A large quantity of trash is distributed across the hillside, some of it broadly scattered informally as household trash and some concentrated into more formal midden areas. Some large terraces were either partially filled with quantities of dark, ashy trash deposits or such material accumulated during their use.

The high visibility of masonry features at Cerro Prieto suggests potentially important facts about this settlement's social organization. Structures were arranged into spatially distinct clusters, perhaps households or groups of households. The larger clusters tended to contain larger and better-constructed structures, which in turn suggests some degree of inequality in the social units composing the clusters. The site is split into two precincts or halves by a pair of boulder walls running vertically up the hill's north slope. The function of this wall is unknown, but we have suggested that it might have divided the settlement into two distinct social groups, perhaps moieties. Similar dividing features are now known to have been present at other hilltop and hillside villages in southern Arizona.

Overall, the features at Cerro Prieto suggest a large, thriving, early Classic period hillside settlement, and not a temporary defensive retreat. There is little evidence that this village had a defensive function, and some of its features, such as trails and cleared access corridors, are actually contrary to the goals of community defense. Terraces, often interpreted at other trincheras sites as explicitly defensive constructions (Hoover 1941; Wilcox 1979), appear at Cerro Prieto to have served multiple functions. Circumstantial evidence indicates that some of the terraces were used as garden plots. They also may have served as extramural courtyards or activity spaces, used in conjunction with nearby clusters of rooms. We have also suggested that the largest terraces, arranged in steplike fashion and visible from a considerable distance, might have had an important symbolic function.

Hillside terraces, along with rockpiles, contour terraces, waffle gardens, check dams, and other presumed agricultural features at lower elevations on the hill slope, indicate that agricultural production was a major activity at Cerro Prieto. A geomorphic evaluation of the agricultural potential of Cerro Prieto's terraces is presented by Keith Katzer below. Another significant pursuit was the manufacture of tabular knives, using an abundant source of raw material at the hill summit. Considering the importance of tabular knives to the harvesting and processing of agave during the early Classic period (S. Fish, P. Fish, Miksicek, and Madsen 1985), it is probable that Cerro Prieto was a regionally prominent source of this artifact.

Important questions remain to be addressed about the village of Cerro Prieto and its place in the Los Robles Community, as well as its role in regional cultural dynamics. Of special interest is the relationship between Cerro Prieto and other sites with trincheras features, including apparently contemporaneous examples in northern Sonora, the Tucson Basin, and central Arizona. These topics are discussed in more detail in Chapter 6, but first we turn to a geomorphic analysis of trincheras terraces, written by the late Keith Katzer.

A GEOMORPHIC EVALUATION OF THE AGRICULTURAL POTENTIAL OF CERROS DE TRINCHERAS

Keith Katzer

The following discussion, written by the late Keith Katzer in 1985, was originally prepared as a paper for a course at The University of Arizona in Culture and Arid Lands Agriculture, taught by Suzanne Fish. It is published here with the permission of his wife, Lisa Ely. Except for a few minor editorial changes ("terrace" has been substituted for his "trinchera") and insertion of additional references, the paper is published as originally written.

Cerros de trincheras are common features in the deserts of southern Arizona and northern Sonora. This study focuses on a particular kind of trincheras feature, consisting of prehistoric coarse to well-made stone walls, up to 4 m in height, occupying the sides and crests of desert hills (cerros). The walls are usually perpendicular to the hill slope and may be linear, curved, or circular, forming a terrace. Upslope of the walls is a layer of earthen fill, generally even with the crest of the wall. Where excavated (S. Fish, P. Fish, and Downum 1984; P.

Fish, S. Fish, Long, and Miksicek 1986), numerous late Hohokam (A.D. 1100–1300) sherds have been recovered, indicating the fill is prehistoric. Terraces are invariably placed on volcanic hills, usually andesitic, the boulders of which are incorporated in the walls.

The majority of investigators (Huntington 1914; Sauer and Brand 1931; Hoover 1941; Fontana and others 1959; Larson 1972; Wilcox 1979) have concluded that terraces were constructed as a defensive measure, although the evidence is less than compelling. Recently, the agricultural hypothesis, first tentatively proposed by Huntington (1914) for the impressive Cerro de Las Trincheras site in northern Sonora, has gained new momentum. Excavations of terraces at Linda Vista Hill (Los Morteros) revealed two distinct patterns of use. Small elliptical terraces were demonstrated to be house pits (Downum 1986). Long linear terraces were found to have been intentionally filled with soil, presumably at the time of construction (S. Fish, P. Fish, and Downum 1984). A test excavation of a linear terrace on Tumamoc Hill (P. Fish, S. Fish, Long, and Miksicek 1986) revealed a layer of fill 40 cm thick. Below this, and dating to a time prior to terrace construction, late Archaic corn was recovered.

Neither the defensive nor the agriculture propositions are easy to substantiate because the two uses may closely parallel each other in the archaeological record. A possible way out of this century-old dilemma comes from evaluating the geomorphic controls present on the hill slopes. These controls include the aspect and gradient of hill slopes, average temperature, soil type, and availability of soil moisture throughout the growing season. Nearly all of these factors might be circumstantial, and could be present but not utilized, in a terrace constructed for defense. The first factor, aspect, is otherwise. If terraces were selectively placed at certain aspects, and hence certain microclimates, at the exclusion of others, a strong case for agricultural use can be made. It is hardly likely that the Hohokam had a tacit agreement with their foes to battle in certain hillside microclimates and not others.

Geomorphic Controls

Cold air drainage along the valley floor often creates a temperature inversion, an observation first documented in the Tucson Basin by Turnage and Hinckley (1938). The investigators monitored two thermographs for a five-year period, one at the base of Tumamoc Hill and one approximately 100 m up the hillside. There was a dramatic difference in the duration of freezing nights between the two stations. On Tumamoc Hill there was an average of 36 days between the first and last freeze of the winter. On the valley floor, the average duration was 157 days. The importance of this dramatic variance in temperature with relief was recently assessed by S. Fish, P. Fish, and Downum (1984), who suggest it was an important factor to prehistoric farmers.

Inversions are not the only significant thermal control on a hillside. The aspect of a hillside is also crucial in determining the resulting temperature. In the northern hemisphere, north-facing slopes are invariably more mesic than their south-facing counterparts, because they are exposed to less direct solar radiation. Reduced solar radiation in turn reduces the evapotranspiration rate of water, thereby conserving soil moisture. The north-south subdivision alone is too coarse for determining microclimates, because even a minor change in aspect has important consequences. The most mesic slopes are those to the north and northeast, whereas the most xeric slope is generally to the southwest, although Hasse (1970) has demonstrated the southeastern slope is the most xeric in the Sonoran desert, because of the often cooler afternoon temperature in late summer when the land is in the shadow of convective thunderstorms. In a study of thermal variation in desert mountain ranges, Logan documented the influence of aspect on temperature. He found that the minimum temperature during the winter varied more than ten degrees Fahrenheit on north- and south-facing slopes of a narrow ridge. He writes (Logan 1961):

> In contrast, the vertical distance of a mile resulted in a difference of 16 [degrees Fahrenheit]. Exposure north or south is of greater effect than altitude; north facing slopes of 5,000 feet may be colder than neutral areas 2,000 feet higher.

The temperature of a hill slope is important for agriculture not only because of the threat of freezing weather and crop loss. During the early summer when temperatures are high and precipitation is at a minimum, cooler aspects reduce evapotranspiration and conserve soil moisture. The availability of soil moisture for longer periods of the year promotes weathering (and hence more soil), and additional plant growth, which discourages soil erosion and gullying during intense thunderstorms.

Aspect

Discussions of trincheras feature aspects in the past have been incomplete, because they were limited to a single hill (Wilcox 1979). Individual sites fail to give fair weight to all aspects because of topographic variation. Tumamoc Hill, for example, is bounded by an abrupt cliff on the south and few, if any, trincheras features could be constructed at this aspect. It is only when a population of *cerros de trincheras* is considered that trends in aspect preference are observable. For this study, nine hills in southern Arizona (five near Sells, and four in the Tucson area) were considered (Fig. 1.1). The sample size was limited by the scarcity of mapped trincheras feature sites. Data for the five sites near Sells (AZ DD:1:1, DD:1:5, DD:1:3, DD:6:1, and DD:2:4) were obtained from Stacy (1974) and for sites in the Tucson Basin (Fig. 4.2) from Wilcox (1979, Tumamoc Hill), S. Fish, P. Fish, and Downum (1984, Los Morteros), Wallace (1983, Rillito Peak), and Downum (Cerro Prieto, see above).

To determine aspect, the hill slopes were first subdivided into eight 45 degree quadrants, centered around the cardinal directions of the compass: a due north quadrant, a northeast quadrant, an east quadrant, and so on. A map wheel was then used to measure the actual length of each terrace in meters. The total meters of a terrace for each aspect was calculated. A long terrace, one that spanned several aspects, was subdivided and the individual segments measured. Thus an extremely long terrace might contribute a portion of its length to two or three different aspects. Only linear terraces were calculated, because there is a strong likelihood that short, crescent-shaped terraces represent house foundations and pits.

Several of the large sites contain many thousands of meters of terraces. To keep these few sites from dominating the combined results, each population was normalized before the sites were averaged together, thereby insuring all sites are given equal weight. Figure 4.34 presents the combined aspects of terraces at nine sites.

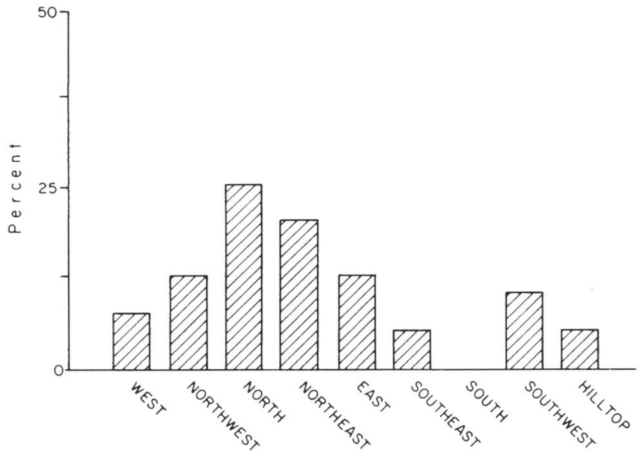

Figure 4.34. Combined aspects of terraces at nine sites discussed in the text.

The results reveal a strong tendency for terraces to be found on northern (NW, N, NE) slopes, equaling 58 percent of all terraces, whereas only 15 percent are on southern (SW, S, SE) slopes. A full 45 percent of all terraces face to the north and northeast, the most mesic microclimate available on a hill. Of the terraces facing south, two-thirds face to the southwest, the aspect suggested by Hasse (1970) to be the most mesic of the southerly directions. Only 5 percent of all terraces face due south or southeast.

Soil Type

Before analyzing the soil moisture-runoff relations, it is important to consider the type of soil present on trincheras feature sites and to compare it both to the natural soil of the hillside and to the soils of the valley floor. Igneous lithologies are rich in minerals that are reduced by weathering into a clay loam. On Tumamoc Hill there is a 40-cm-thick, clay-rich B, or argillic horizon. Directly below it is an impervious layer of calcium carbonate, the calcic horizon, more commonly known as caliche. Below Tumamoc Hill and above the floodplain are a series of small alluvial fans. This deposit is derived from alluvium transported off the surrounding hills and is coarser grained than the fine clay of the hill slope. Often these deposits are relatively recent and do not contain soil profiles. The floodplain of the Santa Cruz varies from a silt loam to a clay loam. The variance represents the primary deposition of silt, clay, and sand by the river and not a soil profile. Aside from clay-rich lenses in the deposit, there are no impervious layers.

Forrest Shreve (1934) summarized some water-holding characteristics of each of these deposits. He found that the alluvial clay would hold 50.4 percent of its dry weight in water. The bajada surface held 32.0 percent and the volcanic soils of the hillside 48.2 percent. Additionally, he determined the wilting point, the point at which soil moisture drops below a threshold that can sustain plants, for each of the deposits. The wilting point is 16.5 percent for the volcanic soil, 7.7 percent for the bajada, and 12.9 percent for the floodplain. Even though the volcanic clay has a slightly lower water-holding capacity than the alluvial clays, Shreve found soil moisture was invariably higher on the volcanic soils. This is due to the water retention capability of clayey soils, coupled with the presence of an impermeable calcic horizon, which concentrates water near the surface.

Textural information on the soils found within terraces is extremely limited and is only available for Tumamoc Hill. Four samples from the test excavation of P. Fish, S. Fish, Long, and Miksicek (1986) were textured by Jeanette Schuster. These four samples span both the fill behind the terrace and the underlying natural hill slope. The texture of the two units is the same, a silty clay loam to a silt loam. Presumably the fill was derived from the adjacent hill slope, although this is not adequately documented at the present time. Nor is it proven the soil retains a high water-holding capacity after redeposition, although it is highly likely.

Catchment

During an intense rainstorm, precipitation exceeds infiltration and runoff occurs. This excess water is transported down slope to a terrace, thus supplementing the contribution of rainfall. The amount of runoff delivered to a terrace is difficult to quantify because of the many variables present in a watershed. These variables include the antecedent soil moisture conditions, the soil type, the vegetation type and density, the slope angle, and the intensity and duration of the runoff event. The actual volume of water can only be accurately determined in an instrumented watershed. Without such quantitative measurements, an investigator must turn to the numerous models utilized by hydrologists and engineers.

The method I have chosen is used by Soil Conservation Survey as adapted to southern Arizona by the Arizona Department of Transportation (Jencsok 1969). This method requires the following information: soil type, vegetation type and density, and antecedent soil moisture conditions. I calculated the volume of runoff that would be generated by four catchment sizes, 10, 100, 500, and 1,000 square meters, and I assumed the drainage to be square and that the terrace occupied a 50-cm-wide strip the length of the base of the catchment. The majority of terraces fit within this range of values. I also tracked three one-hour-long storms of varying intensity: 3 cm, 2.5 cm, and 1.3 cm (1.2 inches, 1.0 inch, and 0.5 inch). The largest value, 3 cm, is the maximum rate for a two-year event. The lowest value, 1.3 cm, commonly occurs each season.

The data are presented as volume of water delivered to the terrace system, and as volume delivered per square meter (Fig. 4.35). The results are impressive. A 1.3-cm rain on a 10-square-meter drainage will produce nearly twice as much water as naturally falls on the terraces. The same rain on a catchment of 500 square meters will deliver more than six times as much water as direct rainfall. Obviously, the presence of a catchment greatly enhances the soil moisture content of a soil.

The volume of water is only one element of the story. If water yield exceeds water storage, then the excess water cannot be used. Shreve (1914) likened the soil to "a gigantic reservoir," and the analogy is apt. As in a reservoir, a soil can store only a certain fixed amount of

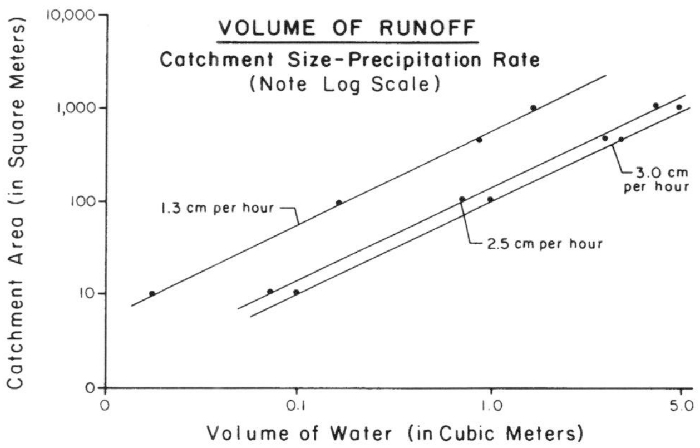

Figure 4.35. Volume of runoff, catchment size-precipitation rate (note log scale).

water, an amount known as the field capacity. Therefore, I have considered data indicating the volume of rain needed to raise soil moisture from 0 percent to field capacity, and from 50 percent to field capacity. The first case required an hour-long rain of 3 cm on a 1,000 square-meter catchment. Dependent on antecedent soil moisture conditions, the majority of all runoff events were retained by the soil in the terrace, assuming the water could be stored on the surface of the terrace while infiltration occurred, perhaps by utilizing a small berm.

The above data cannot be considered to be quantitative. Many variables were not addressed, or were considered in a superficial manner. The model assumes water was delivered evenly to all parts of the terrace, an assumption that is obviously too simplistic. Additionally, water catchments were treated as squares, not as typical drainage basins. This tends to overestimate the areal extent of a terrace, and consequently underestimate the volume of water per square meter. Another complication is the type of storm modeled, which is an intense one-hour-long event. Although such storms undoubtedly occur, it is far more common to have storms of longer duration and more variable rainfall. No doubt the results could be refined, but the results will always be of questionable value. Approximations such as the SCS runoff model indicate the magnitude of the contribution of runoff, but nothing more. To go further in these investigations, catchments and terrace systems must be instrumented and monitored over several seasons.

Discussion

This study has not proven an agricultural use for *cerros de trincheras* sites; that proof, if it is to be found, remains in the ground. However, it has demonstrated that certain geomorphic parameters are favorable to agriculture. The most telling of these controls is the pronounced skewness of trincheras features toward northern aspects, precisely those aspects most favorable for agriculture. The other parameters such as slope, catchment size, soil type, and soil temperature are more favorable for nonirrigated agriculture on hill slopes than on the valley floor.

A hill offers a farmer a choice of aspects, catchment sizes, and slopes, which in turn control soil temperature and moisture. On the valley floor these choices do not exist. Here a farmer has no control over air temperature and can only control soil moisture by direct irrigation. In the Tucson Basin, trincheras terraces may have offered insurance in cases of flooding or down cutting along the Santa Cruz River. No doubt there are pitfalls and tradeoffs in utilizing either strategy, and it is possible both environments were exploited by the same farmers, in the hope that at least one would deliver a crop.

Although the majority of trincheras terraces are concentrated on the northern flanks, they are present in every aspect, even extremely xeric ones such as due south. This may represent the preferred orientation for extremely early crops during the late winter and early spring. In these seasons, soil moisture is still high, but freezing nights exclude planting on the floodplain. Alternatively, the scattering of trincheras terraces to the east, south, and west may represent fringe agricultural areas, utilized only in the wetter years.

The catchment size-water yield relationships calculated here suggest significant amounts of excess water are delivered to the terraces, but this relationship is impossible to quantify without field observations. What is needed is several instrumented watersheds on different aspects of a single hill where it is possible to monitor rainfall, soil surface temperature, and soil moisture. The study could be simplified by monitoring soil moisture at various aspects, both on and off terraces. This study is crucial if we are to understand how trincheras features functioned. Most interesting would be the soil moisture content in May and June, the time of maximum soil moisture deficit in the Sonoran desert. Several other studies might also offer insight into functional questions. A catchment can deliver a great deal of water to a terrace, but naturally this water will be concentrated unevenly along the surface of the terrace, thus reducing its usefulness. Catchments should be mapped in detail to determine if small-scale water-spreading systems were constructed to maximize the effectiveness of the runoff. It would also be interesting to determine the origin of the fill in the terraces. If it is derived from the hill slope directly above the terrace, as would appear logical, then its removal may have enhanced the runoff potential of the hill slope.

Although all of the evidence is not yet in hand, trincheras terraces may prove to be relatively sophisticated agricultural features. If so, the Hohokam had a clear understanding of both soil-runoff relations and the crop-growing potential of the various microclimates present on individual hills.

CHAPTER FIVE

Rock Cairn and Talus Pit Features in the Los Robles Community

John H. Madsen

In the region of southern Arizona once occupied by the Hohokam culture, the transition from the prehistoric to the historic period spans approximately 250 years. This era, commonly referred to as the protohistoric, covers the period from about A.D. 1450 to 1700 (Masse 1981). In southern Arizona, the first 90 years of this transition encompass the end of the Hohokam cultural tradition and the abandonment of sprawling rancheria communities, large towns, and massive public work projects (platform mounds, big houses, and large canal systems). In the following 150 years (A.D. 1539–1691), European expeditions entered southern Arizona, and by A.D. 1700 a series of missions had been established along the upper Santa Cruz River by the Jesuit explorer Father Eusebio Kino. Mid-sixteenth- and seventeenth-century journals written during these expeditions and during the later mission period record important information on local Native American populations, most of whom spoke the Piman language.

Recent protohistoric overviews (Masse 1981; Doelle 1984) combine information from translated Spanish journals and previous archaeological research. These data provide invaluable knowledge on riverine settlement patterns, irrigation and floodwater farming, and social organization of native populations in southern Arizona. It is apparent from the literature, however, that there are many more questions to be answered. As Doelle (1984: 197) points out, unless new documents are discovered, the existing protohistoric data base can be expanded only with new archaeological findings. The recent discovery on the Los Robles survey of seven sites associated with Pima-style pottery provides this kind of understanding and expands our knowledge of the transition from the protohistoric to historic period in southern Arizona.

Talus pits are commonly found on steep hillsides in natural geological formations referred to as talus slides. Such formations occur on most of the volcanic hills throughout the countryside near the Classic period trincheras site of Cerro Prieto (Chapter 4). Each of these sites represents an area where talus had been removed to create numerous small open pits on the rock slopes. Interspersed among the talus pits are features that appear to have been pits originally, but are now filled with rock. The largest talus sites recorded (AZ AA:7:158, AA:7:187, and AA:7:188) are located in a cluster on a volcanic hill just north of Cerro Prieto (Fig. 2.2, sites R-70, R-83, and R-84 respectively). These three sites contain the highest number of pits with Piman pottery in the survey area and therefore serve as the best examples for more intensive study. There are 38 pits at AZ AA:7: 158, 56 pits at AA:7:187, and 15 pits at AA:7:188. The discovery of these features in association with Piman-style ceramics further supports accounts in early Spanish journals, which place two Piman rancherias on the Santa Cruz River in the vicinity of Picacho Peak.

Prompted by the early historic pottery found on these sites, I made a search of the literature to determine if ethnographic information was available that might explain how the pits were used, when they were used, and by what groups of Native Americans. The only features described and shown in early photographs that vaguely resembled the talus pits in the Los Robles area were Tohono O'odham (Papago) cairn burials near San Xavier Mission south of Tucson and talus pit burials in other regions of the western United States. The ensuing field work and additional archival studies herein described were conducted to test the proposition that the Los Robles talus pits represented possible locations of Piman cemeteries dating to the late seventeenth, eighteenth, and early nineteenth centuries.

TALUS PITS

Wallace (1983: 198–199) coined the term "talus pit," suggesting it be applied to open pits caused by the removal of loose rock from hillside talus slopes (see also

Hartmann and Hartmann 1979: 58–60; Martynec 1987: 6). A review of ASM site files indicates that prior to the Los Robles survey, talus pits were recorded in at least nine locations west of the Santa Cruz River. A variety of functions has been suggested for these features, including hunting blinds, defensive works, or the unintentional result of digging in search of water seeps.

Although it is difficult to determine what these pits were used for, it is just as difficult to know when they were constructed, because most have no diagnostic remains. They probably represent a host of different activities that vary by region and time, and it is probable that the Hohokam, in addition to later Piman-speaking groups, built such features.

TALUS PITS AS CEMETERIES

To evaluate the possibility that some talus pit sites might have served as cemeteries, I reviewed much of the literature on Pima (Akimel O'odham; see Fontana 1983) and Papago (Tohono O'odham) culture. An article on Quitobaquito, a Sand Papago (Hiaced O'odham) cemetery in southwest Arizona (Anderson and others 1982) cited several articles on Pima cemeteries, including Lange and Riley's (1970) notes on Bandelier's (1884) description of a Papago hillside cemetery near San Xavier Mission. Lumholtz (1971) and Densmore (1929) described the San Xavier cemetery, and Densmore provided the first early photographs of these cryptlike graves. There were enough similarities between the early Papago cemeteries and the talus sites discovered on the Los Robles survey to hypothesize that they might represent cemeteries.

Using early historical records, Brew and Huckell (1987) itemized Piman burial practices. They concluded that the mortuary complex generally consisted of interment in a shaft grave roofed at ground level without earth to cover the deceased, provision of sustenance for the dead that included water and pinole (either in or outside the grave), and interment of personal property. Variations did exist, possibly on a regional basis, most markedly in the form of hillside crypt burials when such locations were accessible.

Primary descriptions of Piman hillside crypts vary slightly from one account to the next. Underhill (1939: 188–190) detailed two methods of burial:

> In the foothills, where digging was difficult, it was placed in a cave or cleft in the rocks, any openings being filled with stones. Where no cave was available, a rudimentary cliff dwelling was made, one side of the hill being used as a wall while a complementary wall was built up out of dry masonry, so the whole formed a circle four feet or so in diameter. The corpse, with his effects, was seated inside and the hole roofed over with boughs and brush, weighted down with stones. . . .

Besides inhumation, cremation was also an acceptable method of disposing of the dead. This practice seems to have been reserved for individuals killed in warfare, "perhaps for decomposing bodies . . . and perhaps for those either 'highly esteemed' or possessing dangerous magic" (Brew and Huckell 1987: 182). There is no indication in the early documents of where these individuals were interred.

Photographs and descriptions of Piman and Papago covered burial crypts suggest that these vaults are about the same diameter as many archaeological talus pits. There is no mention, however, of interment in open hillside pits. Assuming that the Los Robles talus pits represent Piman cemeteries, it is difficult to explain why 70 percent (78 of 111) of the pits considered here were open. However, in a late nineteenth-century account of Pima cemeteries, Grossman (1873) indicated that a grave was sometimes prepared prior to a sick person's death. If the sick person for whom the grave was dug recovered, the grave was left open. Grossman indicates he saw several open graves in Piman burial grounds.

It is difficult to imagine that each open talus pit represents one person near death that recovered. Three possibilities are suggested as alternative explanations of the open pits. The first is vandalism. Evidence for vandalism was found in some cases where broken jar fragments had been included in light-colored rubble cast downslope. As discussed below, pioneer rancher Yjinio Aguirre has written of removing pottery jars from volcanic hills in this vicinity, perhaps the same sites discussed herein.

Second, the pits may have been covered with wooden timbers or other perishable materials that have long since decayed. Underhill (1939: 188) noted that the Papago were placed in their cryptlike graves and then covered with wood or brush weighted down with rocks. After two or more centuries of exposure, the wooden cap, human remains, and perishable grave goods may have completely decomposed, leaving an open pit. The only items remaining would be nonperishable grave goods such as ceramic vessels. The rocks holding down the brush roof most likely tumbled inside the crypts once the superstructure began to decay.

Finally, the pits may have been dug in anticipation of casualties from Apache raiding that never came. During the mid to late eighteenth century, the Piman-speaking populations on the lower Santa Cruz River between Tucson and Picacho Peak were being harassed by Apaches.

By 1800, the Picacho villagers had taken refuge among the Pima on the Gila River, among the Papago at San Xavier del Bac, and at villages farther west. Talus pits, therefore, might have been dug in the Los Robles area, but not used, during these unsettled times.

Variability in talus pit size is an interesting issue, but one that the ethnographic evidence addresses only indirectly. One possible suggestion is that this variability might reflect age-group mortality rates. For instance, 39 percent of the open pits on site AZ AA:7:157 are between 0.5 m and 1.0 m in diameter. It is noteworthy that during a measles epidemic in 1770, many more children died than adults (Coues 1900), a situation not uncommon to the Papaguería during the seventeenth and eighteenth centuries. Alternatively, talus pit size may reflect cremation versus inhumation. Close examination of partially buried sherds from two small vandalized pits revealed what appeared to be minute layers of ash on the interior surfaces of the jars.

Interestingly, talus pit cemetery sites have been found throughout the western states. Fredin (1981) recorded 51 talus slope sites containing human burials located along the Columbia River in Washington. Harlan Smith's (1910) description and photographs of rock slide graves of the Yakima Valley in Washington are comparable to talus pits found in southern Arizona. Smith indicated that the graves occur from the top to the bottom of the talus slides.

SURFACE APPEARANCE OF THE LOS ROBLES TALUS PITS

Two kinds of talus pits were identified based on surface indications: pits with an "open" appearance, and "rock-filled" pits that seemed to have been refilled after original excavation. Open talus pits are circular to semicircular features, measuring from 0.5 m to 3.0 m in diameter, and ranging from 0.5 m to 1.5 m in depth (Fig. 5.1*a-c*). Sometimes the basalt talus rocks removed during the construction (or perhaps reopening) of a pit were either discarded down slope or reused to form a low wall around the circumference of the pit, giving the feature a cairnlike appearance.

The rock-filled pits are shallow, concave depressions with low mounds of light colored rock. Like the open pits, these features also measure between 0.5 m and 3.0 m in diameter (Fig. 5.1*d-f*). They appear to be pits that were refilled with the rock that was originally removed from the hill surface. The lighter-colored, unweathered rocks from the subsurface that are now on top of the feature contrast sharply with the undisturbed patinated surface rocks surrounding them. In at least two instances, broken fragments of plain ware vessels were visible through the cracks and crevices, leading to a decision to call them rock-filled pits. From the surface, it cannot be ascertained whether the jars were placed in the pits, which were then filled with light-colored talus, or whether the rock fill once covered a wood roof that eventually decayed and collapsed.

MODERN DISTURBANCE OF TALUS PITS

One important source of modern disturbance of the Los Robles talus pits is known. In 1892 the Aguirre family settled at Red Rock, establishing the Aguirre Ranch. The following account, by Yjinio Aguirre, suggests that the Los Robles talus pits were visited and damaged during ranch construction activities:

> In 1921, when Don Higinio was rebuilding his house in Cerro Prieto with black malapai rock, my brother and I as boys would ride in the wagon that was hauling stones from the black hills. Often, the wagon driver would find large 'Ollas,' jars made of red clay among the rocks. We would take them to the rancho and make them into water jars. Most of the Indian relics, rocks with hieroglyphics, have been removed and destroyed by visitors from the cities (Aquirre 1983: 91).

TALUS PIT EXCAVATIONS

Much of the fundamental information required to determine if the Los Robles talus pit sites actually represent Piman cemeteries was not available on the surface. The open pits do not contain visible human remains and the only artifacts consist of broken plain ware bowls and jars. Nine open pits and one rock-filled pit were selected at site AZ AA:7:187 for detailed study (Fig. 5.2). The objective was to identify materials that might support or disprove the notion that pit clusters were cemeteries. Primary evidence would include burned or unburned human bone and paraphernalia that might be interpreted as gifts or personal belongings of the deceased.

The talus slide on which AZ AA:7:187 is located is 1.0 m to 3.0 m thick and is composed of loose basalt boulders and cobbles. Excavation techniques included mapping and carefully removing loose rocks from the pits in an attempt to find cultural remains. Wind-blown and water-deposited soil had accumulated at the bottoms of some pits and these deposits were inspected for archaeological remains by sifting the soil through 1/8-inch and 1/4-inch mesh screens. A few pits were shallow and did not penetrate completely through the rocky talus

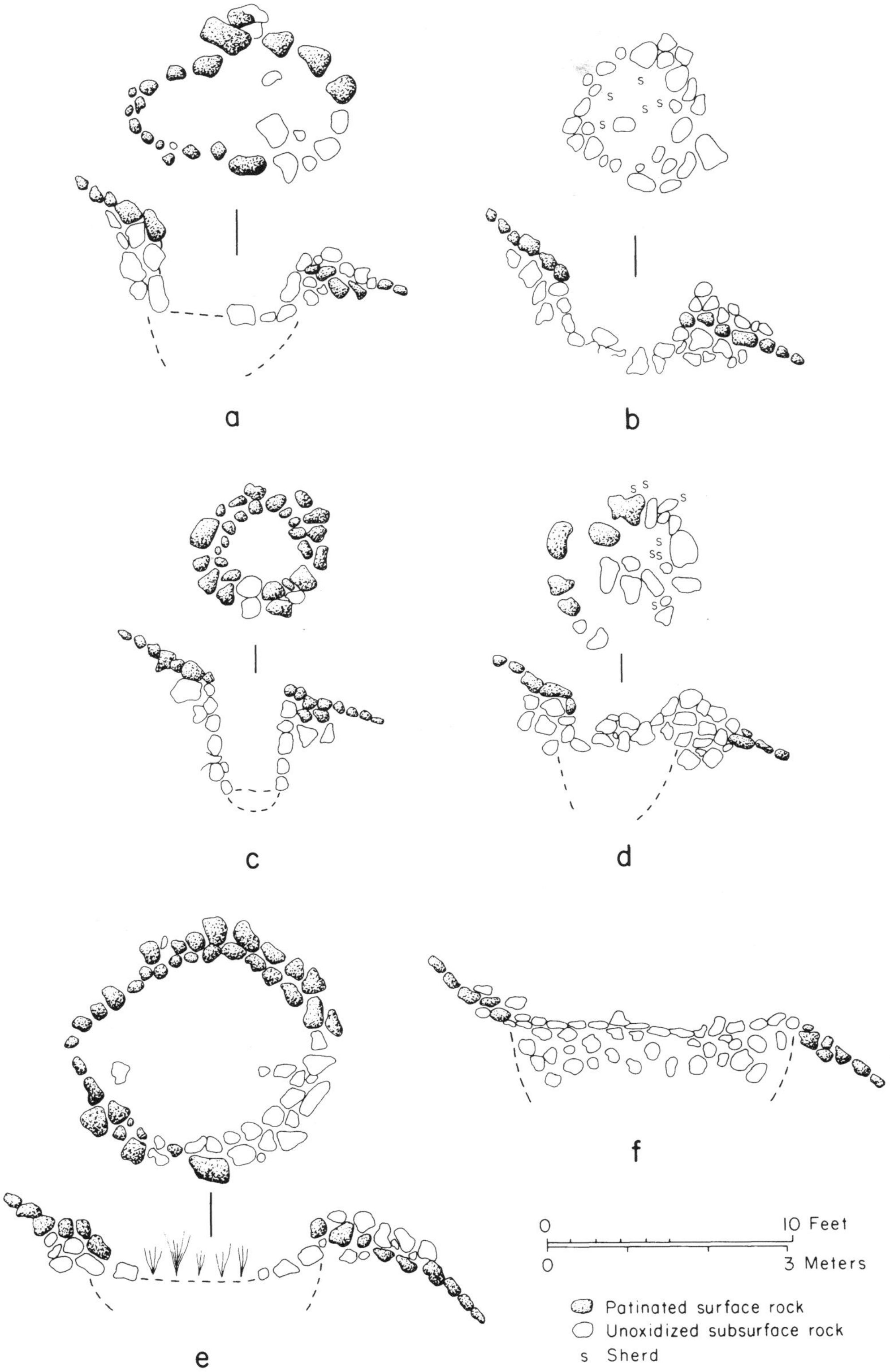

Figure 5.1. Plans and profiles of open pits (*a–c*) and rock-filled pits (*d–f*) at the Los Robles talus pit sites.

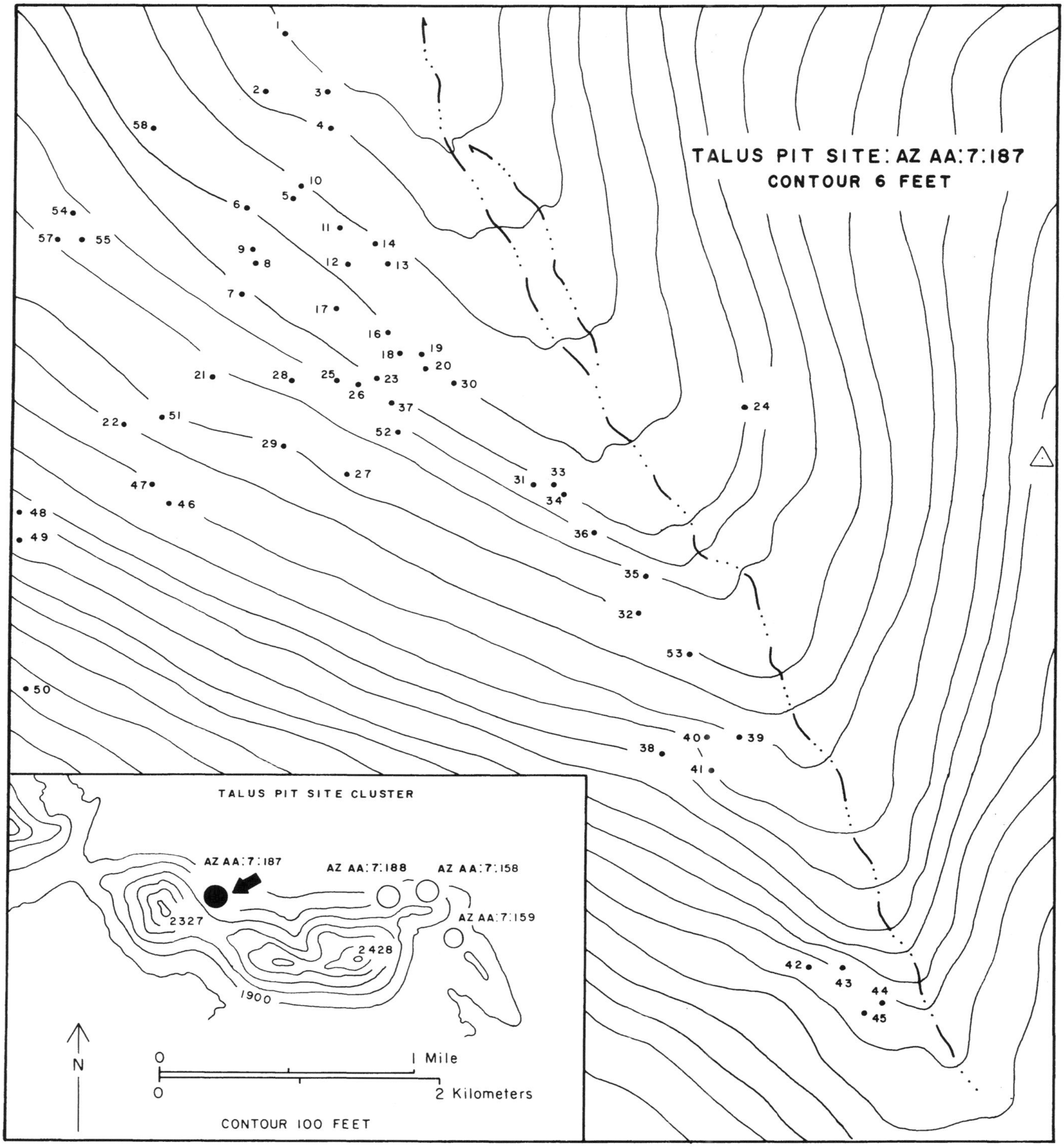

Figure 5.2. Distribution of talus pits at site AZ AA:7:187. Pits originally numbered 15 and 56 were later determined to be noncultural features.

slope. There was a possibility in such instances that fragmented human bone and small artifacts had fallen through the porous talus pit bottoms and had been deposited on the hardpan below. Therefore, once the maximum depth of the shallow pits was defined, additional rocks were removed to allow inspection of the stable ground surface underneath the talus deposits. At the feature we thought might be a rock-filled pit, we removed all rock in a 2.0-square-meter area down through the talus slide to hardpan. In addition, soil samples were taken from the tops, mid-levels, and bottoms of pits that had sufficient soil deposits, and from the hardpan surface below the pits.

Excavations produced no human remains, and except for Piman-style bowl and jar fragments, no other kinds of artifacts were present. However, this lack of primary evidence does not rule out use of the pits as graves. Because of the porousness of the talus slope, perishable materials, including human bone, were undoubtedly subject to disintegration from water, changing temperature and humidity, and consumption by rodents and other scavenging animals.

CERAMICS FROM THE LOS ROBLES TALUS PITS

Plain ware bowl and jar fragments, evidently of historic Piman affiliation, occur in two to five percent of the talus pits on sites AZ AA:7:158, 187, and 188. Pottery fragments were observed in a similar proportion at five other talus pit loci visited during this study. Altogether, seven partially restorable jars, two bowls, and dozens of vessel fragments were collected from the Los Robles talus pit sites. These fragmented vessels are unlike local prehistoric Hohokam pottery that predates A.D. 1450, and are noticeably different from the late nineteenth- and early twentieth-century carbon-cored Papago plain ware and red ware found throughout the northern Tucson Basin.

The majority of talus pit pottery ranges from 4 mm to 6 mm in thickness, with obvious anvil marks on an orange, tan, or gray interior (Fig. 5.3). The exterior surface is brown, gray, or tan and is often wiped horizontally; exteriors are also smoothed (not polished), and can be slightly rough with minute beads and patches of clay. Some vessels have vertical striations evenly spaced on the exterior surface as if combed downward with a brush. The talus pit vessels contain a light brown to gray, platy clay paste, with subangular quartz-feldspar, micaceous schist, and possibly granite temper. Two variants exist, one with large inclusions of crushed micaceous schist, and the other with small micaceous particles that are probably a natural part of the paste.

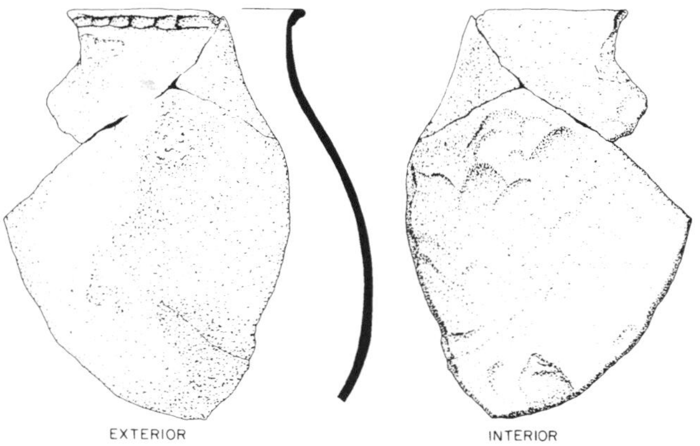

Figure 5.3. Rim and body of a partial jar recovered from talus pit site AZ AA:7:158. Rim diameter is 15 cm.

The most distinctive attribute of the pottery from the Los Robles talus pits is the treatment of vessel rims and necks. All of the bowl and jar fragments analyzed from the pits contain either rims or neck bands (Figs. 5.4, 5.5). Numerous vessel rims were examined under a high-magnification microscope; it appears that there were at least two methods of molding rims. In one method a rope of clay was rolled and compressed into a band. The band was then folded along its narrow axis and attached to the top of the vessel like a coil of clay (Fig. 5.4*b*). The

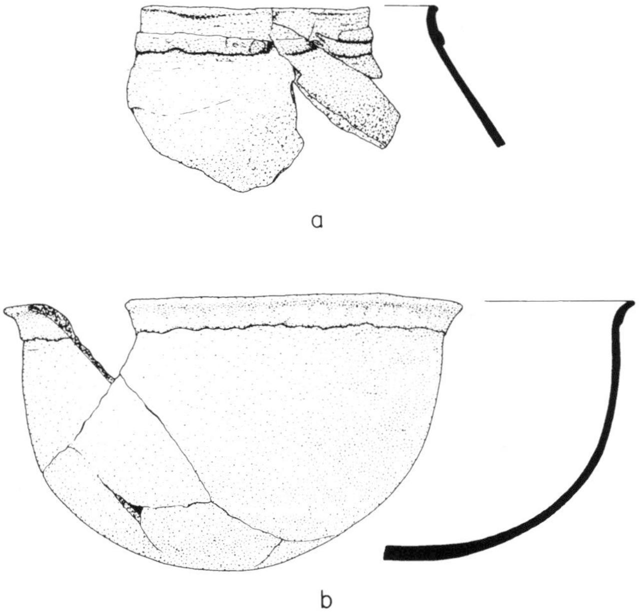

Figure 5.4. Jar rim and neck (*a*; rim diameter, 10 cm) and bowl (*b*; rim diameter, 14 cm) recovered from site AZ AA:7:158.

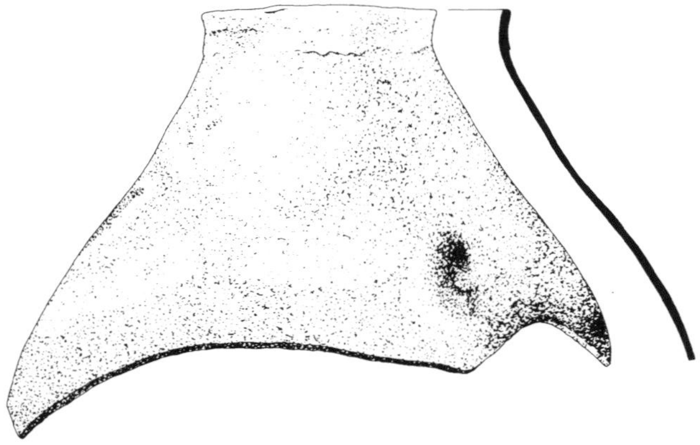

Figure 5.5. Rim-banded jar from talus pit site AZ AA:7:158. Rim diameter is 12 cm.

fold in the band can be seen under a microscope on some vessels. In the most common method of banding, a clay band of single thickness was wrapped around the outside of the rim. This type of band was probably integrated into the rim by pinching and smoothing. In the collection of vessels studied, most jars have straight rims and the bowl rims are flared slightly outward. On one jar the band was smeared vertically at even intervals to form a vertical design. This kind of rim banding may have been practiced to strengthen the vessel orifice. Neck banding, although not common, probably serves the same purpose as rim banding. This treatment consists of wrapping a clay band around the neck of the vessel a few centimeters below the rim (Fig. 5.4*a*).

COMPARATIVE CONTEXT OF LOS ROBLES TALUS PIT CERAMICS

Because the rim styles of the Los Robles talus pit ceramics were so strikingly distinctive, it seemed that much could be learned about the builders of the talus pits from a careful comparative analysis of these rims. Specifically, it seemed likely that the rim styles would be relatively restricted in time, and might also provide important information on cultural affiliation.

Rim-banded pottery is widely distributed across southern Arizona from the lower Colorado River basin, east to the San Pedro River (Fig. 5.6). The terms rim-coiling, reinforced rim band, and folded rim are all used to describe the applied bands around the necks and rims of pottery vessels. This attribute has been found on pottery within the territories of the Yuma, Mojave, Cocopa, and Maricopa tribes (Yuman subgroups), and within the territories of the Gila River Pima, Tohono O'odham (Papago), Sobaipuri, Sand Papago, and Kohatk (Upper Pima subgroups). In order to assess the possible temporal and cultural affinities of the ceramics from the Los Robles talus pits, the form and temporal distributions of rim-banded pottery from three, geographically distinct ceramic traditions are described: (1) the Lower Colorado Buff Ware series; (2) the Sobaipuri plain ware of southeast Arizona, and (3) the Papago-Pima plain wares of south-central Arizona.

The Lower Colorado Buff Ware Series

Rim-banded pottery is described by Mallouf (1980), Rogers (1945), Schroeder (1952), and Waters (1982). Banded vessels are generally assigned to the Patayan III, or ethnographic Yuman period, dated by Waters (1982) as A.D. 1500 until after 1900. Rim bands occur on two basic categories of Patayan III ceramics: Palomas Buff and Colorado Buff.

Patayan III pottery is constructed by coiling tempered clay into the desired shape and thinning the walls with a paddle and anvil. The thin- to medium-walled vessels are then fired in an oxidizing atmosphere. Variation in southwestern Arizona clay sources and the firing technique create a broad range of light colored vessels. Palomas Buff grades through tan, gray, buff, to buff-gray. Colorado Buff is usually pinkish buff to tan. Temper inclusions, surface treatment, and other pottery attributes vary between these two wares (Waters 1982: 568–569).

Waters (1982) indicates that Palomas Buff is found on the lower Gila River as far east as Agua Caliente, immediately north of the river in the Horn and Kofa Mountains, and as far south as Sierra Pinacate, Sonora. Colorado Buff sherds with "reinforced" rim bands occur mainly along the Colorado River from the southern tip of Nevada to the delta, and along the lower Gila River (Waters 1982: 568–570). Colorado Buff pottery was traded as far east as Phoenix, Arizona, as far west as San Diego, California, and as far south as Sierra Pinacate, Sonora.

Seven radiocarbon samples of materials associated with Palomas Buff Ware have been recently dated. The two earliest conventional dates are 280 ± 50 BP (Cable 1987; Bayman and Ryan 1988). Colorado Buff is only roughly dated, from A.D. 500 through post-1900.

Sobaipuri Plain Ware

Along the San Pedro River in southeastern Arizona, Di Peso (1953) found "rim-coiled" pottery within stratified trash deposits at the Spanish-Colonial Presidio of Quiburi. He suggested that this Sobaipuri Plain Ware persisted through the three phases of occupation at Quiburi, from 1692 through 1798.

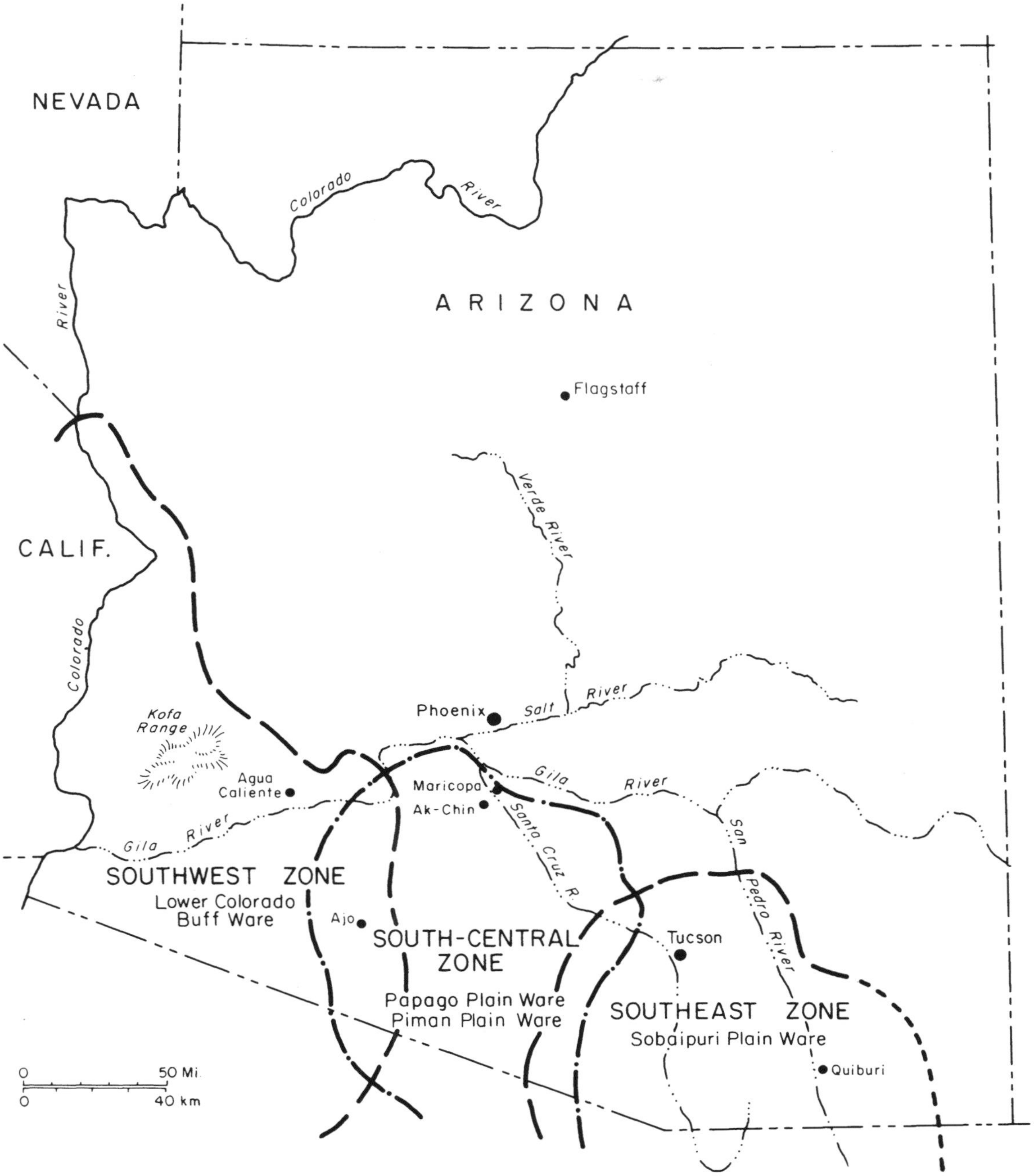

Figure 5.6. Ceramic zones of rim-banded pottery in southern Arizona.

Sobaipuri Plain Ware is a thick- to medium-walled, poorly made pottery shaped by paddle and anvil. The paste is predominantly black to reddish-brown with a carbon streak that is often completely carbonized. Body surface colors range from buff to brown to black (Di Peso 1953: 147–159). A similar pottery is found on the upper Santa Cruz River from Tubac, downstream to Tucson. Jack Williams informed me in 1988 that scores of sherds with reinforced rim bands have been excavated in trash deposits at Tubac (a presidio dating from 1701 to 1864) and at the Tucson Presidio (dating from 1776 to 1865). Inspection of the extensive collections made by Jack Williams suggests that many of these wares are similar to the Sobaipuri Plain Ware described by Di Peso.

Papago Plain Ware

The vast south-central region of Arizona is bounded on the east by Picacho Peak and on the west by the town of Ajo. The Gila River, near Maricopa, probably delineates the northern limit of indigenous rim-banded pottery, and the southern boundary is somewhere south of the International Border. The Tohono O'odham Nation covers about three-fourths of the south-central region. The Los Robles talus pit complex is on the eastern edge of this geographical area.

Rim-banded pottery is found throughout the Tohono O'odham Nation; it has been described by Fontana and others (1962), Haury (1950), and Mallouf (1980). I examined the pottery from Ventana Cave (AZ Z:12:5 ASM) and Batki (AZ Z:16:6) and the survey collections from Santa Ana de Cuiquiburitac (AZ AA:9:2) and numerous other sites within the south-central zone. The Los Robles talus pit pottery is allied closely with the rim-banded Papago pottery found throughout the south-central zone. This resemblance is seen not only in the characteristic rim bands, but also in interior and exterior finish, the distinctive but wide-ranging interior and exterior body color, and vessel thickness, which is generally thin to medium. Much of the Papaguería pottery examined from the Tohono O'odham Nation contained micaceous temper similar to the temper found in the talus pit assemblage. Noteworthy, however, is that many rim-banded pieces examined and classified as Papago Plain on and off the Nation in the south-central zone were nonmicaceous. This diversity in temper is not surprising when one considers the diverse geological strata that form the south-central portion of Arizona.

Historic Papago pottery has been classified into three ceramic complexes (Fontana and others 1962). The earliest complex begins at A.D. 1700 and extends through 1860, followed by an introduction of new pottery types and a continuation of older wares between A.D. 1860 and 1930. The third ceramic period represents modern Papago pottery made from 1930 to 1962.

Two types of Papago Plain are identified by Fontana and others (1962) as having "rim coils" (rim banding). "Variant 1" is a medium to thick nonmicaceous pottery resembling prehistoric Sells Plain. This particular Papago pottery type lasted into the early twentieth century, but Haury (1950) suggests that the rim coil attribute faded out by 1875. A thin pottery with rim coils was identified at Batki. This Tohono O'odham town was in existence in the 1690s and was visited by Father Kino; it was abandoned between 1850 and 1852, when it was destroyed by Apaches (Haury 1950: 19; Russell 1908: 45). Batki is important because it firmly places the use of thin rim-banded pottery prior to 1850 in south-central Arizona.

CLASSIFICATION OF THE LOS ROBLES TALUS PIT CERAMICS

There is no appreciable difference between the Los Robles talus pit pottery and the thin Papago pottery that was found at Batki. For consistency, therefore, following Fontana and others (1962), the talus pit assemblages are referred to as a variant of Papago Plain. The thin Papago pottery with rim bands shares some traits with Pima pottery and Lower Colorado River Buff Ware, but does not resemble Sobaipuri Plain. Except for rim banding, there are no physical characteristics shared between the Patayan III pottery and Sobaipuri Plain Ware.

PROPOSED DATES

The consistent presence of thin-walled, Papago Plain pottery is the best evidence for inferring the dates of use for the Los Robles talus pit sites. Being able to place a beginning and ending date on thin-walled Papago Plain is an important step in determining when the talus pits were used, and by whom. We are faced, however, with insufficient research and specimens for the interval between A.D. 1450 and 1860. Only three collections of thin, rim-banded pottery from south-central Arizona can be placed in time by archaeological evidence or by diaries, those from Batki on the Tohono O'odham Nation, from Santa Ana de Cuiquiburitac just off the Nation, and from the Ak-Chin Indian Community near the town of Maricopa.

As Fontana and others (1962: 102) indicate, it is anyone's guess as to how long Batki was occupied prior to Father Kino's visit in the 1690s, but because there is no observable prehistoric component, the rim-coiled pottery at this site probably postdates A.D. 1450. Batki was destroyed by the mid-nineteenth century, so it provides a reliable surface collection of rim-banded pottery that does not date later than 1852.

Santa Ana de Cuiquiburitac was a short-lived Spanish visita 20 km southwest of the Samaniego Hills, occupied between A.D. 1810 and 1830 (Fontana 1987). Archaeological excavation at Ak-Chin near the town of Maricopa produced a set of whole and broken vessels with rim banding. Although the Ak-Chin collection represents Pima or Maricopa pottery, it resembles the thin-walled Papago pottery in many ways. The Ak-Chin collection was found in association with various materials in house fill that were radiocarbon dated from A.D. 1709 ± 50 through A.D. 1859 ± 60 (conventional dates, from Cable 1987).

The thin-walled, rim-banded pottery of south-central Arizona thus appears to have evolved between A.D. 1450 and 1850. I believe that it will not be found in any datable context much later than 1860. Two additional factors support this proposed date range (1450-1860). First, several historic sites were found during the Northern Tucson Basin Survey; glass fragments and other artifacts were used to place these sites between 1870 and 1890. Although some of these historic sites contained carbon-cored Papago Plain, none of the sites had rim-banded Papago pottery. Second, it is known that from as early as 1775 through 1870, European settlers and established Upper Pima populations were reluctant to occupy the area between Tucson and the Gila River because of the danger imposed by Apache raids; several diary entries support this observation.

Because none of the Los Robles talus pits contain carbon-core Papago pottery or other historic artifacts, and because there is evidence that the Upper Pima were being routed from their Picacho Peak villages as early as 1775, it is reasonable to believe that the talus pits and the associated ceramic assemblage date between A.D. 1450 and 1860, probably before the 1780s.

CULTURAL AFFILIATION OF THE LOS ROBLES TALUS PIT SITES

The basin and range country on either side of the lower Santa Cruz River between Marana and Picacho Peak contains the remnants of over a thousand Hohokam sites clustered around three sprawling rancherias referred to as the Marana, McClellan, and Los Robles mound communities (P. Fish, S. Fish, and Madsen 1986). Whereas the areas surrounding these communities may have been settled as early as A.D. 600, it was not until the twelfth century that they flourished. Platform mounds, terraced hillside villages, reservoirs, prehistoric gardens covering thousands of hectares, and villages covering from 2 hectares to over 7.8 square kilometers (3 square miles) attest to a year-round occupation of this region.

The Piman settlement pattern described in the late 1690s, however, contrasts sharply with the archaeological record from a few centuries before. Unlike the three Hohokam communities that existed prior to A.D. 1450, the diaries of Father Eusebio Francisco Kino and Lieutenant Juan Mateo Manje mention only one Piman village in this vast desert region along the lower Santa Cruz River between present-day Rillito and Coolidge, a distance of about 103 km (64 miles).

This seemingly isolated protohistoric village was named Santa Catarina de Cuituabaga by Kino, and although its exact location is unknown today, most researchers using Kino's and Manje's diaries place the village west of Picacho Peak near the Santa Cruz River (Bolton 1948; Karns 1954). Manje describes Santa Catarina in 1697 as having 200 persons and 40 houses (Karns 1954: 91). Two years later on 2 November 1699, Kino and Manje rode fifteen leagues (about 37.5 miles)

> to reach the rancheria of Santa Catarina de Cuituabaga, where the Indians met them with crosses and cleanly swept roads. Manje counted 300 male adults. According to the Indians, the settlement had over a thousand inhabitants. Its lands were very fertile, as could be seen from the produce given to the visitors: various kinds of cantaloupes and watermelons, and roasting ears which the natives were picking at the time. Manje observed: "So rich is the land that, although they plant only in favorable seasons, they harvest two crops every year" (Burrus 1971: 253).

There are at least six additional references to Santa Catarina from the 1690s (including Burrus 1971: 376, 429; Smith 1966a: 43-44; Smith 1966b: 14). However, after 1699 the rancheria of Santa Catarina fades from the records. It is not until the expedition of Lieutenant Colonel Don Juan Bautista de Anza in 1775 that the lower Santa Cruz River in the vicinity of Picacho Peak is mentioned again (Bolton 1930: 30-31). Fray Pedro Font, who traveled with the Anza expedition in 1775, gives a detailed description of this journey. After leaving the northern Tucson Basin in the vicinity of Rillito, the expedition traveled "six long leagues west-northwest and at times west, at half past one in the afternoon we halted at some lagoons of rain water which the Indians call Oytaparts, site of a village of Papago Pimans which the Apache destroyed" (Bolton 1930: 30). Bolton's footnotes indicate that "Oitpar" means "old town." Font goes on to say that on the next day (29 October 1775):

> Half a league beyond the place whence we set out there is an abandoned pueblo of Papagos, of some thirty huts, called Cuitoa, which at times they are accustomed to occupy, a little further on there is a lagoon which is the seepage or rising of the river of El Tuquison and San Xavier, which disappears and ends in these plains (Bolton 1930: 30-32).

Traveling four and one-half leagues farther the same day, the Anza expedition camped a little west of Picacho de Tacca (Picacho Peak).

Fontana (1987) cites an unpublished manuscript written by Father Bonaventure from San Xavier Mission. This Franciscan missionary indicates that:

> The Kwahatk people form the Papago Band, which is part "Dohono Ootam" [Tohono O'odham] (Desert People), and part "Akimal Ootam" [Akimel O'odham] (River People). Their village of origin,

> the Pueblo of Quajote [Kohatk], is located in the desert region, but a great part of the people resided along the Santa Cruz River, from Akchin, southwest of Picacho Peak, and upstream as far as the Tucson Mountains (Fontana 1987: 150-151).

Father Bonaventure also suggests that:

> the Piman Indians who lived in settlements along the Santa Cruz River north of Tucson in the 18th century were driven from these places as a result of Apaches attacking from the northeast and east. The principal farming or "field" village of this group seems to have been that of Akchin (often rendered "Aquituni"; O'odham for "Arroyo Mouth"), whose population of 134 men and women were assembled in Tucson in 1796.... This Akchin should not be confused with the Akchin village much farther to the west in Papago country... (Fontana 1987: 152-153).

Based on the writings of Dobyns (1974) and Hackenberg (1974: 274-276), Doelle (1984: 203) concludes that the late seventeenth- and eighteenth-century villages in the vicinity of Picacho Peak, particularly Santa Catarina, were affiliated with the "Kohatk Pima," and not with the Sobaipuri of the middle and upper Santa Cruz and San Pedro rivers. Fontana (1987) also indicates that Father Bonaventure, who was fluent in the Piman language, suggested the Kwahatk (Kohatk) were displaced Papago living among the Pima.

To summarize, this information suggests there was a Piman occupation in the vicinity of Picacho Peak and the Samaniego Hills at least until the mid-eighteenth century. There are conflicting interpretations on whether these rancherias were seasonal or permanent settlements, but in any case there were numerous families living in the area. The presence of thin-walled, rim-banded pottery similar to Papago Plain supports the inference that the Los Robles talus pits were of historic Upper Pima affiliation. Because of the absence of human remains and burial paraphernalia, their use as cemeteries remains uncertain. However, the porousness of the talus slope could have promoted rapid decomposition of bone and other perishable materials. There were no items other than plain ware bowls and jars that could be interpreted as grave goods, but this lack could be the result of burial custom, particularly if the pits were used for cremation crypts rather then for inhumations. We can conclude with some certainty, however, that the talus pits were probably built prior to A.D. 1800 by the Kohatk Papago, who once occupied the lower Santa Cruz River Basin in the vicinity of Picacho Peak.

Note: This study was made possible through support from the U.S. Department of the Interior, Bureau of Reclamation, Arizona State Land Department (Grant 4-CS-30-1380) and the Arizona State Museum, as part of the Hohokam Platform Mound study being conducted along the Tucson Aqueduct, Phase A.

CHAPTER SIX

Land Use and Hohokam Settlement in the Los Robles Community

The Los Robles archaeological survey and the Cerro Prieto mapping project have provided significant new information on the nature of Hohokam, protohistoric, and historic period settlement and land use in the lower Santa Cruz River Basin. Probably the main contribution of these studies has been documentation of Preclassic and Classic period Hohokam communities extending along the Los Robles Wash and reaching westward into the Samaniego Hills. Traditionally, it was thought that secondary streams such as Los Robles Wash drained a sparsely occupied hinterland intermediate between the riverine Hohokam of the Phoenix and Tucson basins. Instead, recent archaeological efforts have established that Los Robles Wash, like many other secondary washes along the lower Santa Cruz River, supported a large and thriving Hohokam community for a period of several centuries. Following a Hohokam abandonment around A.D. 1300, the area was later used by protohistoric Piman groups, probably those living in and around the village of Santa Catarina.

In this chapter I consider the information from the Los Robles survey and the Cerro Prieto mapping project from two complementary perspectives: (1) the cumulative record of land use, as revealed by the spatial distribution and environmental associations of significant site categories, and (2) the sequence of cultural change along Los Robles Wash, as indicated by the spatial and temporal distribution of the sample of relatively well-dated sites.

CUMULATIVE LAND USE PATTERNS

One way to maximize available survey information is to consider what the area's archaeological sites reveal about long-term patterns of prehistoric land use. In such an analysis, it is assumed that known prehistoric sites represent a cumulative record of habitation, resource extraction, and other activities conducted on the landscape surrounding Los Robles Wash. The analysis begins by considering broad patterns of prehistoric site distributions, organized by functional and formal site categories.

Habitation Sites

The Los Robles survey documented 17 habitation sites, each of which had some form of ceramic evidence indicating a Hohokam-period component (Fig. 6.1). Although the intensity of occupation at individual sites is unclear for any particular time period, the Hohokam occupation left a considerable imprint on the landscape in the form of structures, trash mounds, artifact scatters, and other features associated with habitation activities. Included are the remains of a presumed Preclassic ballcourt (the Hog Farm Ballcourt Site), an early Classic period mound, probably a platform mound (the Los Robles Mound Site), and a large trincheras village (AZ AA:7:11, Cerro Prieto).

The history and organizational structure of habitation sites are considered below. From the more general perspective of long-term land use, the following observa-

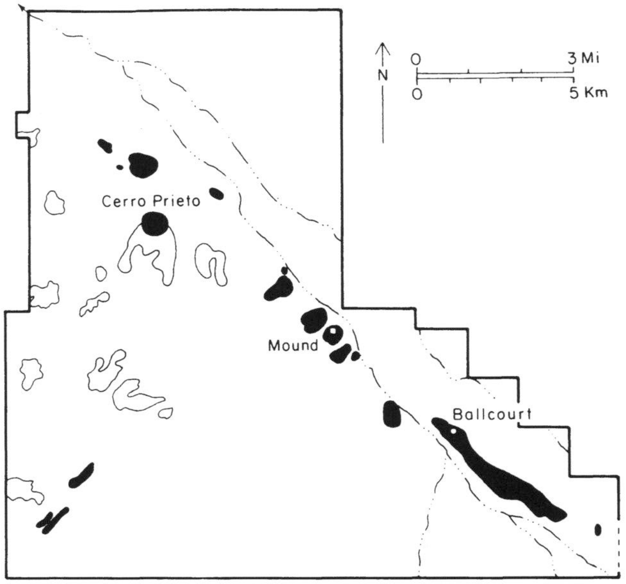

Figure 6.1. Prehistoric habitation sites (site types 1, 2, 3, and the trincheras village of Cerro Prieto). Contours indicate major hills.

tions can be made. First, settlements were concentrated along Los Robles Wash; most sites are less than 1 km from the wash channel, and most of these are within only a few hundred meters. This pattern was probably determined by a number of environmental factors, the most obvious being proximity to a reliable source of domestic water. As discussed in Chapter 2, Los Robles Wash certainly flowed at times during the rainy seasons, and the wash channel and adjacent alluvial deposits must have provided opportunities for the construction of reservoirs, walk-in wells, or other catchments. Agricultural land in and along the wash would have been another important attraction for settlements, and it is likely that the floodplain and adjacent alluvial deposits, well watered and periodically replenished with sediment and organic matter, were heavily cultivated.

Second, most of the large settlements are located along the west bank of the wash. This may be partly a result of survey coverage as the east bank of the wash was largely unsurveyed and the true density of sites in this zone remains unknown. However, other factors suggest that the west bank of the wash might indeed have been favored for settlement. This area has numerous low gravel ridges that probably offered protection from overbank flooding. The east side of Los Robles Wash is lower than the west side and is subject to frequent flooding, as shown by thick deposits of alluvium there. Also, the best locations for ak chin farming occur just west of the channel of Los Robles Wash, where alluvial fans are crossed by numerous small drainage channels depositing sand, silt, and organic debris washing down from the Samaniego Hills (Wilson 1980, 1981; see also Chapter 1).

Exceptions to these general patterns are provided by seven settlements of varying size located some distance from Los Robles Wash. One was the large, early Classic period hillside village of Cerro Prieto (AZ AA:7:11). As discussed in Chapter 4 and in more detail below, there may have been important nonenvironmental reasons for locating this village on a volcanic hillside. The three settlements just north of Cerro Prieto may have been satellite villages of Cerro Prieto, or they may have been situated to take advantage of the dry and floodwater farming opportunities afforded by the alluvial fans and ridges in this vicinity.

In the far southwest corner of the study area, three other habitation sites also deviate from the general pattern of settlement location. Factors that would explain the location of these sites so far from the wash include seasonal habitation, perhaps during the summer when washes or water catchments would have provided sufficient drinking water. It is also possible that these sites were not components of the Los Robles Community, but rather belonged to a prehistoric settlement system extending west of the survey area boundaries. The largest of these sites, AZ AA:11:79 (R-151), dated only to the late Pioneer and early Colonial periods, and it may represent part of the initial colonization of the Los Robles area by Hohokam populations originating perhaps from the Tucson Basin. The remaining two sites in the southwest corner of the survey area are undated, but they, too, could have been among an initial set of settlements occupied early in the Hohokam sequence. Only further investigation of these sites, and adequate inspection of the area west of the Los Robles survey boundary, can resolve the issue.

Farmsteads, Fields, and Water Diversion Sites

Farmsteads, agricultural field sites, and the single site with a water diversion feature are concentrated on rocky, bajada ridges within a few kilometers of Cerro Prieto. However, it is suspected that the pattern shown in Figure 6.2 is primarily due to visibility factors. The upland zone where agricultural sites are most heavily concentrated is also the zone where features such as stone structures, rockpiles, alignments, and clearings are most highly visible. Although it is clear the area surrounding Cerro Prieto was used for prehistoric dry farming, this does not mean that agricultural activities were confined to this zone. Therefore, it is likely that additional farmsteads, fields, and water control features were located elsewhere in the study area, but that these are much less

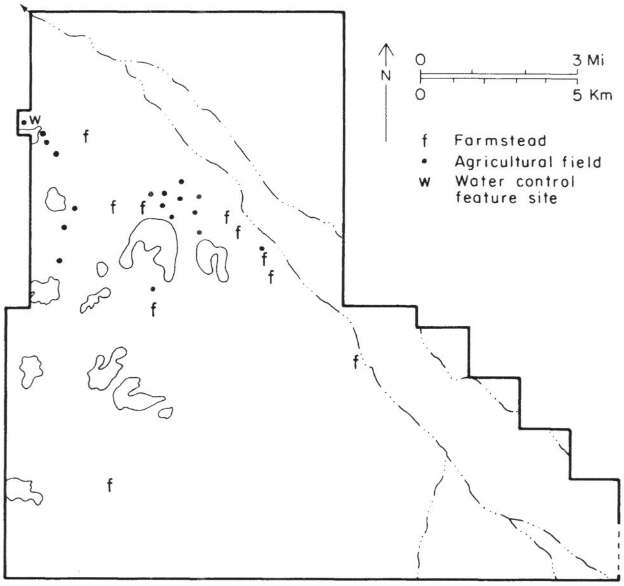

Figure 6.2. Prehistoric farmsteads (site type 4), agricultural fields (site type 5), and water control feature (site type 7).

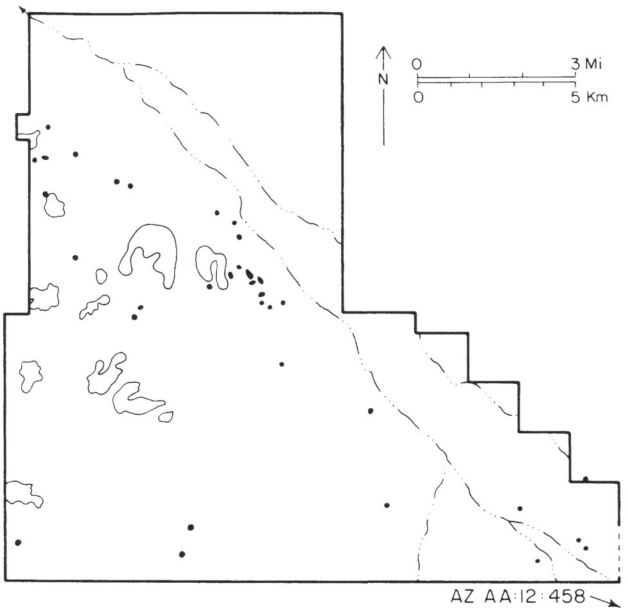

Figure 6.3. Prehistoric limited activity plant or animal food processing sites (site type 9).

visible because of alluviation and because the sites themselves were more ephemeral. Additional surveys, test excavations, and special analyses (for example, remote sensing, pollen studies, and examination of soil chemistry) would be required to disclose the locations of these sites (Gasser 1990).

In spite of these interpretive limitations, the sites recorded in Figure 6.2 show that diverse prehistoric agricultural strategies were probably practiced in the Los Robles survey area. Most of the sites so far identified seem to have been used for dry farming activities involving the construction of rock features such as rockpiles and alignments. Because of a lack of excavation data, the crops that might have been grown in such features are at present unknown. However, in the area surrounding the Marana platform mound, immediately east of the Los Robles survey area, similar constructions were used for the cultivation of agave (S. Fish, P. Fish, Miksicek, and Madsen 1985; S. Fish, P. Fish, and Madsen 1992). Discovery of tabular knife fragments, steep-edged scrapers, and other fiber-processing tools at some of the Los Robles sites suggests an analogous function for the rock features there. Although the Los Robles farmstead and field sites are poorly dated, comparison with the Marana agave fields suggests that most were probably constructed and used during the early Classic period (about A.D. 1150–1300).

Limited Activity Plant and Animal Food Processing Sites

The widespread distribution of plant and animal food processing sites indicates that hunting and food collecting activities took place in a variety of environmental zones (Fig. 6.3). A lack of information regarding the specific nature of these activities at individual sites precludes detailed analysis. It is presumed that the majority of plant and animal food processing sites were used by residents of the settlements along Los Robles Wash, and that the Samaniego Hills were part of the immediate sustaining hinterland of the greater Los Robles Community.

Rock Shelters

All four rock shelter sites are in the west-central portion of the survey area (Fig. 6.4). The locations of rock shelters obviously depend on the presence of hillsides or mesas, so it is not surprising that such sites would be concentrated in a part of the survey area dotted with volcanic hills. Because none of these sites have yet been excavated, it is difficult to determine how they were used and how they fit into the round of prehistoric off-settlement activities. Considering their position in the western portion of the survey area, they might have been associated with hunting, food gathering, or quarrying activities in the surrounding hills. If so, perhaps these sites were used for overnight camping on prolonged resource-gathering forays.

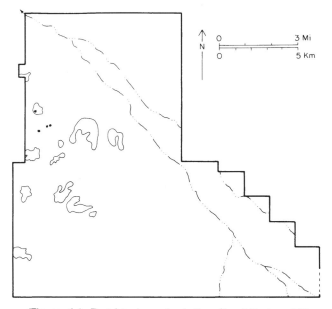

Figure 6.4. Prehistoric rock shelter sites (site type 10).

Trincheras Feature Sites

This site category was defined on the basis of morphological criteria, namely, the presence of stacked rock features on volcanic hills. Hence, its analytical utility is limited, and consideration of this site category is best achieved on a case-by-case basis. The largest and most impressive trincheras feature site in the Los Robles survey area is Cerro Prieto (Fig. 6.5), a *cerro de trincheras* built and occupied during the Tanque Verde phase (Chapter 4). Its role in the Los Robles Community is discussed below under "Early Classic Period."

The remaining set of sites presents a mixed group of rock features, the functions of which remain largely unknown. Such sites are confined to volcanic hills providing suitable building material. Trincheras feature sites were scattered widely across the Los Robles survey area (Fig. 6.5), and the unimpressive nature of their constructions would seem to preclude use as defensive fortifications.

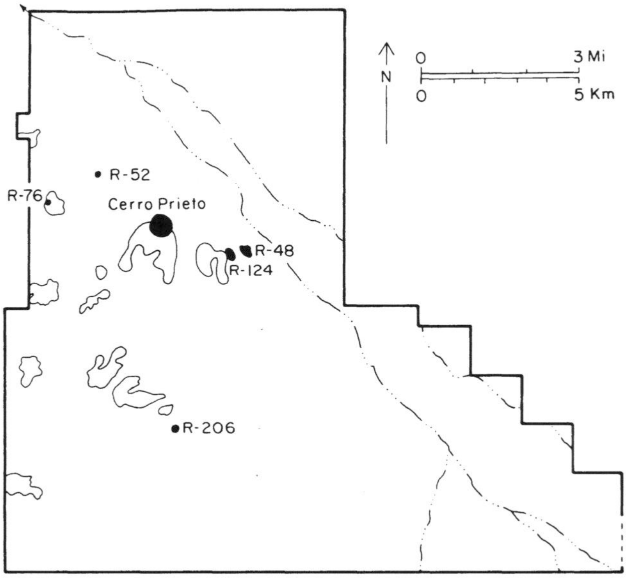

Figure 6.5. Prehistoric trincheras feature sites (site type 6).

Quarry Sites

The distribution of quarry sites (Fig. 6.6), concentrated largely in the western portion of the survey area, matches the natural distribution of suitable raw materials for the manufacture of chipped stone tools. Quarries are poorly dated, but assuming that at least some date to the ceramic period, these sites provide evidence that inhabitants of prehistoric Los Robles settlements often accomplished at least preliminary reduction of chipped stone tools at or near the geological source of lithic material.

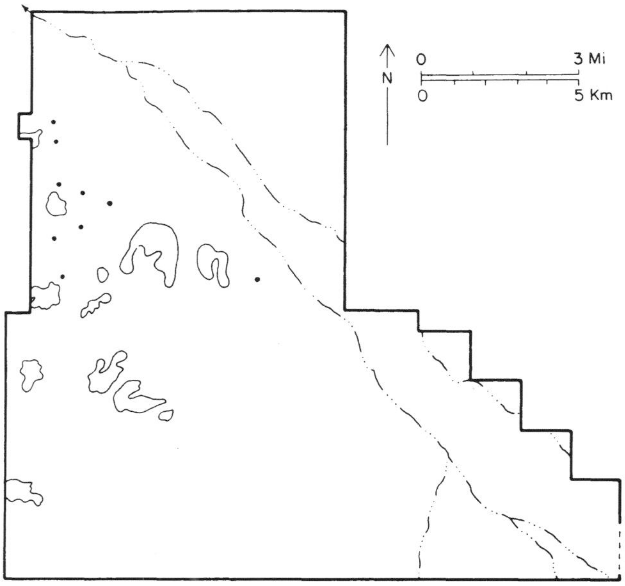

Figure 6.6. Prehistoric quarry sites (site type 12).

The recovery of chipped stone tools and debitage from non-quarry sites would probably contribute substantially to our understanding of the full range of lithic procurement activities.

Petroglyph Sites

The locations of petroglyph sites are obviously constrained by the locations of rock outcrops or boulders suitable for manufacturing petroglyphs. However, not all outcrops suitable for petroglyphs were used, so the distribution of petroglyph sites may reveal important patterns relevant to social boundaries, transportation routes, and ceremonial activities. On the basis of style and patination, most of the petroglyphs in the Los Robles survey area appear to date to the late Hohokam period, but as noted in Chapter 3, a few also may belong to the Archaic period, and some may date to protohistoric and historic times.

Within the Los Robles survey area, the largest concentrations of petroglyphs are on or near Cerro Prieto and Pan Quemado, with the highest number of glyphs on Inscription Hill (AZ AA:7:8; Fig. 6.7), a low, isolated volcanic peak. Pan Quemado and Inscription Hill are the volcanic peaks nearest the course of Los Robles Wash. The concentration of petroglyphs here may be related to the use of petroglyphs to convey important symbolic information to a large number of people. If Los Robles Wash served as a transportation corridor, then the petroglyphs on these hills would have been visible to travelers moving north and south along the west bank of the wash.

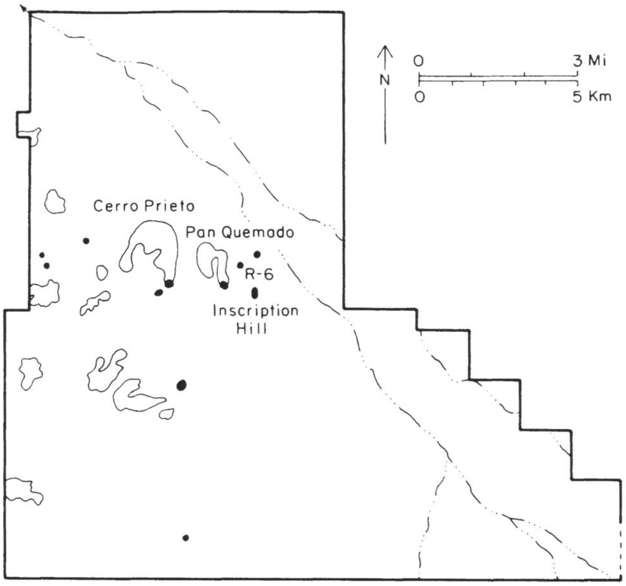

Figure 6.7. Petroglyph sites (site type 8).

An additional factor in the clustering of petroglyphs here may have been the presence of a prehistoric reservoir at AZ AA:7:43, Locus 4. People coming to the reservoir from the large settlements farther south along Los Robles Wash would have passed close to the petroglyphs at Inscription Hill. Likewise, petroglyph sites at the southern ends of Cerro Prieto and Pan Quemado would have been seen by travelers skirting the tips of these volcanic masses. Wallace and Holmlund (1986: 176) have noted that petroglyphs in such prominent locations can be conceived of as "signalling devices," situated for maximum visibility to passersby. The social context and symbolic meaning of these messages remain unknown, but the prominent locations of the petroglyphs in the vicinity of Cerro Prieto and Pan Quemado leave little doubt that they were created to be seen and "read."

The remaining petroglyph sites are relatively small and widely scattered. Three are in the western portion of the survey area, one is a few kilometers south of Cerro Prieto, and one is near the southern boundary of the survey area. None of these sites show an obvious relationship to important resources or routes of travel, but further analysis or the discovery of additional petroglyph sites might disclose such patterning.

Artifact Scatters

The final site category to be considered from the perspective of long-term land use patterns is the poorly understood set of remains classified as artifact scatters. These sites are abundant and widespread (Fig. 6.8), and they evidently reflect a wide range of prehistoric activities (Chapter 3). Unfortunately, lacking a firmer understanding of individual site functions, it is not possible to confidently identify significant patterns in the placement or characteristics of these sites. It would appear that most artifact scatters mark the locations of resource gathering activities by residents of floodplain settlements, probably including the hunting and processing of wild game animals and the harvesting and cooking of wild plant foods such as cactus fruits and mesquite beans. Considering the general trends in settlement history along Los Robles Wash (discussed below), most scatters probably date to the Sedentary and Classic periods.

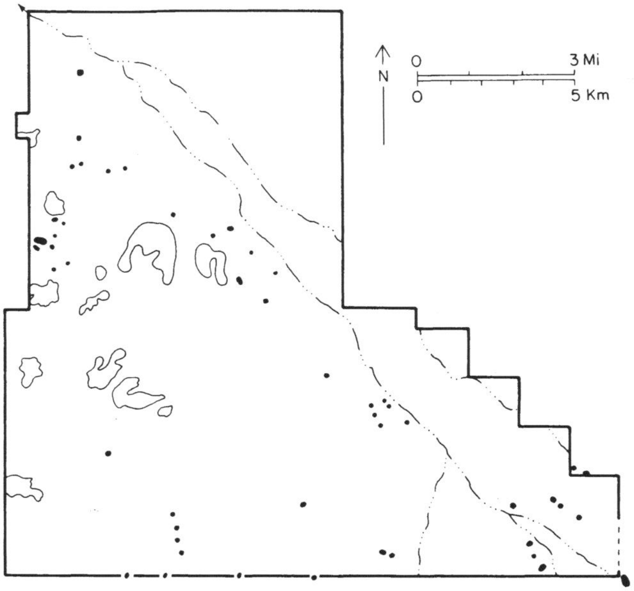

Figure 6.8. Prehistoric artifact scatters (site type 13).

TEMPORAL PATTERNS OF SETTLEMENT AND LAND USE

One of the most important goals of a regional archaeological study is to reconstruct sequences of cultural change, including shifts in the sizes and locations of settlements and changing patterns of land use. The ability to accomplish this task for the Los Robles Wash area is complicated by the incomplete nature of the available data base. Few excavations have been conducted in the survey area, so most inferences must be based on surface appearances of archaeological sites, and we know that surface remains in the Los Robles area are potentially deceptive. In particular, most sites along the course of

Los Robles Wash and some in upland settings are partially obscured by recent alluvium. Other sites have been disturbed by erosion and modern farming, livestock raising, and construction activities. In addition, many sites were not intensively mapped, and surface collections were limited in terms of the number of artifacts recovered and the area that was collected. Consequently, it is difficult to understand the internal growth sequences of individual sites, some of which cover hundreds of thousands of square meters and must surely have changed considerably through time in extent and intensity of occupation. It is equally difficult to reconstruct overall patterns of settlement and land use, because such reconstructions must be based ultimately on knowledge of individual sites.

In spite of these handicaps, which are common to most archaeological surveys, the data from the Los Robles archaeological survey do support a number of intriguing, albeit preliminary, conclusions. Perhaps most important, the general growth trends of prehistoric settlement along Los Robles Wash are similar to other areas in southern Arizona and correlate roughly with important cultural transformations across a broad area of the Southwest. Like adjacent areas watered by secondary washes, large-scale settlement of the Los Robles area apparently did not begin until sometime during the seventh or eighth centuries A.D., and like many areas of the southern Southwest, the Los Robles Wash settlement system witnessed considerable population growth and settlement expansion in the eighth through twelfth centuries. Furthermore, paralleling general organizational trends throughout the Hohokam world, the Los Robles Wash settlement system seems to have crystallized into an integrated Preclassic period community, organized around a ballcourt village (AZ AA:11:12). Further, as was generally true for the entire Hohokam cultural system, the twelfth century brought major changes for Hohokam populations along Los Robles Wash. These changes are evident not in a disruption of settlement patterns or apparent subsistence pursuits, but in the reorientation of the community around a mound settlement (AZ AA:11:25) and a large *cerro de trincheras* (Cerro Prieto, AZ AA:7:11).

The cultural sequence along Los Robles Wash also departs from that of many Hohokam settlement systems, but parallels that of the nearby Marana Community (S. Fish, P. Fish, and Madsen 1992). No Gila Polychrome or other Salado pottery was recovered or observed in the Los Robles survey area, and therefore there is no evidence of a Tucson or Civano phase component to the Los Robles Wash settlement system. The entire length of Los Robles Wash was abandoned before the Hohokam late Classic period, and it is reasonable to propose complete abandonment of this area by no later than about A.D. 1325, if not before.

Finally, the survey has revealed some important aspects of the post-Hohokam period in southern Arizona. After an apparent hiatus of two centuries or more, the Los Robles Wash area was reused and perhaps reoccupied. The first evidence of post-Hohokam land use is provided by a poorly understood set of protohistoric Pima sites, most of which are concentrated in the rocky uplands in the north half of the survey area. These sites, some of which might have been hillside cemeteries (Madsen, Chapter 5), were associated with Pima settlements along the lower Santa Cruz, perhaps the "lost" village of Santa Catarina documented first by Father Kino but never relocated by archaeologists. Remains of this settlement may be somewhere within the Los Robles survey area, perhaps in the unsurveyed northeast portion.

The sequence of cultural changes in the Los Robles survey area, discussed below, can be organized by five relevant time periods: Archaic, Preclassic Hohokam, Classic Hohokam, protohistoric, and historic. Patterns of settlement and land use are considered for each time period, and the implications of these patterns are explored with respect to current research issues.

Archaic Period

Somewhat surprisingly, the survey produced scant traces of Archaic period sites. The most convincing evidence of an Archaic presence was a set of heavily patinated, geometric petroglyphs at site AZ AA:7:43, near the southern tip of Pan Quemado. Unfortunately, these petroglyphs were not associated with a detectable Archaic site. This is unusual, because the surrounding terrain was covered with soft, aeolian deposits of silt and sand, a geomorphic setting often preferred by Archaic period groups for camping or settlement in other areas of southern Arizona (for example, Bayham and others 1986). Perhaps Archaic period sites are present in the vicinity, but are now buried beneath recent deposits of aeolian or alluvial sediments (Roth 1992: 305).

Other than these petroglyphs, there was little evidence of a substantial Archaic presence anywhere in the survey area. The only physical remains that could be reliably attributed to Archaic populations were a handful of isolated San Pedro style or concave-based projectile points and bifaces (Roth and Huckell 1992). One San Pedro style projectile point was recovered from the surface of the Los Robles Mound Site, but the unquestionable Tanque Verde phase age of the mound indicates that the artifact was either an heirloom or a Classic period Hohokam point rendered in an Archaic style. It is possible that some of the quarry or artifact scatter sites date to the Archaic period, but if so the scarcity of diagnostic projectile points throughout the survey area seems unusual.

The lack of Archaic period remains is puzzling and raises important questions about the origins of later Hohokam period populations in the survey area. It is possible that Archaic period sites are present but have not yet been discovered, that some of the supposed ceramic period quarry sites in fact are Archaic special activity sites or campsites, or that many ceramic period sites contain unrecognized underlying Archaic period components. However, the obtrusive nature of late Archaic sites in the Tucson Basin and elsewhere in southern Arizona renders this implausible. If there was a substantial late Archaic presence in the Los Robles survey area, it likely would have been discovered by now. The marked absence of such remains, coupled with the lack of early Pioneer period ceramics, suggests that the area of Los Robles Wash was not settled until perhaps the seventh or eighth centuries A.D.

Preclassic Hohokam

Pioneer Period

As in many other areas of southern Arizona, the first evidence of a significant Hohokam presence in the Los Robles survey area dates to the Snaketown phase of the late Pioneer period. No Vahki, Estrella, or Sweetwater phase ceramics were recovered or observed, but Snaketown Red-on-buff sherds were recovered from the surfaces of two sites (Fig. 6.9), a farmstead (AZ AA:11:21) in an alluvial setting, and a habitation site (AA:11:79) in an upland setting. Conceivably, these sites could have been components of a local Pioneer period settlement system, or they could have been sites within the seasonal round of a larger settlement system, perhaps one centered in the Tucson Basin. More is said below about the possible origins of Snaketown phase settlements.

Late Pioneer to Late Colonial Periods

Although the exact growth trends for the late Pioneer through late Colonial periods are not yet known, by late Colonial times a number of settlements had been established along Los Robles Wash (Figs. 6.10–6.12). This settlement system apparently originated with the Hog Farm Ballcourt Site. The small sample of surface ceramics from this site precludes a detailed understanding of its growth history, but the presence of Gila Butte Red-on-buff sherds indicates it was founded at least as early as the Gila Butte or Cañada del Oro phase (about A.D. 775–900). It is unknown whether this ballcourt was present in Rillito phase times (Wilcox 1991b: 106–107). However, the existence of a similar ballcourt at the western Avra Valley site of Water World, unquestionably dated to the Rillito phase (Ravesloot and Czaplicki 1989; Vokes 1989: 132–139), suggests that the Hog Farm ballcourt might date to this time as well. If so, the site was probably the original or "parent" settlement of what would later become a substantial Preclassic community spread along Los Robles Wash.

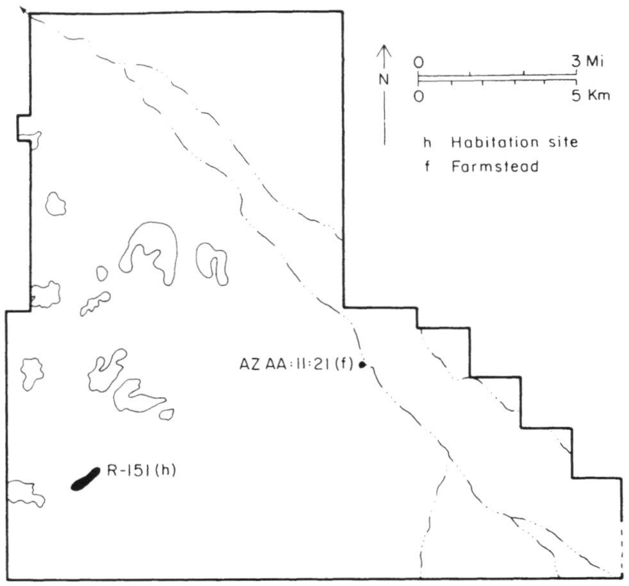

Figure 6.9. Late Pioneer period sites.

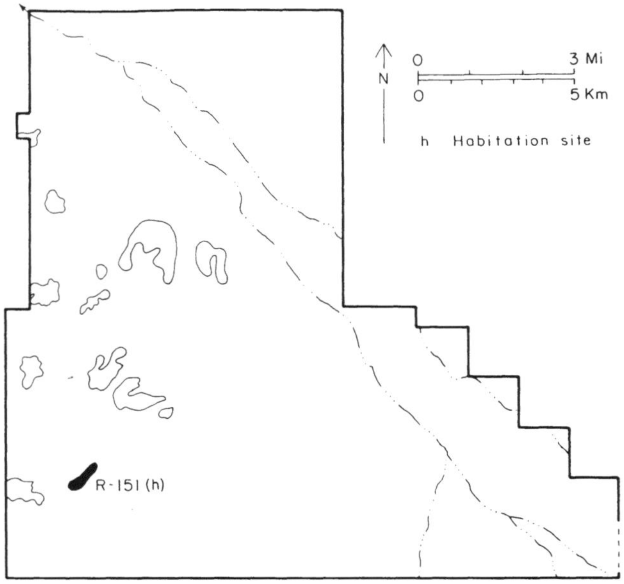

Figure 6.10. Late Pioneer–Early Colonial period sites.

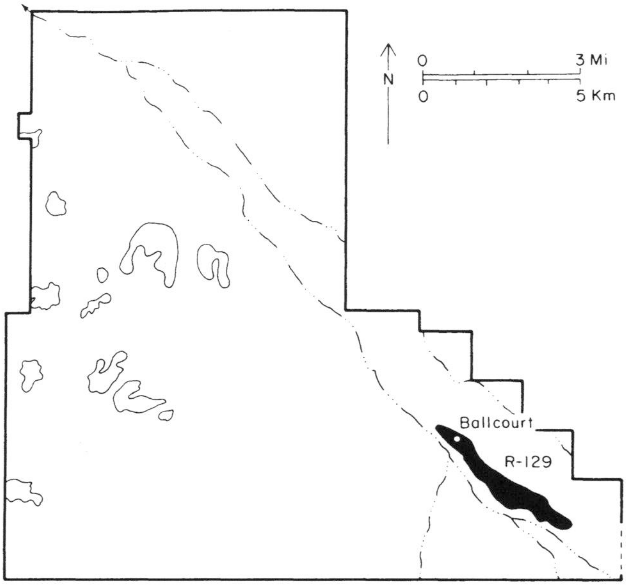

Figure 6.11. Early Colonial period sites.

By late Colonial times, the middle portion of Los Robles Wash supported a number of settlements extending northward from the Hog Farm Ballcourt village (AZ AA:11:12). Their even spacing hints that individual settlements were established by autonomous social groups intent on maintaining territorial rights to particular segments of the wash. These settlements may have been founded by people whose ancestors had originally inhabited the Hog Farm Ballcourt village, or they may have been established by immigrants from beyond the Los Robles Wash area. Several sites were dotted with substantial late Colonial trash middens or mounds, often spread over a considerable area, suggesting that these were sizable habitation villages and not merely seasonal farmsteads.

Late Colonial-Sedentary Period to Sedentary-Early Classic Period

During the Late Colonial-Sedentary to Sedentary-Early Classic interval there was an apparent growth in the number of settlements, and the settlement system expanded both upstream and downstream along Los Robles Wash (Figs. 6.13–6.15). With the exception of AZ AA:7:145 (Site R–57), all the habitation sites dating to the late Colonial period survived into the Sedentary, and several new settlements were established. This seems to imply a substantial increase in the area's population. There was also a proliferation of farmsteads, plant or animal food processing sites, and artifact scatters along Los Robles Wash and extending westward into the upland zone. Farmsteads in the west portion of the survey area indicate that Sedentary period agricultural efforts diversified to include dry farming or ak chin cultivation beyond the alluvial fans along the west bank of Los Robles Wash. Probably during this interval, the reservoir at Pan Quemado was constructed, perhaps to serve the domestic water needs of a growing population along the middle portion of Los Robles Wash.

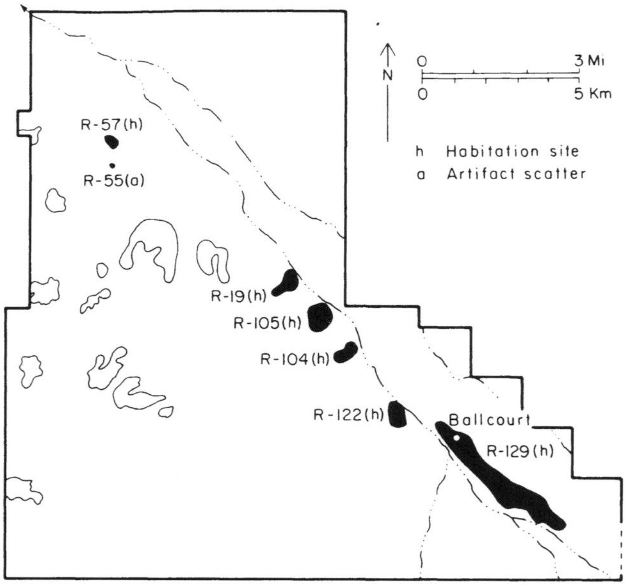

Figure 6.12. Late Colonial period sites.

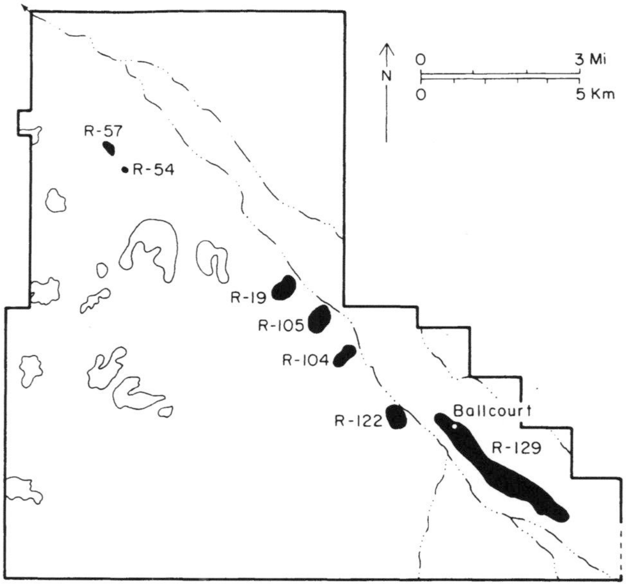

Figure 6.13. Late Colonial-Sedentary period sites. All are habitation sites.

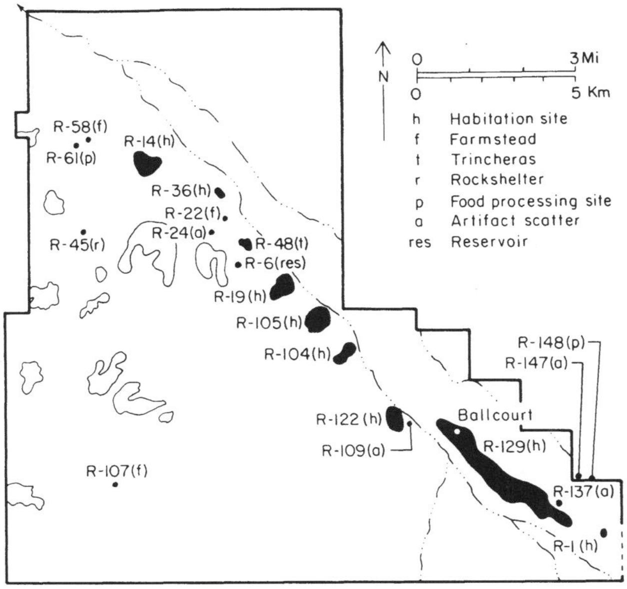

Figure 6.14. Sedentary period sites.

During the Sedentary period, the Hog Farm Ballcourt Site (AA:11:12) apparently maintained its status as the dominant settlement along Los Robles Wash. The large size of this site and the presence of a ballcourt mark it as a probable community center for the Los Robles Wash area (Wilcox and Sternberg 1983: 189–217; Doelle and Wallace 1991: 302–305). In functional terms, the Hog Farm Ballcourt Site thus may have been a ceremonial focal point, integrating the Los Robles settlements into a larger Preclassic community spread along both banks of Los Robles Wash and extending westward into the Samaniego Hills. The precise boundaries of this community are not yet clear, but may have conformed roughly to the limits of the survey area. The postulated community probably did not extend much to the east and south, because those areas appear to have been within the boundaries of another Preclassic community centered on the ballcourt village of Los Morteros, located at the north tip of the Tucson Mountains (Doelle and Wallace 1991: 299, 304; S. Fish, P. Fish, and Madsen 1992: 21).

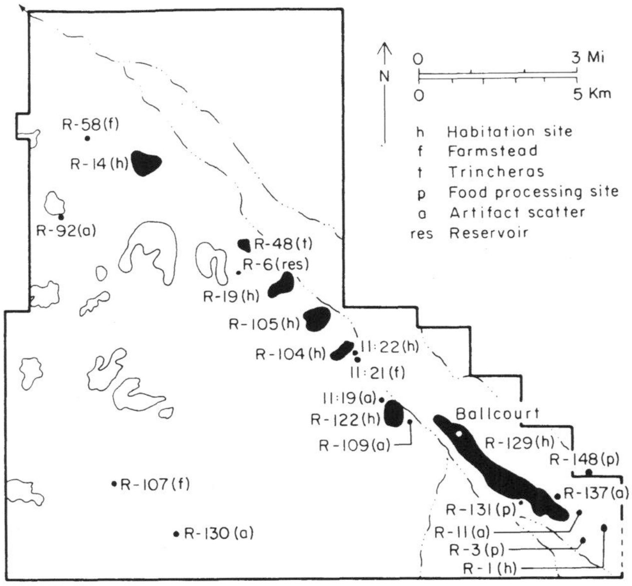

Figure 6.15. Sedentary-Early Classic period sites.

Discussion

The establishment and growth of Preclassic settlements along Los Robles Wash reflect a process of Preclassic Hohokam expansion that unfolded across a broad area of the northern Sonoran Desert and beyond. The inferred growth trends of the Los Robles Preclassic community, the locational stability of its individual settlements, and the emergence of a ballcourt village are all hallmarks of late Pioneer to Sedentary period settlement processes in a number of subareas of the Hohokam tradition (Doelle and Wallace 1991). In more general terms, the timing and nature of changes for the Preclassic Los Robles Community fit the stages of Initiation, Expansion, and Differentiation identified by Cordell and Gumerman (1989) for cultural expressions across much of the U.S. Southwest during the interval from about A.D. 200 to 1150. Though many specific questions remain about its growth and development, it is clear that the Preclassic Los Robles Community was but one aspect of a much larger set of demographic and cultural changes spread across the Southwest.

When viewed in such a broad framework, the Los Robles survey area may someday give important insights into how and perhaps why these changes took place. One paramount issue involves the spread of the Hohokam cultural pattern into nonriverine environments such as the Los Robles Wash area. If decorated sherds are a reliable indicator, Hohokam settlement in the survey area first appears during the Snaketown phase, without a clear transition from a late Archaic cultural base. A crucial question is, therefore, by what process was the area along Los Robles Wash incorporated into the Hohokam cultural pattern? There are two possibilities: (1) that Hohokam subsistence practices, residential patterns, ceremonial systems, and other cultural attributes were adopted by an indigenous population, or (2) that Los Robles Wash was colonized by "Hohokam" populations from beyond the immediate area. The lack of Archaic period remains indicates the second process was more likely.

If the Los Robles Wash settlement system was indeed initiated during the Snaketown phase by a migrant population, then a natural question involves the geographical and cultural origins of this population. Using relative proportions of decorated ceramics, Doelle and Wallace (1991: 282–290) have tentatively identified the Los Robles Wash area as part of the greater Tucson Basin Hohokam cultural tradition. Although it must be acknowledged that such archaeological measures of cultural affiliation or ethnic identity are fraught with potential problems, on the basis not only of ceramic proportions but also geographical proximity, the Tucson Basin provides a likely source population for the Los Robles area.

Conclusions about the specific nature of this colonization must await the collection of much additional information. However, because the survey recorded only two Snaketown phase sites, and one of them was identified as a farmstead, it may be suggested that the Los Robles Wash area was first staked out with a few seasonal agricultural settlements. Perhaps the floodwater farming potential of the wash was a sufficient attraction to draw farmers from the northern end of the Tucson Basin. Interestingly, the earliest clear evidence for a Hohokam presence in the Avra Valley south of Los Robles Wash also dates to the Snaketown phase, and also seems to have involved seasonal floodwater farming (Czaplicki and Ravesloot 1988, 1989). It may be that the Los Robles Wash area, like the adjacent Avra Valley, was sought out by late Pioneer farmers from the Tucson Basin who were seeking additional floodwater farming opportunities along secondary drainages of the Santa Cruz River. Why these people would have been motivated to explore these zones is at present unknown and is a question that is probably best answered with data from the Tucson Basin itself.

The Snaketown phase Hohokam efforts at exploration or small-scale settlement were followed during the early Colonial by a more substantial occupation. By Gila Butte or Cañada del Oro times (about A.D. 775–900), the Hog Farm Ballcourt village had been established. In the Rillito phase (about A.D. 900–1000), the Los Robles settlement system was greatly expanded with the establishment of at least five habitation villages.

Considering the association between settlements and Los Robles Wash, it is likely that the growth of the Preclassic community was fostered by the agricultural potential of the wash environment. As noted in Chapter 2, historically the floodplain of the wash was extremely well suited to floodwater farming, and there is reason to believe that this was the case in prehistoric times as well. Alluvial fans west of the wash probably offered good opportunities for ak chin cultivation. Further, double cropping might have been practiced prehistorically along Los Robles Wash, as it apparently was by seventeenth-century Pima farmers (Wilson 1985; compare with Gasser 1990: 9). This favorable combination of agricultural conditions could have encouraged both natural population increase and in-migration from surrounding areas.

To put these processes into a larger perspective, Doelle and Wallace (1991: 301) have observed that during the Rillito phase, Tucson Basin Hohokam populations expanded into adjacent areas such as the foothills of the Tortolita Mountains and the Avra Valley (see also Dart 1987: 286–287). Paralleling the situation along Los Robles Wash, Rillito phase ballcourt villages were established in each of these areas. Doelle and Wallace suggest that this pattern was the outcome of a population resource imbalance in the Tucson Basin. In their view, "there are suggestions that the prime areas along the major river systems [of the Tucson Basin] had been used by the Rillito phase, thereby forcing further expansion to occur in less optimal environmental zones." If this was in fact the case, perhaps the Los Robles Wash area was one of the most productive of the so-called "less optimal environmental zones," and perhaps at least some of the apparent population growth here was due to out-migration from the Tucson Basin.

Whatever the factors underlying the apparent success of the Los Robles settlement system, during the Sedentary period the number and distribution of habitation sites continued to expand. There is some evidence for diversification of agricultural strategies during the Sedentary, but the continued occupation of late Colonial villages or hamlets and the concentration of new settlements along the west bank of Los Robles Wash suggest that floodplain and ak chin farming continued as important subsistence practices. Though the dating of both the construction and abandonment of the Los Robles ballcourt is still unclear, it is presumed that during the Sedentary period this village continued to be the social, ceremonial, and perhaps political center for the settlement system as a whole.

In all likelihood, the growth of the Los Robles settlement system was not due to agricultural productivity alone. As they have been in historic times, Los Robles Wash and the nearby Santa Cruz River undoubtedly were used as prehistoric overland transportation corridors connecting the Phoenix Basin with the Tucson Basin and Avra Valley. The Preclassic Los Robles Community was strategically located and would have been a critical link in local exchange networks. Literally thousands of red-on-buff ceramics were traded into the Tucson Basin from the Gila and Salt River valleys (Doelle and Wallace 1991: 284), and large quantities of shell moved from the Gulf of California northeast into the Phoenix Basin

(McGuire 1991: 353; McGuire and Howard 1987; Crown 1991b). The importance of the Preclassic Los Robles settlements in such transactions cannot be judged until these sites are excavated. However, it can be postulated that people along Los Robles Wash were favorably situated to participate in both the ceramic and shell exchange networks, and that this position made them valued trading partners to both the Tucson Basin and Phoenix Basin Hohokam populations.

It is also conceivable that residents of the Preclassic Los Robles Community were directly involved in the production of specialized artifacts for export. There is strong evidence for the manufacture of ground stone tools and tabular knives at various outcroppings on and around Cerro Prieto and Pan Quemado. Most of these sites apparently date to the Classic period, but the possibility remains that such craft specializations began in the Preclassic period.

Early Classic Period

The early Classic period represents the peak of prehistoric occupation along Los Robles Wash, not only in terms of the number and size of individual settlements, but also their geographic distribution (Fig. 6.16). All but two of the settlements dating to the Sedentary period show an early Classic period component, and several new settlements, farmsteads, and special activity locations were established during the early Classic. Most importantly, two large settlements were added: (1) a village with a (platform?) mound on the west bank of Los Robles Wash (AZ AA:11:25), and (2) Cerro Prieto (AA:7:11), an extensive village on the slopes of the area's largest volcanic hill, about 6 km northwest of AA:11:25.

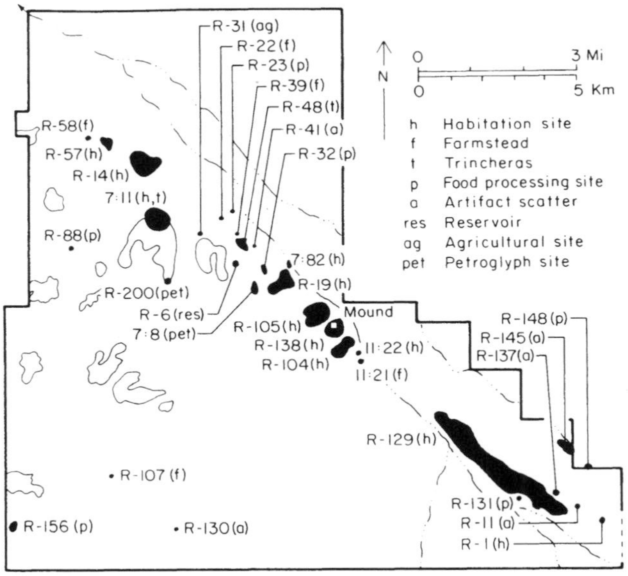

Figure 6.16. Early Classic period sites.

This expansion of the Los Robles settlement system coincided with widespread organizational changes referred to generally as the Hohokam Sedentary to Classic transition. In many areas, these changes were reflected in the apparent replacement of the ballcourt with the platform mound as the most prominent and central form of monumental architecture, and in changes in architecture, subsistence pursuits, ceremonial activities, mortuary practices, and exchange networks (Gregory 1991: 165–169; Crown 1991a: 150–153; Doyel 1991: 253–258). Although the specific abandonment date of the ballcourt at Hog Farm (AA:11:12) remains unknown, it is reasonable to propose that it, like other ballcourts throughout the Hohokam regional system, ceased to be used sometime around the late Sedentary to early Classic period boundary. If so, the Hog Farm ballcourt was probably replaced as a community focal point by the Los Robles mound. Surface sherds from this site dated only to the early Classic period, and it appears that an entirely new settlement accommodated the mound.

At approximately the same time that the Los Robles mound settlement began, a large *cerro de trincheras* was founded at Cerro Prieto. Regarding the function and organization of this settlement, and its place in a regional context of other trincheras sites, the following conclusions are offered, summarized from Chapter 4.

1. Cerro Prieto was a large hillside village with more than 230 oval and rectangular stone house foundations, abundant trash deposits, large and small terraces, an elaborate network of trails, and numerous other features such as check dams, waffle gardens, rockpiles, petroglyphs, and rock walls.
2. Many structures at Cerro Prieto were arranged into coherent clusters that apparently reflected households or groups of households. Differences in size and construction techniques suggest that some households were larger and wealthier than others.
3. Cerro Prieto does not appear to have been constructed and used primarily as a defensive retreat. This conclusion is based on the following evidence and arguments (see also P. Fish and S. Fish 1989: 121–122).
   (a) On the basis of formal, associational, and distributional criteria, few of the terraces seem built to serve a defensive function; agricultural, ceremonial, residential, or perhaps even symbolic functions seem more likely.
   (b) Clusters of structures were designed without apparent regard for defense (for example, groups of

houses were usually not fortified with enclosing walls, and doorways normally opened downslope, toward potential attackers).

(c) A network of trails and cleared corridors provided easy access into the heart of the village, certainly a design flaw for a defensive refuge.

(d) The flanks and back sides of Cerro Prieto were unprotected by rock works, leaving the village vulnerable to attack from the south, southeast, and west.

(e) The most easily defended portions of the hill (the upper talus slopes and the flat-topped summit) showed no rock constructions that could be interpreted as defensive features.

(f) The majority of Tanque Verde phase floodplain settlements in the Los Robles Community were located several kilometers away from Cerro Prieto, diminishing its usefulness as an emergency retreat. Pan Quemado, closer to Los Robles Wash, would have been a feasible location for a defensive refuge to protect floodplain villages, had one been needed, but there is no evidence that it was ever used for this purpose.

(g) There was no natural source of water nor any evidence of a structure for storing drinking water at Cerro Prieto, a potentially fatal flaw if attackers wished to lay siege to the village. Again, Pan Quemado would have made a more likely spot for a defensive refuge, because it has within its interior valley a probable reservoir. Access to this reservoir was never blocked by walls or other features. In fact, the southern end of the valley leading to the reservoir was completely open, and access over a volcanic ridge to the north would have been eased by a trail that appears to lead in the direction of Cerro Prieto.

(h) A comparative analysis by Keith Katzer of trincheras terraces across southern Arizona revealed a preference for north and northeast slopes, and an aversion to south-facing slopes. This pattern makes sense if terraces were sited to take advantage of the cooler and wetter environmental conditions offered by these aspects, but cannot be easily explained if they were constructed for defense.

4. There were numerous features at Cerro Prieto that may have served a ceremonial or symbolic function. Included were massive terraces, up to 4 m high, on the eastern slopes of the hill; a set of large, stone-walled compounds on the northern slopes; and a double row of boulders, splitting the site into two segments or precincts. The functions of these features remain unknown, but they bespeak symbol and ceremony rather than defense. All could have been seen from a considerable distance, and their form and arrangement on the hillside imply formal demarcation and spatial segregation of diverse activities, rather than a unitary function such as defense of the community. It is suggested that the double boulder wall might have split the village into two distinct social groups. Similar dividing walls occur at other early Classic period *cerros de trincheras* or trincheras feature sites, including Linda Vista Hill and Tumamoc Hill in the Tucson Basin, and Fortified Hill near Gila Bend.

5. The residents of Cerro Prieto appear to have been involved in at least two economically important activities, (a) the cultivation of crops in hillside terraces and waffle gardens, and (b) the manufacture of tabular knives from an excellent source of raw material at the hill summit. The latter activity was potentially quite significant, because tabular knives were commonly used and presumably were in great demand across southern Arizona during the early Classic period. Each of these activities may have contributed substantially to the size, power, and prestige of the Cerro Prieto village, both within the Los Robles Community and at a greater geographical scale.

6. Architectural features at Cerro Prieto show specific similarities to two widely separated trincheras feature sites: Fortified Hill near Gila Bend, Arizona and the massive site of Cerro de Las Trincheras at Trincheras, Sonora. The construction techniques, shapes, sizes, and arrangements of structures at Cerro Prieto provide an impressive match with the structures at Fortified Hill. Both sites were occupied during the early Classic period, and both have similar ceramic assemblages, with decorated sherds dominated by Tanque Verde Red-on-brown. Both are split by massive walls. The large terraces of Cerro Prieto, though vastly fewer in number and not nearly as long, are similar in form to those at Cerro de Las Trincheras. Though it remains to be established if Cerro Prieto and Cerro de Las Trincheras were contemporaneous, both sites are similar in having one or more large, rectangular enclosures on their lower slopes (see Fig. 4.7) and each site has an extraordinarily large structure at its summit. A number of specific matches in masonry construction styles, and some general resemblances in site layouts, can also be observed between Cerro Prieto and at least roughly contemporaneous hilltop or hillside sites extending north from the Phoenix Basin into the Agua Fria and New River valleys, and even as far north as the Prescott area. These far-flung similarities may indicate that the builders of such sites shared general concepts of the structural layout and symbolic importance of the appearance of trincheras features, but that individual sites were made up of elements chosen from a regional mix of construction styles (see also Wasley and Johnson 1965: 81).

These conclusions about Cerro Prieto raise important questions about its role in the greater Los Robles Community. It is difficult to imagine that this settlement was designed as an emergency defensive refuge for residents of floodplain villages, or even that it could ever have served this purpose, regardless of why it was built. It is equally difficult to interpret Cerro Prieto as an alternative residential choice for some inhabitants of the Los Robles mound community (that is, some people chose to build and live in a terraced hillside village equipped with massive terraces, compounds, and dividing walls, whereas others chose adobe rooms and pit houses near the floodplain). Organizationally and ceremonially, Cerro Prieto must have played a much greater role in the Los Robles Community than previously suspected (Stacy 1974; Doelle and Wallace 1991: 330).

Discussion

An early Classic period reorganization of the Los Robles settlement system is indicated by the founding of a new settlement featuring a rectangular, earthen mound (AZ AA:11:25) and the construction of a large trincheras village at Cerro Prieto (AZ AA:7:11). These changes came at a time of widespread transitions not only for the Hohokam (Doyel 1981: 47-63), but for other prehistoric Southwestern cultural systems as well. Cordell and Gumerman (1989: 11) have referred to the interval from about A.D. 1130-1150 to 1275-1300 as the "Reorganization Period" of the prehistoric Southwest. In their view, this period was "in general,... a time of apparent instability, with changes in the nature of the previously strong large systems, some local abandonments, and the development of new centers."

Certainly, the Los Robles Wash settlement system fits this characterization, as sometime around the end of the Sedentary period the Hog Farm ballcourt settlement was apparently abandoned as a community center and the major expressions of public architecture shifted to the Los Robles mound and Cerro Prieto villages. Many other Hohokam settlement systems in southern Arizona, including the adjacent Marana Community, underwent similar changes (S. Fish, P. Fish, and Madsen 1992: 20-40).

The reasons for such transformations, at any level of geographical scale, remain elusive. Cordell and Gumerman (1989: 11-12) have proposed that changing precipitation patterns, resulting in lowered water tables and increased erosion, might have disrupted the operation of cultural systems in some areas of the Southwest. However, they acknowledge that "the Hohokam area... cannot be assumed to have undergone the same environmental problems," and they point out that for the Hohokam, changes often came in the form of community reorganization rather than abandonment (p. 12). Data from the Los Robles survey indicate that settlement locations remained stable throughout the late Sedentary to early Classic transition, suggesting in turn that environmental changes, if they did occur, brought no significant disruption of settlement patterns and subsistence pursuits. It is difficult, therefore, to postulate that the Sedentary to Classic period transition was precipitated by a changing environment.

Considering present difficulties involved in generalizing about the causes of the Sedentary to Classic period transition, it might be more appropriate to concentrate first on understanding the nature of the transition itself. Increasingly, it appears that the decline of the Preclassic Hohokam regional system did not embody abrupt change followed by cultural stasis. Rather, this transition entailed a relatively long period of reorganization and adjustment. One persistent source of confusion in Hohokam archaeology has been the tendency to conflate the early and late Classic periods, and to emphasize the important differences between the late Preclassic Sacaton phase and the late Classic period Civano phase. Certainly, when compared in this fashion, the contrast between the Preclassic and Classic periods seems especially sharp. The problem in this comparison, however, is that the transition from Preclassic to Classic periods was not abrupt, but instead unfolded over the course of more than a century. As McGuire (1991: 370) has noted,

> the [Sedentary to Classic] transformation was not sudden but rather a matter of small quantitative changes building up to a major qualitative shift at the end of the Sedentary *followed by a hundred years or more of reorganization* (emphasis added; see also Crown 1991a: 153).

This conclusion implies that the years spanning the late twelfth through thirteenth centuries were a time of experimentation and organizational diversity, not of stability and normative pattern. Much of the archaeological record in southern Arizona from this period, including the sites along Los Robles Wash, supports this viewpoint.

For example, the early Classic period settlement system along Los Robles Wash shows a rather eclectic mix of monumental architectural forms. What does this situation imply about the early Classic period in southern Arizona? One hypothesis is that the Los Robles mound settlement and Cerro Prieto were constructed by two societal segments with differing organizational and ideological principles, drawn from distinct geographical and cultural sources. Specifically, the Los Robles mound settlement may reflect a platform mound-centered belief system originating from the Gila and Salt River valleys, whereas Cerro Prieto may reflect "trincheras" concepts drawn from a source area in northern Sonora.

In this scenario, the early Classic period is viewed as a time of ideological and organizational flux, set into motion by whatever forces were responsible for the breakup of the Hohokam regional system and the rejection of concepts and principles associated with the late Preclassic Hohokam ballcourt network (Wilcox and Sternberg 1983; Wilcox 1991b). In response to these events, some populations in southern Arizona apparently reorganized during the early Classic period into communities encompassing at least two different types of settlements exhibiting monumental architecture: the platform mound village, and the *cerro de trincheras*. The belief systems underlying both types ultimately may have been derived from the northern Mesoamerican frontier (Haury 1976: 343-348; Feinman 1991), but the more local origin of *cerros de trincheras* appears to have been northern Sonora (Sauer and Brand 1931; McGuire 1991), whereas platform mounds were first developed and achieved their most elaborate expression in the Phoenix Basin (Doyel 1981: 53-55, 1991: 254-255).

Perhaps lending some support to these ideas, it is of considerable interest to note that the communities having *both* platform mounds and *cerros de trincheras* lie in a zone intermediate between northern Sonora and the Phoenix Basin. In addition to the Los Robles Community, the early Classic period Marana (S. Fish, P. Fish, and Madsen 1992) and Martinez Hill (Gabel 1931) communities of the Tucson Basin (Fig. 4.2) may be counted as examples of this phenomenon. Further west, the Arizona Papaguería is known to have examples of both platform mounds (Scantling 1940; Dart and others 1990) and *cerros de trincheras* (Hoover 1941; Hayden 1942; Stacy 1974). However, because we know little about early Classic period settlement patterns in the Papaguería, and because early Classic period platform mounds there are relatively small and might be easily overlooked, at present it is not possible to determine whether or not these types of villages were incorporated into the boundaries of a single community. Nonetheless, the generally overlapping distribution of platform mounds and *cerros de trincheras* in the Tucson Basin and the Papaguería suggests that these were intermediate zones, where certain elements of early Classic period society emulated the cultural traditions of both north (Phoenix Basin) and south (northern Sonora).

This process of organizational and ideological change might not have been particularly radical or disruptive. Neither of the prominent early Classic period forms of monumental architecture (platform mounds and *cerros de trincheras*), nor the concepts presumably associated with them, were entirely new or exotic. Small, palisaded platform mounds had been within the Hohokam architectural repertoire since at least the Sedentary period, and perhaps before (Wasley 1960; Haury 1976: 82-94). *Cerros de trincheras* apparently had existed in northern Sonora since at least the ninth century A.D. (McGuire and others 1992). Thus, in the post-ballcourt era, populations in the Tucson Basin and Papaguería may have filled an ideological vacuum by adopting or elevating to new prominence a set of concepts and ceremonies with which they had at least some familiarity. In the process, certain segments of society may have aligned with one or the other belief systems, with the material outcome being the contemporaneous existence of two manifestly different types of settlements exhibiting monumental constructions (that is, platform mounds versus the terraces, compounds, and large hilltop and hillside enclosures of *cerros de trincheras*).

This hypothesis, of course, depends on the identification of platform mounds and *cerros de trincheras* as important symbolic and ceremonial (and by extension, political; see Knight 1986: 685) components of early Classic period communities. What evidence in fact indicates that they served such functions? Few if any scholars of Hohokam prehistory would deny that platform mounds served as the loci of important ritual or ceremonial activities. Numerous lines of evidence point to such a use. Included are analogy with Mesoamerican mounds and pyramids (Ferdon 1955; Wasley 1960; Haury 1976: 93, 346-347; Bostwick 1992); the presence of high, enclosing compound walls that restrict access to the mound or control foot traffic around it (P. Fish and S. Fish 1991: 167; Neitzel 1991: 214; Jacobs 1992; Howard 1992); the presence of extremely large, elaborately constructed, and thick-walled rooms on the mound top (Doyel 1981: 31; Downum 1993); the exclusive association of platform mounds with unusual architectural elements such as adobe and stone "columns" and "altars" (Hayden 1957: 85-89; Downum 1993); the presence of multiple large cooking pits and storage facilities on the platform mounds and within their compounds (Doyel 1981: 29-33; Lindauer 1992; Downum 1993); and the consistent associations between platform mounds and rare artifacts such as quartz crystals, carved stone effigies, and shell trumpets (Fewkes 1912b; Scantling 1940; Nelson 1991; Downum 1993). In addition, Paul Fish has informed me that excavations at the Marana platform mound have produced potsherds from multiple vessels made in the form of a *Datura* seed pod. Considering the hallucinogenic properties and ethnographically documented religious significance of the *Datura* plant, this may provide evidence of a previously unsuspected use of platform mounds for vision quests or similar rituals.

Evidence for a ritual or ceremonial use of *cerros de trincheras* is less firmly established. However, many features at Sonoran *cerros de trincheras*, including dozens or even hundreds of terraces, rectangular hillside enclosures, and hilltop "corrales" or massive-walled structures, suggest elaborate, labor-intensive, and highly visible public architecture (Huntington 1913, Plate 3). No ballcourts, platform mounds, or other monuments have yet been identified in Sonora, so the terraces and large enclosures of *cerros de trincheras* appear to have been the only candidates for ceremonial architecture during a period extending from at least the ninth to perhaps as late as the sixteenth centuries A.D. The Sonoran *cerros de trincheras* have not yet been excavated, so the nature of activities conducted on them, and the form of ritual or ceremonial artifacts possibly associated with their features, remain unknown. Ongoing work by Randall McGuire and Elisa Villalpando at the site of Cerro de Las Trincheras in Sonora promises to add considerably to our understanding of such sites, and their possible symbolic, ceremonial, and organizational role in the prehistory of northern Mexico.

In the U.S. Southwest, evidence for ritual or ceremonial activities on *cerros de trincheras* is circumstantial, provided largely by surface evidence of architectural forms and artifacts and features recovered in a handful of scattered excavations. As reviewed in Chapter 4, we now know that some of the Southwest's largest *cerros de trincheras* (including Cerro Prieto, Linda Vista Hill, and probably Tumamoc Hill and Martinez Hill as well) were used for habitation. However, mixed among residential structures were apparently nonresidential stone features such as walled and artificially leveled compounds, large terraces, and broad, cleared corridors or trails. Smaller examples of *cerros de trincheras* show variable combinations of structure foundations, terraces, walls, and enclosures (Stacy 1974) that replicate the forms found at the larger sites. The reasons for interpreting many of these constructions as symbolic or ceremonial features, and not defensive fortifications, have already been discussed. Also as reviewed in Chapter 4, artifacts that may reasonably be interpreted as having been used in rituals or ceremonies were recently recovered from a walled compound or plaza at the summit of the Linda Vista Hill Site, a *cerro de trincheras* at the northern end of the Tucson Basin. Of possible additional significance, a shell trumpet was found in a stone compound near the summit of Site AZ T:4:8 (ASM), a "fortified" or trincheras feature site along the New River.

Two additional lines of evidence may be mentioned briefly with respect to the possible religious and ceremonial importance of *cerros de trincheras*. First, these sites are often accompanied by abundant prehistoric petroglyphs (Fontana and others 1959: 44–46; Ferg 1979; Wallace 1983), including examples at Tumamoc Hill of individuals holding staffs and wearing headdresses, and a group of five people holding hands as if engaged in a sort of line dance (Ferg 1979: 105). That such petroglyphs might commemorate ceremonial activities associated with *cerros de trincheras* certainly seems a plausible hypothesis (compare with Ferg 1979). Second, among contemporary Piman groups in southern Arizona (the O'odham), the summits and rocky outcrops of volcanic hills are common locations for shrines, and some (including *cerros de trincheras*) are associated with legends that tell of powers and beings inhabiting the hills (Russell 1908: 254–256, Plates 40–41; Hartmann and Hartmann 1979: 64; Hartmann 1989: 47). Assuming that the O'odham are the descendants of the Hohokam, it seems at least possible that such beliefs reflect ancient concepts and realities, perhaps even the twelfth- and thirteenth-century use of volcanic hillsides as *cerros de trincheras*.

Three final points can be made about the preceding scenario. First, the idea that early Classic period social and ceremonial life in all communities was controlled by a single, ruling elite seems, even on theoretical grounds, a probable oversimplification. Throughout the century or more of reorganization that characterized the early Classic, it is more likely that there would have been multiple religious, social, and political institutions, some perhaps roughly congruent with individual settlements, and others cross-cutting settlement or even community boundaries (see also Doyel 1981: 51, 63). Knight (1986) has proposed a model of religious pluralism and multiple cult institutions for Mississippian societies in the eastern United States, and this concept may have some utility for the early Classic period Hohokam. At the least, the hypothesis of multiple ideologies or cult institutions (Wallace 1966: 84–96), signified by distinctive architectural forms, ceremonial artifacts, and perhaps burial practices, provides a useful way to structure future investigations of platform mound and trincheras sites.

Second, this scenario also may provide a productive way to consider other puzzling aspects of the early Classic period, for example, the multiple Soho phase platform mounds of Compound B at Casa Grande (Fewkes 1912b), Pueblo Grande (Downum 1993), and perhaps other Phoenix Basin sites, and the proliferation of early Classic period mounds in the Tonto Basin. Such phenomena are untidy anomalies if early Classic period communities are viewed as integrated polities tightly controlled by a single religious and political elite, but make considerably more sense if seen as the architectural symbols and ceremonial facilities of multiple cult organizations or priesthoods (Knight 1986: 679–682; Anderson 1990). Precisely how such organizations might have been related to each other, how they might have corresponded with political offices or other community leadership roles, and how they might have changed during the late

Classic period, remain to be understood (see also Wilcox 1991a: 268).

Finally, the hypothesis of multiple religious institutions during the early Classic period may hold implications for late Classic period developments. Several lines of evidence seem to point to important changes in Hohokam communities during the late Classic, perhaps toward greater consolidation of religious and political leadership. Two well-known examples are the widespread appearance of Salado polychrome vessels, thought by some to represent integrative icons or symbols, and an increase in the number of structures placed atop platform mounds, perhaps indicating participation in mound-top activities by increasingly larger groups of people. Other aspects of platform mound development suggest more inclusive ceremonial activities as well. For example, at the onset of the late Classic period at Casa Grande, the double platform mound configuration of Compound B apparently is abandoned and the "big house" of Compound A is constructed. At Pueblo Grande, it appears that a configuration of two smaller platform mounds is enclosed by a single retaining wall, creating one very large mound with a single surface supporting multiple sets of self-contained adobe compounds (Downum 1993). A similar process of late Classic period mound consolidation may account for the enormous platform mound at Mesa Grande. In the Tonto Basin, the late Classic period apparently brings abandonment of multiple early Classic period platform mounds, and aggregation of the Basin's population into a more limited number of settlements with larger and more elaborate mounds. At the onset of the Late Classic, the Tucson Basin witnesses an apparent abandonment of the *cerros de trincheras*, abandonment of outlying communities like Marana and Los Robles, and aggregation of the local population into a smaller number of more densely inhabited compound settlements. If the early Classic period was indeed a time of religious pluralism and multiple cult institutions, then perhaps the late Classic period or "Salado" developments cited above, as well as a general abandonment of *cerros de trincheras* across southern and central Arizona, reflect the development of fewer, more inclusive, and possibly more powerful institutions.

Comparison of the Los Robles and Marana Communities

The early Classic period Los Robles Community and the adjacent Marana Community, located on the east side of the Santa Cruz River, show important similarities and differences. Like Los Robles, the early Classic period Marana Community was the outcome of reorganization at the end of the Sedentary period. The Marana platform mound site (AZ AA:12:251), like the Los Robles Mound (AA:11:25), was founded during the Tanque Verde phase as a village to accommodate a platform mound. As with Los Robles, the Marana platform mound was also established north of a Sedentary period ballcourt settlement, in this case the extensive Preclassic and early Classic village of Los Morteros (AZ AA:12:57). The Marana Community also encompassed both a platform mound and a large *cerro de trincheras* village, the latter located on Linda Vista Hill, just west of the village of Los Morteros (Downum 1986). Finally, like Los Robles, Marana was abandoned at the end of the early Classic period.

There are important differences as well. Unlike Los Robles, much of the early Classic Marana Community was spread over an area that previously had been avoided for settlement. Rather than existing in relative isolation along a secondary drainage, the Marana Community seems to have been directly connected to the north end of the Tucson Basin with a canal originating from the Santa Cruz River. Possibly, there were differences in subsistence practices as well. Whereas farming efforts of the Los Robles Community appear to have been largely focused around the floodplain of Los Robles Wash, the Marana Community encompassed a wide diversity of agricultural strategies, including floodplain, ak chin, and dry farming efforts. In the Marana Community, there is an extensive system of rockpile fields along the bajadas of the Tortolita Mountains, evidently used for the cultivation of agave. Although some rockpile feature sites are known, fields of this extent are not matched in the immediate hinterlands of the Los Robles Community.

Similarities between Marana and Los Robles, as well as geographical proximity, suggest that these two communities were closely related. Differences in their form and developmental trajectories indicate that they were also independent and were shaped by slightly different historical and cultural processes. Synchrony of abandonment hints that the ultimate fates of both Marana and Los Robles were linked to larger processes of cultural change, namely widespread consolidation of regional populations at the beginning of the late Classic period.

Late Classic Period

One of the clearest patterns to emerge from the Los Robles archaeological survey was the absence of late Classic period remains. Among all the sherds collected or seen at all sites, and among all the isolated artifacts observed, not a single fourteenth-century Salado polychrome sherd was recorded. Thus, much like the Marana Community on the east side of the Santa Cruz River, the Los Robles Wash area seems to have been abandoned sometime before the late Classic period.

This simple observation raises the question of why this entire area should have been abandoned after so many centuries of apparent success. As yet, there is no answer. Environmental change is an obvious possibility, but no relevant environmental data have yet been collected, and the hypothesis has little a priori appeal. It has been noted previously that settlement locations along the west bank of Los Robles Wash generally remained stable from the Colonial through early Classic periods. This stability in turn was attributed to the ongoing farming potential of the Los Robles Wash floodplain and the alluvial fans adjacent to the west. It is difficult, therefore, to imagine environmental changes that could have affected the farming potential of both areas to the extent that complete abandonment would have been necessary. Perhaps, as has been proposed for the Santa Cruz River in the southern Tucson Basin (Doelle and others 1987; Waters 1987; Ellis and Waters 1991), entrenchment of Los Robles Wash was an insurmountable problem during the latter part of the early Classic period. If so, the Los Robles area populations might have relocated downstream along the Santa Cruz River, where abundant late Classic period remains have been found. However, the Marana Community, directly across the river from the Los Robles Community, was also abandoned toward the end of the early Classic. Marana, though, does not seem to have been susceptible to the effects of arroyo down-cutting, at least on a scale that might have forced complete abandonment. Hence, it is difficult to propose that a single environmental process could have caused the abandonment of both the Marana and Los Robles early Classic period communities.

Social causes for abandonment are even more elusive. Various authors (for example, Doelle and Wallace 1991) have proposed scenarios involving intercommunity or interregional conflict as a cause of Classic period abandonments. Yet, the empirical basis for inferring conflict is slim and relies almost entirely on trincheras sites, ceramic distributions, and the interpretation of uninhabited areas as prehistoric "buffer zones" (following P. Fish and S. Fish 1989). However, if trincheras sites are not viewed as defensive constructions, then there is little evidence of prehistoric conflict in the lower Santa Cruz River Basin. It is possible, of course, that the abandonment of the Los Robles Wash area was due to factionalism or some other internal social process. If, as proposed, the early Classic period Los Robles Community accommodated at least two major ideological systems, perhaps the leaders associated with each engaged in competition that ultimately led to a community breakup (see Johnson and Earle 1987: 17-21; Anderson 1990). It is possible also that both the Marana and Los Robles communities were abandoned as part of a large-scale consolidation of Tucson Basin-area populations at the onset of the late Classic (Doelle and Wallace 1990). If so, both the process and its motivation remain obscure.

Perhaps the only solid conclusion that can be offered is that the Los Robles Wash area was completely abandoned by no later than about A.D. 1325. Whether this abandonment involved a local downstream shift in settlement or a more widespread relocation of the community's population is unknown. Additional survey information from adjacent areas is required to understand the nature of this abandonment, and hence its possible cause and consequences. More detailed environmental evidence from the Los Robles Wash area would also be desirable to test for possible environmental changes during the transition from the early to late Classic periods.

Protohistoric Period

As discussed by Madsen in Chapter 5, three of the protohistoric sites (AZ AA:7:158, 187, and 188; Fig. 6.17) dated exclusively to the protohistoric and exhibited hillside rock cairn or open pit features that might represent the remains of burial pits. However, the limited investigations conducted by Madsen were inconclusive, and the only solid judgment is that these pits served as caches of some sort containing bowls and jars manufactured between about A.D. 1450 and 1860, and probably before the 1780s. The cairns and pits were severely vandalized and few ceramic artifacts (most of which were collected) and no human remains were left

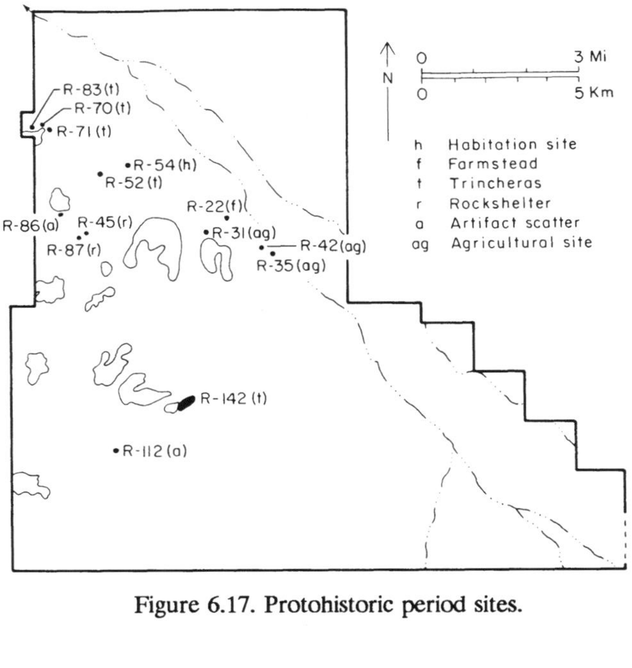

Figure 6.17. Protohistoric period sites.

in them. The remaining sites are a mixed group of rock constructions classified as trincheras feature sites, habitation sites, farmsteads, agricultural fields, rock shelters, and artifact scatters, all assigned a protohistoric component on the basis of sherds resembling the type Whetstone Plain. Only one of these sites had Whetstone Plain(?) sherds in the absence of Hohokam plain or decorated sherds. All the others had Whetstone Plain(?) sherds along with prehistoric types, and none had sherds showing the distinctive rim coils and other attributes of the ceramics seen at the cairn and pit sites described in Chapter 5.

The assignment of sites AZ AA:7:158, 187, and 188 to the protohistoric or early historic period is sound. As discussed by Madsen, sherds recovered from these sites were certainly not within the range of Hohokam ceramics, and most resembled the ceramics recovered from known protohistoric or early historic Piman sites. Dating of the other sites is less certain. First, there are the ambiguities involved in correctly identifying the type Whetstone Plain. Second, even with its restricted definition, its temporal distribution is poorly understood; did some prehistoric Hohokam ceramics resemble Whetstone Plain? Finally, even if this type was represented, there is the problem of how to interpret the low frequency of later sherds at sites known or suspected to have been primarily prehistoric in age. Perhaps some protohistoric sites were reoccupied or reused in a manner congruent with prehistoric use, but perhaps not. The most obvious possibility in this regard is that low frequencies of Whetstone Plain(?) sherds at predominantly prehistoric sites indicate that these sites were reused for resource gathering or other limited activities during protohistoric times.

The picture of protohistoric activities within the survey area is at present unclear. The rock cairn and pit sites in the northwest corner of the survey area suggest the presence of a nearby protohistoric village, but such a site has not yet been identified. Sherds resembling Whetstone Plain at a variety of prehistoric sites across the survey area indicate that the Samaniego Hills served as the immediate hinterland for a set of habitation sites, but again, where these sites were located is problematic. From the standpoint of archaeological research into the effects of European contact on Piman-speaking peoples, this situation is especially unfortunate. The time during which these villages were occupied was a traumatic one for the native inhabitants of Pimería Alta, marked by death from disease, Apache raiding, and devastating assaults on native systems of belief, settlement, and subsistence (Ezell 1961, 1983; Doelle 1981, 1984; Fontana 1983; Doyel 1989; McGuire and Villalpando 1989; Doelle and Wallace 1990). Our historical and archaeological understanding of these events and processes is meager, and any information that might be provided by remaining material evidence would contribute greatly to documenting the post-Contact history of the O'odham people (see also McGuire 1982b: 196–199). It is possible that protohistoric villages have survived modern erosion and land use along the Los Robles Wash and Santa Cruz River, and that they someday will be located. Until they are, the meaning of protohistoric sites in the survey area will remain something of a puzzle.

Historic Period

The few late historic period sites within the survey area appear to have been homesteads and camps. On the basis of artifacts and site locations, most were associated with the mining town of Sasco, which existed from about 1907 to the mid 1920s. Papago Plain and Papago Red sherds suggest that some of the sites were built and used by Tohono O'odham people. An informed understanding of this period would involve more extensive field and documentary studies than was feasible for the Los Robles survey. These sites may contain an important record of everyday life for the inhabitants of Sasco and its immediate environs. Such people are poorly represented in written documentation, so further study of these sites perhaps could clarify some details of the living conditions and activities of workers in Arizona's early twentieth-century mining and smelting industry.

SUMMARY, SUGGESTED RESEARCH, AND PRESERVATION FOR THE FUTURE

The Los Robles Archaeological survey and the Cerro Prieto mapping project have succeeded in filling in the rough outlines of prehistoric, protohistoric, and historic period settlement and land use across a large area of the lower Santa Cruz River Basin. As a result of these studies and others (for example, Teague and Crown 1984; Downum and others 1986; Rice 1987; Ciolek-Torrello and Wilcox 1988; S. Fish, P. Fish, and Madsen 1992), the regional picture of archaeology in the desert Southwest has been made clearer. Entirely new and, to some extent, unanticipated settlement systems have been discovered and their boundaries mapped. The most important result has been the greatly enhanced knowledge of regional demographic trends and of the formal, functional, and environmental variability of Hohokam settlement. Traditional models of Hohokam prehistory, phrased in terms of a core-periphery contrast, are now known to be far too simplistic to characterize the complexity of the Hohokam world and its individual communities (Wilcox 1980, 1991b; Crown 1990; McGuire 1991). The Los Robles Community, lying in an area once thought to be intermediate between the Hohokam core of the Salt-Gila river valleys and the peripheries of the Tucson Basin and Papaguería, illustrates the point. We now know that large Hohokam communities extended north from the northern end of the Tucson Basin, into the Santa Cruz Flats, and on to the Gila River. Where on such a complex and seemingly continuous cultural landscape did the core end and the periphery begin?

In spite of the excitement that has been justifiably created by the recent expansion of information about such communities, much work remains. Most of our knowledge about the prehistoric communities between the Tucson and Phoenix basins comes from surface observations. Although this report has proposed some rather specific inferences regarding the timing and dynamics of growth and abandonment for the Los Robles Community, it should be emphasized again these propositions are only first approximations to be tested with further field research and analysis. Considering the vagaries of erosion and deposition, the large numbers of poorly dated and functionally ambiguous artifact scatters, and the almost intractable problems of dating and characterizing Hohokam demographic trends from surface data, there is little doubt that the Los Robles Community holds further surprises and significant discoveries. Three particularly important problems concern the dates for the foundation and abandonment of the ballcourt at AZ AA:11:12, the morphology and function of the mound at AZ AA:11:25, and the activities associated with the large terraces and compounds at Cerro Prieto. Much of the interpretive scenario presented in this volume hinges on the outcome of investigations directed toward these problems, and until additional data are forthcoming, many of the ideas presented herein will remain hypotheses only.

Future research, of course, depends on the continuing existence and integrity of the individual sites that compose the Los Robles Community. If past reaction to threats are any indication, there is good reason to be optimistic about the future. When developers attempted to lease part of the State Trust lands surrounding Cerro Prieto and Pan Quemado for the purpose of building a guest ranch and shooting range, response from the public and archaeologists was swift and decisive. As a consequence, the Arizona State Parks Board recommended the area become a state park and it was so designated in 1986. The Los Robles Archaeological District has now been added to the State (1988) and National (1989) Registers of Historic Places (Downum 1988). Nomination of this District, a joint effort by the Arizona State Museum, the Arizona State Land Department, and the Arizona State Historic Preservation Office, was made possible through the information gathered during the USBR Los Robles Archaeological Survey. The final outcome of these efforts is a 12,894 acre Archaeological District that encompasses 119 archaeological sites containing information relating to the foundation, growth, and abandonment of the Classic period Los Robles Community.

As a result of this nomination, the U.S. Bureau of Land Management (Phoenix District) is now considering acquiring the Los Robles Archaeological District for management as a Resource Conservation Area. Because the Phoenix District of the BLM recently (1988) completed its Resource Management Plan (RMP) and Final Environmental Impact Statement, acquisition of the Los Robles Archaeological District is being considered as an amendment to the 1988 RMP. Notice of Intent to pursue an amendment to the RMP was issued in the Federal Register of 24 March, 1989, and public meetings were held on April 11–12, 1989, in Sonoita and Tucson. The BLM has so far received a favorable public response to its proposed acquisition of the Los Robles District, and additional studies are underway to assess the feasibility and impacts of such an action. Conceivably, acquisition of the Los Robles District by the BLM could facilitate the creation of an Arizona State Park in this area by allowing the state to lease the property from the BLM at a rate much reduced from the fee the State Land Department is now required to charge. However, as of this writing (December 1992), the voters of Arizona turned down for the second time an amendment to the state's constitution that would permit such exchanges of state and federal land. Thus, the status of the Los Robles Community as either a Resource Conservation Area or a state park remains unclear. In the meantime, steps have been taken to insure against the further degradation of the Los Robles sites by vandalism and theft. Rangers from Picacho Peak State Park patrol the area, and, through an agreement worked out between the Arizona State Land Department and the Army Reserve National Guard, aerial surveillance is provided by helicopter overflights originating from the Pinal Air Park. In addition, a network of local professional and amateur archaeologists regularly visit and monitor the condition of archaeological sites, especially Cerro Prieto and petroglyph sites near Pan Quemado.

In the final analysis, however, the continued existence and a more informed understanding of these sites will depend on their permanent designation as an archaeological monument and full-time monitoring and enforcement of antiquities legislation. We can only hope that the people of Arizona will someday insist that these remarkable places be preserved and carefully managed. There could be no more fitting expression of respect for the Hohokam who lived between desert and river.

References

AGUIRRE, YJINIO
1983 *Echoes of the Conquistadores: History of a Pioneer Family in the Southwest.* Privately printed. Copy on file in Arizona State Museum Site Files, University of Arizona, Tucson.

ANDERSON, DAVID GEORGE
1990 Political Change in Chiefdom Societies: Cycling in the Late Prehistoric Southeastern United States. MS, Doctoral dissertation, Department of Anthropology, University of Michigan, Ann Arbor.

ANDERSON, KEITH M., FILLMAN BELL, AND YVONNE G. STEWART
1982 Quitobaquito: A Sand Papago Cemetery. *The Kiva* 47(4): 215–237.

ARIZONA DAILY STAR
1985 July 13, "Multisport Resort Planned for Red Rock," Section E, p. 1.
1985 September 1, "Archaeologists Fear Resort's Impacts on Prehistoric Sites," Section B, p. 1.
1991 July 27, "Relics Recovered: Search of home turns up ancient Indian carvings," Section A, p. 1.

BAHR, DONALD M.
1983 Pima and Papago Social Organization. In *Handbook of North American Indians*, Vol. 10, *Southwest*, edited by Alfonso Ortiz, pp. 178–192. William G. Sturtevant, General Editor. Washington: Smithsonian Institution Press.

BANDELIER, ADOLPH F.
1884 Reports by A. F. Bandelier on His Investigations in New Mexico During the Years 1883–84. *Annual Report of the Executive Committee of the Archaeological Institute of America* 5: 55–98. Cambridge: John Wilson and Son.
1892 Final Report of Investigations Among the Indians of the Southwestern United States, Carried on Mainly in the Years from 1880 to 1885. Part II. *Papers of the Archaeological Institute of America, American Series* 4. Cambridge: Cambridge University Press.

BAYMAN, JAMES M., AND RICHARD M. RYAN
1988 Lower Colorado Buffware and the Protohistoric Period in Southern Arizona. *Pottery Southwest News, Queries and Views on Archaeological Ceramics* 15(1). Albuquerque.

BAYHAM, FRANK E., DONALD H. MORRIS, AND M. STEVEN SHACKLEY
1986 Prehistoric Hunter-Gatherers of South-Central Arizona: The Picacho Reservoir Project. *Arizona State University Anthropological Field Studies* 13. Tempe: Arizona State University.

BERNARD-SHAW, MARY
1983 The Stone Tool Assemblage of the Salt-Gila Aqueduct Project Sites. In "Hohokam Archaeology Along the Salt-Gila Aqueduct Central Arizona Project: Material Culture," edited by Lynn S. Teague and Patricia L. Crown, pp. 373–443. *Arizona State Museum Archaeological Series* 150(8), Parts 2, 3, 4, and 5: 373–443. Tucson: Arizona State Museum, University of Arizona.
1989a Archaeological Investigations at the Redtail Site, AA:12:149 (ASM), in the Northern Tucson Basin. *Center For Desert Archaeology Technical Report* 89-8. Tucson: Desert Archaeology.
1989b Archaeological Investigations at Los Morteros, AZ AA:12:57 (ASM), Locus 1, in the Northern Tucson Basin. *Institute for American Research Technical Report* 89-9. Tucson: Institute for American Research.
1990 Archaeological Excavations in the Lonetree Site, AZ AA:12:120 (ASM) in the Northern Tucson Basin. *Center for Desert Archaeology Technical Report* 90-1. Tucson: Desert Archaeology.

BERNARD-SHAW, MARY, AND FREDERICK W. HUNTINGTON (Editors)
1990 Rincon Phase Seasonal Occupation in the Northern Tucson Basin. *Center for Desert Archaeology Technical Report* 90-2. Tucson: Desert Archaeology.

BOLTON, HERBERT E.
1930 *Font's Complete Diary: Anza's California Expeditions*, Vol. 4. Berkeley: University of California Press.
1948 *Kino's Historical Memoir of Pimería Alta, 1683–1711.* Berkeley and Los Angeles: University of California Press.

BOSTWICK, TODD W.
1992 Platform Mound Ceremonialism in Southern Arizona: Possible Symbolic Meanings of Hohokam and Salado Platform Mounds. In "Proceedings of the Second Salado Conference," edited by Richard C. Lange and Stephen Germick. *Occasional Paper*. Phoenix: Arizona Archaeological Society.

BRANIFF, BEATRIZ
1990 The Identification of Possible Elites in Prehispanic Sonora. In *Perspectives on Southwestern Prehistory*, edited by Paul E. Minnis and Charles L. Redman, pp. 173–183. Boulder: Westview Press.

BREW, SUSAN A., AND BRUCE B. HUCKELL
1987 A Protohistoric Piman Burial and a Consideration of Piman Burial Practices. *The Kiva* 52(3): 163–191.

BROWN, DAVID E. (Editor)
1982 Biotic Communities of the Southwest--United States and Mexico. *Desert Plants* 4(1–4).

BRYAN, KIRK
1925 The Papago Country, Arizona: A Geographic, Geologic, and Hydrologic Reconnaissance with a Guide to Desert Watering Places. *U.S. Geological Survey Water Supply Paper* 499. Washington.

BURRUS, ERNEST H., S.J.
1971 Kino and Manje: Explorers of Sonora and Arizona. *Sources and Studies for the History of the Americas* 10. Rome and St. Louis: Jesuit Historical Institute.

CABLE, JOHN S.
1987 Who Were the Protohistoric Occupants of Ak-Chin?: A Study Concerning the Relationship Between Ethnicity and Ceramic Style. Ak Chin Final Report. MS on file, Soil Systems, Inc., Phoenix.

CIOLEK-TORRELLO, RICHARD (Editor)
1987 Hohokam Settlement Along the Slopes of the Picacho Mountains: The Picacho Area Sites, Tucson Aqueduct Project. *Museum of Northern Arizona Research Paper* 35(3). Flagstaff: Museum of Northern Arizona.

CIOLEK-TORRELLO, RICHARD, AND DAVID R. WILCOX
1988 Hohokam Settlement Along the Slopes of the Picacho Mountains: Synthesis and Conclusions. *Museum of Northern Arizona Research Paper* 35(6). Flagstaff: Museum of Northern Arizona.

CORDELL, LINDA S., AND GEORGE J. GUMERMAN
1989 Cultural Interaction in the Prehistoric Southwest. In *Dynamics of Southwest Prehistory*, edited by Linda S. Cordell and George J. Gumerman, pp. 1–17. Washington: Smithsonian Institution Press.

COUES, ELLIOTT
1900 *On the Trail of a Spanish Pioneer: Garces Diary 1775–6*. New York: Francis P. Harper.

CRAIG, DOUGLAS B., AND JOHN E. DOUGLAS
1984 Architectural Variability and Community Structure at Cerro Prieto (AZ AA:7:11 ASM). Paper presented at the 49th annual meeting, Society for American Archaeology, Portland, Oregon.

CROWN, PATRICIA L.
1985 Morphology and Function of Hohokam Small Structures. *The Kiva* 50(2–3): 75–94.
1990 The Hohokam of the American Southwest. *Journal of World Prehistory* 4(2): 223–255.
1991a The Hohokam: Current Views of Prehistory and the Regional System. In *Chaco and Hohokam: Prehistoric Regional Systems in the American Southwest*, edited by Patricia L. Crown and W. James Judge, pp. 135–157. Santa Fe: School of American Research Press.
1991b The Role of Exchange and Interaction in Salt-Gila Basin Hohokam Prehistory. In "Exploring the Hohokam: Prehistoric Desert Peoples of the American Southwest," edited by George J. Gumerman. *Amerind Foundation New World Studies Series* 1: 383–415. Albuquerque: University of New Mexico Press.

CZAPLICKI, JON S., AND JOHN C. RAVESLOOT
1988 Hohokam Archaeology Along Phase B of the Tucson Aqueduct, Central Arizona Project. Excavations at Fastimes (AZ AA:12:384), A Rillito Phase Site in the Avra Valley. *Arizona State Museum Archaeological Series* 178(2). Tucson: Arizona State Museum, University of Arizona.
1989 (Editors) Small Sites and Specialized Reports. Hohokam Archaeology Along Phase B of the Tucson Aqueduct, Central Arizona Project. *Arizona State Museum Archaeological Series* 178(4): Tucson: Arizona State Museum, University of Arizona.

DART, ALLEN
1984 Environment of the Study Area. In "A Class III Survey of the Tucson Aqueduct Phase A Corridor, Central Arizona Project," compiled by Jon S. Czaplicki. *Arizona State Museum Archaeological Series* 165: 5–6. Tucson: Arizona State Museum, University of Arizona.
1987 Archaeological Studies of the Avra Valley, Arizona, for the Papago Water Supply Project. Vol. I: Class III Archaeological Surveys on the Tohono O'odham Indian Reservation. *Institute for American Research Anthropological Paper* 9. Tucson: Institute for American Research.

DART, ALLEN, AND WILLIAM R. GIBSON
1988 The Western Extent of the Tucson Basin Hohokam: Evidence from Recent Surveys in the Avra Valley. In "Recent Research on Tucson Basin Prehistory: Proceedings of the Second Tucson Basin Conference," edited by William H. Doelle and Paul R. Fish. *Institute for American Research Anthropological Paper* 10: 253–276. Tucson: Institute for American Research.

DART, ALLEN, JAMES P. HOLMLUND, AND HENRY D. WALLACE
1990 Ancient Hohokam Communities in Southern Arizona: The Coyote Mountains Archaeological District in the Altar Valley. *Center for Desert Archaeology Technical Report* 90-3. Tucson: Desert Archaeology.

DEAN, JEFFREY S.
1991 Thoughts on Hohokam Chronology. In "Exploring the Hohokam: Prehistoric Desert Peoples of the American Southwest," edited by George J. Gumerman. *Amerind Foundation New World Studies Series* 1: 61–149. Albuquerque: University of New Mexico Press.

DENSMORE, FRANCES
1929 Papago Music. *Bureau of American Ethnology Bulletin* 90. Washington: Smithsonian Institution.

DI PESO, CHARLES C.
1953 The Sobaipuri Indians of the Upper San Pedro River Valley, Southeastern Arizona. Collaborators Arthur Woodward, Rex E. Gerald, and Virginia Gerald. *Amerind Foundation* 6. Dragoon, Arizona: Amerind Foundation.

DITTERT, ALFRED E., JR., AND DONALD E. DOVE (Editors)
1985 Proceedings of the 1983 Hohokam Symposium, Parts I and II. *Arizona Archaeological Society*

Occasional Paper 2. Phoenix: Phoenix Chapter, Arizona Archaeological Society.

DOBYNS, HENRY F.

1974 The Kohatk: Oasis and Ak-Chin Horticulturalists. *Ethnohistory* 21: 317–327.

DOELLE, WILLIAM H.

1981 The Gila Pima in the Seventeenth Century. In "The Protohistoric Period in the North American Southwest, A.D. 1450–1700," edited by David R. Wilcox and W. Bruce Masse. *Arizona State University Anthropological Research Paper* 24: 57–70. Tempe: Arizona State University.

1984 The Tucson Basin During the Protohistoric Period. *The Kiva* 49(3–4): 195–211.

DOELLE, WILLIAM H., AND HENRY D. WALLACE

1990 The Transition to History in Pimería Alta. In *Perspectives on Southwestern Prehistory*, edited by Paul E. Minnis and Charles L. Redman, pp. 239–257. Boulder: Westview Press.

1991 The Changing Role of the Tucson Basin in the Hohokam Regional System. In "Exploring the Hohokam: Prehistoric Desert Peoples of the American Southwest," edited by George J. Gumerman. *Amerind Foundation New World Studies Series* 1: 279–345. Albuquerque: University of New Mexico Press.

DOELLE, WILLIAM H., FREDERICK W. HUNTINGTON, AND HENRY D. WALLACE

1987 Rincon Phase Community Reorganization in the Tucson Basin. In "The Hohokam Village: Site Structure and Organization," edited by David E. Doyel. *American Association for the Advancement of Science Publication* 87-15: 71–95.

DONKIN, R. A.

1979 Agricultural Terracing in the Aboriginal New World. *Viking Fund Publications in Anthropology* 56. Tucson: University of Arizona Press.

DOWNUM, CHRISTIAN E.

1986 The Occupational Use of Hill Space in the Tucson Basin: Evidence from Linda Vista Hill. *The Kiva* 51 (4): 219–232.

1988 Hohokam Platform Mound Communities of the Lower Santa Cruz River Basin, ca. A.D. 1050–1450. National Register of Historic Places Multiple Property Documentation Form. MS on file, Arizona State Historic Preservation Office, Phoenix.

1991 The Los Robles Survey: Archaeological Investigations of the Lower Santa Cruz River Basin, from Marana to Redrock, Arizona. MS on file, Arizona State Museum Library, University of Arizona, Tucson.

1993 (Editor) Archaeology of the Pueblo Grande Platform Mound and Surrounding Features. *Pueblo Grande Museum Anthropological Papers* 1. Phoenix: Pueblo Grande Museum.

DOWNUM, CHRISTIAN E., AND ALLEN DART

1984 Hohokam Sites: Reach 2. In "A Class III Survey of the Tucson Aqueduct Phase A Corridor, Central Arizona Project," compiled by Jon S. Czaplicki. *Arizona State Museum Archaeological Series* 165: 95–145. Tucson: Arizona State Museum, University of Arizona.

DOWNUM, CHRISTIAN E., AND JOHN H. MADSEN

1989 Classic Period Platform Mounds South of the Gila River. In "The Northern Tucson Basin Survey: Research Directions and Background Studies," edited by Paul R. Fish, Suzanne K. Fish, and John H. Madsen. MS on file, Arizona State Museum, University of Arizona, Tucson.

DOWNUM, CHRISTIAN E., JOHN E. DOUGLAS, AND DOUGLAS B. CRAIG

1985 Community Structure and Agricultural Strategies at Cerro Prieto (AZ AA:7:11). In "Proceedings of the 1983 Hohokam Symposium, Part II," edited by Alfred E. Dittert, Jr., and Donald E. Dove. *Arizona Archaeological Society Occasional Paper* 2: 545–556. Phoenix: Phoenix Chapter, Arizona Archaeological Society.

DOWNUM, CHRISTIAN E., ADRIANNE G. RANKIN, AND JON S. CZAPLICKI

1986 A Class III Archaeological Survey of the Phase B Corridor, Tucson Aqueduct, Central Arizona Project. *Arizona State Museum Archaeological Series* 168. Tucson: Arizona State Museum, University of Arizona.

DOYEL, DAVID E.

1981 Late Hohokam Prehistory in Southern Arizona. *Contributions to Archaeology* 2. Scottsdale, Arizona: Gila Press.

1984 From Foraging to Farming: An Overview of the Preclassic in the Tucson Basin. *The Kiva* 49(3–4): 147–165.

1989 The Transition to History in Northern Pimería Alta. In *Columbian Consequences*, Vol. 1, *Archaeological and Historical Perspectives on the Spanish Borderlands West*, edited by David Hurst Thomas, pp. 139–158. Washington: Smithsonian Institution Press.

1991 Hohokam Cultural Evolution in the Phoenix Basin. In "Exploring the Hohokam: Prehistoric Desert Peoples of the American Southwest," edited by George J. Gumerman. *Amerind Foundation New World Studies Series* 1: 231–278. Albuquerque: University of New Mexico Press.

ELLIS, G. LAIN, AND MICHAEL R. WATERS

1991 Cultural and Landscape Influences on Tucson Basin Hohokam Settlement. *American Anthropologist* 93(1): 125–137.

ELSON, MARK D.

1986 Archaeological Investigations at the Tanque Verde Wash Site, a Middle Rincon Settlement in the Eastern Tucson Basin. *Institute for American Research Anthropological Paper* 7. Tucson: Institute for American Research.

EZELL, PAUL H.

1961 The Hispanic Acculturation of the Gila River Pimas. *American Anthropological Association Memoir* 90.

EZELL, PAUL H. (*continued*)
1983 History of the Pima. In *Handbook of North American Indians*, Vol. 10, *Southwest*, edited by Alfonso Ortiz, pp. 125–136. Washington: Smithsonian Institution Press.

FARMER, T. REID
1984 A Cultural Resources Survey for the Western States Microwave Tower System in Southern and Central Arizona: Greenlee, Cochise, Pinal, Maricopa, and La Paz Counties. Report prepared for Times Mirror Microwave Communications by Gilbert/Commonwealth, Englewood, Colorado. MS, Arizona State Museum Site Files, University of Arizona, Tucson.

FEINMAN, GARY M.
1991 Hohokam Archaeology in the Eighties: An Outside View. In "Exploring the Hohokam: Prehistoric Desert Peoples of the American Southwest," edited by George J. Gumerman. *Amerind Foundation New World Studies Series* 1: 461–483. Albuquerque: University of New Mexico Press.

FERDON, EDWIN N., JR.
1955 A Trial Survey of Mexican-Southwestern Architectural Parallels. *School of American Research Monograph* 21. Santa Fe: Museum of New Mexico.

FERG, ALAN
1979 The Petroglyphs of Tumamoc Hill. *The Kiva* 45(1–2): 95–118.

FEWKES, J. WALTER
1909 Prehistoric Ruins of the Gila Valley. *Smithsonian Miscellaneous Collections* 52(1873): 403–436. Washington: Smithsonian Institution.
1912a Antiquities of the Upper Verde River and Walnut Creek Valleys, Arizona. *Twenty-Eighth Annual Report of the Bureau of American Ethnology, 1906–1907*, pp. 181–220. Washington: Smithsonian Institution.
1912b Casa Grande, Arizona. *Twenty-Eighth Annual Report of the Bureau of American Ethnology, 1906–1907*, pp. 25–179. Washington: Smithsonian Institution.

FIELD, JOHN J.
1992 An Evaluation of Alluvial Fan Agriculture. In "The Marana Community in the Hohokam World," edited by Suzanne K. Fish, Paul R. Fish, and John H. Madsen. *Anthropological Papers of The University of Arizona* 56: 53–63. Tucson: University of Arizona Press.

FIELD, JOHN J., KEITH KATZER, JAMES LOMBARD, AND JEANETTE SCHUSTER
1989 A Geomorphic Survey of the Picacho and Northern Tucson Basins. In "The Northern Tucson Basin Survey: Research Directions and Background Studies," edited by Paul R. Fish, Suzanne K. Fish, and John H. Madsen. MS on file, Arizona State Museum, University of Arizona, Tucson.

FISH, PAUL R., AND SUZANNE K. FISH
1989 Hohokam Warfare from a Regional Perspective. In "Cultures in Conflict: Current Archaeological Perspectives," edited by Diana C. Tkaczuk and Brian C. Vivian, pp. 112–129. *Proceedings of the 20th Annual Chacmool Conference*. Calgary: Archaeological Association of the University of Calgary.
1991 Hohokam Political and Social Organization. In "Exploring the Hohokam: Prehistoric Desert Peoples of the American Southwest," edited by George J. Gumerman. *Amerind Foundation New World Studies Series* 1: 151–175. Albuquerque: University of New Mexico Press.

FISH, PAUL R., SUZANNE K. FISH, AND JOHN H. MADSEN
1986 Spatial, Functional, and Social Differentiation in a Tucson Basin Classic Community. MS on file, Arizona State Museum, University of Arizona, Tucson.
1988 Differentiation in Bajada Portions of a Tucson Basin Classic Community. In "Recent Research on Tucson Basin Prehistory: Proceedings of the Second Tucson Basin Conference," edited by William H. Doelle and Paul R. Fish. *Institute for American Research Anthropological Paper* 10: 22–239. Tucson: Institute for American Research.
1989 An Introduction to Research Goals and Perspectives. In "The Northern Tucson Basin Survey: Research Methods and Background Studies," edited by Paul R. Fish, Suzanne K. Fish, and John H. Madsen. MS on file, Arizona State Museum, University of Arizona, Tucson.

FISH, PAUL R., SUZANNE K. FISH, AUSTIN LONG, AND CHARLES H. MIKSICEK
1986 Early Corn Remains from Tumamoc Hill, Southern Arizona. *American Antiquity* 51(3): 563–572.

FISH, PAUL R., SUZANNE K. FISH, STEPHANIE WHITTLESEY, HECTOR NEFF, MICHAEL D. GLASCOCK, AND J. MICHAEL ELAM
1992 An Evaluation of the Production and Exchange of Tanque Verde Red-on-brown Ceramics in Southern Arizona. In "Chemical Characterization of Ceramic Pastes in Archaeology," edited by Hector Neff. *Monographs in World Archaeology* 7: 233–254. Madison: Prehistory Press.

FISH, SUZANNE K.
1984 Agriculture and Subsistence Implications of the Salt-Gila Aqueduct Project Pollen Analysis. In "Hohokam Archaeology Along the Salt-Gila Aqueduct, Central Arizona Project, Environment and Subsistence," edited by Lynn S. Teague and Patricia L. Crown. *Arizona State Museum Archaeological Series* 150(7): 111–138. Tucson: Arizona State Museum, University of Arizona.

FISH, SUZANNE K., AND GARY P. NABHAN
1991 Desert as Context: The Hohokam Environment. In "Exploring the Hohokam: Prehistoric Desert Peoples of the American Southwest," edited by George J. Gumerman. *Amerind Foundation New World Studies Series* 1: 29–60. Albuquerque: University of New Mexico Press.

FISH, SUZANNE K., PAUL R. FISH, AND CHRISTIAN E. DOWNUM
1984 Hohokam Terraces and Agricultural Production in the Tucson Basin, Arizona. In "Prehistoric Agri-

cultural Strategies in the Southwest," edited by Suzanne K. Fish and Paul R. Fish. *Arizona State University Anthropological Research Paper* 33: 55–71. Tempe: Department of Anthropology, Arizona State University.

FISH, SUZANNE K., PAUL R. FISH, AND JOHN H. MADSEN (Editors)

1992 The Marana Community in the Hohokam World. *Anthropological Papers of The University of Arizona* 56. Tucson: University of Arizona Press.

FISH, SUZANNE K., PAUL R. FISH, CHARLES H. MIKSICEK, AND JOHN H. MADSEN

1985 Prehistoric Agave Cultivation in Southern Arizona. *Desert Plants* 7(2): 107–112, 102.

FONTANA, BERNARD L.

1983 Pima and Papago: Introduction. In *Handbook of North American Indians*, Vol. 10, *Southwest*, edited by Alfonso Ortiz, pp. 125–136. William G. Sturtevant, General Editor. Washington: Smithsonian Institution Press.

1987 Santa Ana de Cuiquiburitac: Pimería Alta's Northernmost Mission. With translations from Spanish documents by Daniel S. Matson. *Journal of the Southwest* 29(2): 133–159.

FONTANA, BERNARD L., J. CAMERON GREENLEAF, AND DONNELLY D. CASSIDY

1959 A Fortified Arizona Mountain. *The Kiva* 25(2): 41–52.

FONTANA, BERNARD L., WILLIAM J. ROBINSON, CHARLES W. CORMACK, AND ERNEST E. LEAVITT, JR.

1962 *Papago Indian Pottery*. Seattle: University of Washington Press.

FREDIN, LARRY

1981 Talus Pit Comparisons: Mt. Tolman Project vs. Creston, Washington Area. MS on file, Archaeological and Historical Services, Eastern Washington University, Cheney.

GABEL, NORMAN E.

1931 Martinez Hill Ruins. MS, Master's thesis, Department of Anthropology, University of Arizona, Tucson.

GASSER, ROBERT E.

1990 Ak-Chin Farming. In "Archaeology of the Ak-chin Indian Community West Side Farms Project: The Land and the People." *Soils Systems Publications in Archaeology* 9(2). Phoenix: Soils Systems.

GELDERMAN, FREDERICK W.

1972 *Soil Survey of the Tucson -Avra Valley Area, Arizona*. Soil Conservation Service in Cooperation with The University of Arizona Agricultural Experiment Station. Washington: U.S. Department of Agriculture.

GLADWIN, WINIFRED, AND HAROLD S. GLADWIN

1929 The Red-on-buff Culture of the Papagueria. *Medallion Paper* 4. Globe, Arizona: Gila Pueblo.

GREENLEAF, J. CAMERON

1975 The Fortified Hill Site Near Gila Bend, Arizona. *The Kiva* 40(4): 213–282.

GREENWALD, DAWN M.

1988 Ground Stone. In "Hohokam Settlement Along the Slopes of the Picacho Mountains: Material Culture," edited by Martha M. Callahan, pp. 127–220. *Museum of Northern Arizona Research Paper* 35(4). Flagstaff: Museum of Northern Arizona.

GREGORY, DAVID A.

1991 Form and Variation in Hohokam Settlement Patterns. In *Chaco and Hohokam: Prehistoric Regional Systems in the American Southwest*, edited by Patricia L. Crown and W. James Judge, pp. 159–193. Santa Fe: School of American Research Press.

GROSSMAN, FREDERICK E.

1873 The Pima Indians of Arizona. *Annual Report of the Smithsonian Institution for 1871*, pp. 407–419. Washington.

GUMERMAN, GEORGE J.

1991 Understanding the Hohokam. In "Exploring the Hohokam: Prehistoric Desert Peoples of the American Southwest," edited by George J. Gumerman. *Amerind Foundation New World Studies Series* 1: 1–27. Albuquerque: University of New Mexico Press.

HACK, JOHN

1942 The Changing Physical Environment of the Hopi Indians of Arizona. *Papers of the Peabody Museum of Archaeology and Ethnology, Harvard University*, 35(1). Cambridge: Peabody Museum.

HACKENBERG, ROBERT A.

1974 Aboriginal Land Use and Occupancy. In "Papago Indians, I," edited by D. A. Horr, pp. 23–308. *American Indian Ethnohistory: Indians of the Southwest*. New York: Garland.

HARTMANN, GAYLE HARRISON, AND WILLIAM K. HARTMANN

1979 Prehistoric Trail Systems and Related Features on the Slopes of Tumamoc Hill. *The Kiva* 45(1–2): 39–69.

HARTMANN, WILLIAM K.

1989 *Desert Heart: Chronicles of the Sonoran Desert*. Tucson: Fisher Books.

HASSE, E. F.

1970 Environmental Fluctuations on South-Facing Slopes in the Santa Catalina Mountains of Arizona. *Ecology* 51: 959–974.

HASTINGS, JAMES R., AND RAYMOND M. TURNER

1964 *The Changing Mile*. Tucson: University of Arizona Press.

HAURY, EMIL W.

1950 *The Stratigraphy and Archaeology of Ventana Cave*. Tucson: University of Arizona Press, and Albuquerque: University of New Mexico Press.

1976 *The Hohokam: Desert Farmers and Craftsmen*. Tucson: University of Arizona Press.

1987 Comments on Symposium Papers. In "The Hohokam Village: Site Structure and Organization," edited by David E. Doyel. *American Association for the Advancement of Science Publication* 87-15: 249-252.

HAYDEN, JULIAN D.
1942 Ash Hill Site, Notes. MS in the Arizona State Museum Archives, University of Arizona, Tucson.
1957 Excavations, 1940, at University Indian Ruin. *Technical Series* 5. Globe, Arizona: Southwestern Monuments Association.

HENDERSON, T. KATHLEEN
1986 Site Structure and Development at La Ciudad: A Study of Community Organization. MS, Doctoral dissertation, Department of Anthropology, Arizona State University, Tempe.

HOOVER, J. W.
1941 Cerros de Trincheras of the Arizona Papaguería. *Geographical Review* 31: 228–239.

HOWARD, JERRY B.
1985 Courtyard Groups and Domestic Cycling: A Hypothetical Model of Growth. In "Proceedings of the 1983 Hohokam Symposium, Part I," edited by Alfred E. Dittert, Jr., and Donald E. Dove. *Arizona Archaeological Society Occasional Paper* 2: 311–326. Phoenix: Phoenix Chapter, Arizona Archaeological Society.
1992 Architecture and Ideology: An Approach to the Functional Analysis of Platform Mounds. In "Proceedings of the Second Salado Conference," edited by Richard C. Lange and Stephen Germick. *Occasional Paper*. Phoenix: Arizona Archaeological Society.

HOWARD, WILLIAM A., AND THOMAS GRIFFITHS
1966 Trinchera Distributions in the Sierra Madre Occidental, Mexico. *Publications in Geography, Technical Paper* 66-1. Denver: Department of Geography, University of Denver.

HUCKELL, BRUCE B., MARTYN D. TAGG, AND LISA W. HUCKELL
1987 The Corona de Tucson Project: Prehistoric Use of a Bajada Environment. *Arizona State Museum Archaeological Series* 174. Tucson: Arizona State Museum, University of Arizona.

HUNTINGTON, ELLSWORTH
1913 The Fluctuating Climate of North America. *Annual Report of the Smithsonian Institution, 1912*, pp. 383–412. Washington: Smithsonian Institution.
1914 The Climatic Factor as Illustrated in Arid America. *Carnegie Institution of Washington Publication* 192. Washington.

HUNTINGTON, FREDERICK W.
1986 Archaeological Investigations at the West Branch Site: Early and Middle Rincon Occupation in the Southern Tucson Basin. *Institute for American Research Anthropological Paper* 5. Tucson: Institute for American Research.

HUNTINGTON, FREDERICK W., AND JAMES P. HOLMLUND
1986 Archaeological Mapping of Two Sections of Site AZ AA:11:12, Marana, Arizona. *Institute for American Research Technical Reports* 86-4. Tucson: Institute for American Research.

IVES, RONALD
1973 Father Kino's 1697 Entrada to the Casa Grande Ruin in Arizona: A Reconstruction. *Arizona and the West* 15: 345–370.

JACOBS, DAVID
1992 Increasing Ceremonial Secrecy at a Salado Platform Mound. In "Developing Perspectives on Tonto Basin Prehistory," edited by Charles L. Redman, Glen E. Rice, and Kathryn E. Pedrick. *Arizona State University Anthropological Field Studies* 26: 45–60. Tempe: Arizona State University.

JENCSOK, E. I.
1969 Hydrologic Design for Highway Drainage in Arizona. MS, Arizona Highway Department, Bridge Division, Phoenix.

JOHNSON, ALFRED E.
1960 The Place of the Trincheras Culture of Northern Sonora in Southwestern Archaeology. MS, Master's thesis, Department of Anthropology, University of Arizona, Tucson.
1963 The Trincheras Culture of Northern Sonora. *American Antiquity* 29(2): 174–186.

JOHNSON, ALLEN W., AND TIMOTHY EARLE
1987 *The Evolution of Human Societies: From Foraging Group to Agrarian State*. Stanford: Stanford University Press.

JONES, STAN
1965 Mystery of the Hohokams. *Desert Magazine*, October, pp. 24–26.

KARNS, HARRY J. (Translator)
1954 *Unknown Arizona and Sonora, 1693–1721, from the Francisco Fernandez de Castillo Version of Luz de Tierra Incógnita*, by Captain Juan Mateo de Manje. Tucson: Arizona Silhouettes.

KELLEY, J. CHARLES
1953 Reconnaissance and Excavation in Durango and Southern Chihuahua, Mexico. *American Philosophical Society Yearbook* (1953). Philadelphia: American Philosophical Society.
1971 Archaeology of the Northern Frontier: Zacatecas and Durango. In *Handbook of Middle American Indians* 11(2): 768–801. General Editor, Robert Wauchope. Austin: University of Texas Press.

KIDDER, ALFRED V.
1924 *An Introduction to the Study of Southwestern Archaeology, with a Preliminary Account of the Excavations at Pecos.* Phillips Academy, Papers of the Southwestern Expedition 1. New Haven: Yale University Press.

KNIGHT, VERNON JAMES, JR.
1986 The Institutional Organization of Mississippian Religion. *American Antiquity* 51(4): 675–687.

LANGE, CHARLES H., AND CARROLL L. RILEY (Editors and Annotators)
1970 *The Southwestern Journals of Adolph F. Bandelier: 1883–1884*. Albuquerque: University of New Mexico Press.

LARSON, STEPHEN M.

1972 The Tumamoc Hill Site Near Tucson, Arizona. *The Kiva* 38(2): 95–101.

1979 The Material Culture Distribution on the Tumamoc Hill Summit. *The Kiva* 45(1–2): 71–81.

LINDAUER, OWEN

1992 Centralized Storage: Evidence from a Salado Platform Mound. In "Developing Perspectives on Tonto Basin Prehistory," edited by Charles L. Redman, Glen E. Rice, and Kathryn E. Pedrick. *Arizona State University Anthropological Field Studies* 26: 33–44. Tempe: Arizona State University.

LOGAN, R. F.

1961 Winter Temperatures of a Mid-Latitude Desert Mountain Range. *Geographical Review* 51: 236–252.

LOMBARD, JAMES P.

1986 Provenance of Sand Temper in Hohokam Ceramics, Arizona. Prepublication Master's Manuscript, on file, Antevs Reading Room, Department of Geosciences, University of Arizona, Tucson.

1987 Provenance of Sand Temper in Hohokam Ceramics. *Geosciences* 2.

LOWE, CHARLES

1977 *Arizona's Natural Environment*. Tucson: University of Arizona Press.

LUMHOLTZ, CARL S.

1971 *New Trails in Mexico*. Glorieta, New Mexico: Rio Grande Press.

MADSEN, JOHN H.

1989 Geology of the Lower Santa Cruz River Drainage Basin: A Pilot Study of Prehistoric Stone Procurement. In "The Northern Tucson Basin Survey: Research Directions and Background Studies," edited by Paul R. Fish, Suzanne K. Fish, and John H. Madsen. MS on file, Arizona State Museum, University of Arizona, Tucson.

MADSEN, JOHN, SUZANNE K. FISH, AND PAUL R. FISH

1989 Field Methods and Techniques. In "The Northern Tucson Basin Survey: Research Directions and Background Studies," edited by Paul R. Fish, Suzanne K. Fish, and John H. Madsen. MS on file, Arizona State Museum, University of Arizona, Tucson.

MALLOUF, MICHAEL G.

1980 *An Archeological Survey of the Ajo Crest, Organ Pipe National Monument, Southwestern Arizona*. Tucson: U.S. National Park Service, Western Archeological and Conservation Center.

MARTYNEC, RICHARD J.

1987 The Black Mountain Trincheras Site. In "The San Xavier Archaeological Project," by Peter L. Steere, Boyd Johns, Aphrodite Ploumis, James Copus, Richard J. Martynec, Henry D. Wallace, Douglas E. Kupel, Linda Roth, and Scott T. Clay-Poole. *Southwest Cultural Series* 1(5). Tucson: Cultural and Environmental Systems.

MASSE, W. BRUCE

1981 A Reappraisal of the Protohistoric Sobaipuri Indians of Southeastern Arizona. In "The Protohistoric Period in the North American Southwest A.D. 1450–1700," edited by David R. Wilcox and W. Bruce Masse. *Arizona State University Anthropological Research Paper* 24: 28–56. Tempe: Department of Anthropology, Arizona State University.

MCCARTHY, CAROL HEATHINGTON

1982 An Archaeological Sample Survey of the Middle Santa Cruz River Basin, Picacho Reservoir to Tucson, Arizona. *Arizona State Museum Archaeological Series* 148. Tucson: Arizona State Museum, University of Arizona.

MCGUIRE, RANDALL H.

1982a Environmental Background. In *Hohokam and Patayan: Prehistory of Southwestern Arizona*, edited by Randall H. McGuire and Michael B. Schiffer, pp. 13–56. New York: Academic Press.

1982b Problems in Culture History. In *Hohokam and Patayan: Prehistory of Southwestern Arizona*, edited by Randall H. McGuire and Michael B. Shiffer, pp. 153–222. New York: Academic Press.

1991 On the Outside Looking In: The Concept of Periphery in Hohokam Archaeology. In "Exploring the Hohokam: Prehistoric Desert Peoples of the American Southwest," edited by George J. Gumerman. *Amerind Foundation New World Studies Series* 1: 347–382. Albuquerque: University of New Mexico Press.

MCGUIRE, RANDALL H., AND ANN VALDO HOWARD

1987 The Structure and Organization of Hohokam Shell Exchange. *The Kiva* 52(2): 113–146.

MCGUIRE, RANDALL H., AND MARIA ELISA VILLALPANDO

1989 Prehistory and the Making of History in Sonora. In *Columbian Consequences I: Archaeological and Historical Perspectives on the Spanish Borderlands West*, edited by D. H. Thomas, pp. 159–177. Washington: Smithsonian Institution Press.

MCGUIRE, RANDALL H., MARIA ELISA VILLALPANDO, AND JOHN MCNIFF

1992 Altar Valley Survey Project, 1988 Season. MS, Draft report submitted to the Instituto Nacional de Antropología e Historia, Hermosillo, Sonora.

NABHAN, GARY P.

1983 Papago Fields: Arid Lands Ethnobotany and Agricultural Ecology. MS, Doctoral dissertation, Arid Lands Resource Sciences, University of Arizona, Tucson.

1986 Ak-chin "Arroyo Mouth" and the Environmental Setting of the Papago Indian Fields in the Sonoran Desert. *Applied Geography* 6(2): 61–75.

NEITZEL, JILL

1991 Hohokam Material Culture and Behavior: The Dimensions of Organizational Change. In "Exploring the Hohokam: Prehistoric Desert Peoples of the American Southwest," edited by George J. Gumerman. *Amerind Foundation New World Studies Series* 1: 177–230. Albuquerque: University of New Mexico Press.

NELSON, RICHARD S.
1991 Hohokam Marine Shell Exchange and Artifacts. *Arizona State Museum Archaeological Series* 179. Tucson: Arizona State Museum, University of Arizona.

RANKIN, ADRIANNE G.
1986 General Environmental Conditions, in Chapter 2, Environment and Geology. In "A Class III Archaeological Survey of the Phase B Corridor, Tucson Aqueduct, Central Arizona Project," by Christian E. Downum, Adrianne G. Rankin, and Jon S. Czaplicki. *Arizona State Museum Archaeological Series* 168: 5-11. Tucson: Arizona State Museum, University of Arizona.

RAVESLOOT, JOHN C., AND JON S. CZAPLICKI
1989 Dating and Site Development. In "Hohokam Archaeology Along Phase B of the Tucson Aqueduct, Central Arizona Project. Excavations at Water World (AZ AA:16:94), A Rillito Phase Ballcourt Village in the Avra Valley," edited by Jon S. Czaplicki and John C. Ravesloot. *Arizona State Museum Archaeological Series* 178(3): 19-44. Tucson: Arizona State Museum, University of Arizona.

RAVESLOOT, JOHN C., AND PATRICIA M. SPOERL
1984 A Fortified Hilltop Site, AZ T:4:8. In "Prehistoric Cultural Development in Central Arizona: Archaeology of the Upper New River Region," edited by Patricia M. Spoerl and George J. Gumerman. *Center for Archaeological Investigations Occasional Paper* 5: 63-100. Carbondale: Southern Illinois University.

REFF, DANIEL T.
1991 Anthropological Analysis of Exploration Texts: Cultural Discourse and the Ethnological Import of Fray Marcos de Niza's Journey to Cibola. *American Anthropologist* 93(3): 636-655.

REICHHARDT, KAREN
1989a A Vegetation Disturbance Pilot Study in the Northern Tucson Basin. In "The Northern Tucson Basin Survey: Research Directions and Background Studies," edited by Paul R. Fish, Suzanne K. Fish, and John H. Madsen. MS on file, Arizona State Museum, University of Arizona, Tucson.
1989b Vegetation of the Northern Tucson and Picacho Basins. In "The Northern Tucson Basin Survey: Research Directions and Background Studies," edited by Paul R. Fish, Suzanne K. Fish, and John H. Madsen. MS on file, Arizona State Museum, University of Arizona, Tucson.

RICE, GLEN E. (Editor)
1987 Studies in the Hohokam Community of Marana. *Arizona State University Anthropological Field Studies* 15. Tempe: Department of Anthropology, Arizona State University.

ROGERS, MALCOLM J.
1945 Final Yuman Pottery Types Nomenclature and Synonyms. MS on file, San Diego Museum of Man, San Diego, California.

ROHN, ARTHUR H.
1965 Postulation of Socio-economic Groups from Archaeological Evidence. In "Contributions of the Wetherill Mesa Archeological Project," assembled by Douglas Osborne. *Memoirs of the Society for American Archaeology* 19: 65-69.

ROTH, BARBARA J.
1992 Sedentary Agriculturalists or Mobile Hunter-Gatherers? Recent Evidence on the Late Archaic Occupation of the Northern Tucson Basin. *Kiva* 57(4): 291-315.

ROTH, BARBARA J., AND BRUCE B. HUCKELL
1992 Cortaro Points and the Archaic of Southern Arizona. *Kiva* 57(4): 353-370.

RUSSELL, FRANK
1908 The Pima Indians. In *Twenty-Sixth Annual Report of the Bureau of American Ethnology, 1904-1905*, pp. 3-389. Washington.

SAUER, CARL, AND DONALD BRAND
1931 Prehistoric Settlements of Sonora, with Special Reference to Cerros de Trincheras. *University of California Publications in Geography* 5(3): 67-148.

SCANTLING, FREDERICK H.
1940 Excavations at the Jackrabbit Ruin, Papago Indian Reservation, Arizona. MS, Master's thesis, Department of Anthropology, University of Arizona,Tucson.

SCHROEDER, ALBERT H.
1940 A Stratigraphic Survey of Pre-Spanish Trash Mounds of the Salt River Valley, Arizona. MS, Master's thesis, Department of Anthropology, University of Arizona, Tucson.
1952 A Brief Survey of the Lower Colorado River from Davis Dam to the International Border. MS, U.S. Bureau of Reclamation, Reproduction Unit, Region Three, Boulder City, Nevada.
1985 Hohokam Material Culture. In "Proceedings of the 1983 Hohokam Symposium, Part II," edited by Alfred E. Dittert, Jr., and Donald E. Dove. *Arizona Archaeological Society Occasional Paper* 2: 733-744. Phoenix: Phoenix Chapter, Arizona Archaeological Society.

SELLERS, WILLIAM D., RICHARD H. HILL, AND MARGARET SANDERSON-RAE
1985 *Arizona Climate: The First Hundred Years*. Tucson: Institute of Atmospheric Physics, University of Arizona.

SHREVE, FOREST
1914 Rainfall as a Determinant of Soil Moisture. *The Plant World* 17: 9-26.
1934 Rainfall, Runoff, and Soil Moisture Under Desert Conditions. *Annals of the Association of American Geographers* 24(3): 131-164.

SIRES, EARL W., JR.
1984 Hohokam Architecture and Site Structure. In "Hohokam Archaeology Along the Salt-Gila Aqueduct, Central Arizona Project: Prehistoric Occupation of

the Queen Creek Delta," edited by Lynn S. Teague and Patricia L. Crown. *Arizona State Museum Archaeological Series* 150(9): 115–139. Tucson: Arizona State Museum, University of Arizona.

SKIBO, JAMES M.
1986 Large Site Reconnaissance in the Lower Santa Cruz Basin. Paper presented at the Second Tucson Basin Conference, Tucson, Arizona.

SMITH, FAY JACKSON (Editor and Translator)
1966a Diary of Lieutenant Cristobal Martin Bernal. In *Father Kino in Arizona*, edited by Fay Jackson Smith, John L. Kessell, and Francis J. Fox, S.J., pp. 35–47. Tucson: Arizona Historical Society.
1966b The Relación Diaria of Father Kino. In *Father Kino in Arizona*, edited by Fay Jackson Smith, John L. Kessell, and Francis J. Fox, S.J., pp. 1–34. Tucson: Arizona Historical Society.

SMITH, HARLAN I.
1910 The Archaeology of the Yakima Valley. *American Museum of Natural History Anthropological Paper* 6(1). New York: American Museum of Natural History.

SPOERL, PATRICIA M.
1984 Archaeological Surveys. In "Prehistoric Cultural Development in Central Arizona: Archaeology of the Upper New River Region," edited by Patricia M. Spoerl and George J. Gumerman. *Center for Archaeological Investigations Occasional Paper* 5: 17–59. Carbondale: Southern Illinois University.

STACY, VALERIA KAY PHERIBA
1974 Cerros de Trincheras in the Arizona Papaguería. MS, Doctoral dissertation, Department of Anthropology, University of Arizona, Tucson.
1977 Activity Patterning at Cerros de Trincheras in Southcentral Arizona. *The Kiva* 43(1): 11–17.

TEAGUE, LYNN S., AND PATRICIA L. CROWN
1984 Hohokam Archaeology Along the Salt Gila Aqueduck, Central Arizona Project, Synthesis and Conclusions. *Arizona State Museum Archaeological Series* 150(9). Tucson: Arizona State Museum, University of Arizona.

TUCSON CITIZEN
1985 July 13, "Red Rock Resort Will Offer Risks and Show Guns to Draw Japanese."

TURNAGE, W. V., AND A. L. HINKLEY
1938 Freezing Weather in Relation to Plant Distribution in the Sonoran Desert. *Ecological Monograph* 8: 529–550.

UNDERHILL, RUTH M.
1939 Social Organization of the Papago Indians. *Columbia University Contributions to Anthropology* 30. New York: Columbia University Press.

VOKES, ARTHUR W.
1989 Architecture, Trash Deposits, Cremations, and Feature Descriptions. In "Hohokam Archaeology Along Phase B of the Tucson Aqueduct, Central Arizona Project. Excavations at Water World (AZ AA:16:94), A Rillito Phase Ballcourt Village in the Avra Valley," edited by Jon S. Czaplicki and John C. Ravesloot. *Arizona State Museum Archaeological Series* 178(3): 45–151. Tucson: Arizona State Museum, University of Arizona.

WALLACE, ANTHONY F. L.
1966 *Religion: An Anthropological View*. New York: Random House.

WALLACE, HENRY D.
1983 The Mortars, Petroglyphs, and Trincheras on Rillito Peak. *The Kiva* 48(3): 137–246.
1988 Ceramic Boundaries and Interregional Interaction: New Perspectives on the Tucson Basin Hohokam. In "Recent Research on Tucson Basin Prehistory: Proceedings of the Second Tucson Basin Conference," edited by William H. Doelle and Paul R. Fish. *Institute for American Research Anthropological Paper* 10: 313–348. Tucson: Institute for American Research.

WALLACE, HENRY D., AND JAMES P. HOLMLUND
1986 Petroglyphs of the Picacho Mountains, South Central Arizona. *Institute for American Research Anthropological Papers* 6. Tucson: Institute for American Research.

WASLEY, WILLIAM W.
1960 A Hohokam Platform Mound at the Gatlin Site, Gila Bend, Arizona. *American Antiquity* 26(2): 244–262.

WASLEY, WILLIAM W., AND ALFRED E. JOHNSON
1965 Salvage Archaeology in Painted Rocks Reservoir, Western Arizona. *Anthropological Papers of The University of Arizona* 9. Tucson: University of Arizona Press.

WATERS, MICHAEL R.
1982 Appendix G: The Lowland Patayan Ceramic Typology. In *Hohokam and Patayan: Prehistory of Southwestern Arizona*, edited by Randall H. McGuire and Michael B. Schiffer, pp. 537–570. New York: Academic Press.
1987 Holocene Alluvial Geology and Geoarchaeology of AZ BB:13:14 and the San Xavier Reach of the Santa Cruz River, Arizona. In "The Archaeology of the San Xavier Bridge Site (AZ BB:13:14), Tucson Basin, Southern Arizona," edited by John C. Ravesloot. *Arizona State Museum Archaeological Series* 171: 39–60. Tucson: Arizona State Museum, University of Arizona.

WILCOX, DAVID R.
1979 Warfare Implications of Dry-Laid Masonry Walls on Tumamoc Hill. *The Kiva* 45(1–2): 15–38.
1980 The Current Status of the Hohokam Concept. In "Current Issues in Hohokam Prehistory: Proceedings of a Symposium," edited by David E. Doyel and Fred T. Plog, pp. 236–242. *Arizona State University Anthropological Research Paper* 23. Tempe: Arizona State University.
1984 Research Problems. In "A Class III Survey of the Tucson Aqueduct Phase A Corridor, Central Arizona Project," compiled by Jon S. Czaplicki. *Arizona State Museum Archaeological Series* 165: 195–208.

WILCOX, DAVID R. (*continued*)
Tucson: Arizona State Museum, University of Arizona.

1991a Hohokam Social Complexity. In *Chaco and Hohokam: Prehistoric Regional Systems in the American Southwest*, edited by Patricia L. Crown and W. James Judge, pp. 253-275. Santa Fe: School of American Research Press.

1991b The Mesoamerican Ballgame in the American Southwest. In *The Mesoamerican Ballgame*, edited by Vernon L. Scarborough and David R. Wilcox, pp. 101-125. Tucson: University of Arizona Press.

WILCOX, DAVID R., AND TERRY SAMPLES
1992 The Wagner Hill Ballcourt and Indian Peak Ruin: Revised Permit Report of the 1990 MNA/NAU/Oberlin Archaeological Field School and Subsequent Studies. Report submitted to Mr. James McKie, Prescott National Forest Archaeologist, and Dr. John A. Hanson, Kaibab National Forest Archaeologist.

WILCOX, DAVID R., AND CHARLES STERNBERG
1983 Hohokam Ballcourts and Their Interpretation. *Arizona State Museum Archaeological Series 160.* Tucson: Arizona State Museum, University of Arizona.

WILCOX, DAVID R., THOMAS R. MCGUIRE, AND CHARLES STERNBERG
1981 Snaketown Revisited. *Arizona State Museum Archaeological Series* 155. Tucson: Arizona State Museum, University of Arizona.

WILSON, JOHN P.
1980 Cultural Resources of the Proposed Tucson Electric Tortolita-South Utility Corridor and Alternative Routes, Pinal and Pima Counties, Arizona. Report No. 21, prepared for the Tucson Electric Power Company, Tucson. MS, Arizona State Museum Site Files, University of Arizona, Tucson.

1981 Archeological Survey of the Proposed Tucson Electric Tortolita-South Relocated Segment, Pinal and Pima Counties, Arizona. Report No. 26, prepared for the Tucson Electric Power Company, Tucson. MS, Arizona State Museum Site Files, University of Arizona, Tucson.

1985 Early Piman Agriculture: A New Look. In "Southwestern Culture History: Collected Papers in Honor of Albert H. Schroeder," edited by Charles H. Lange. *The Archaeological Society of New Mexico* 10: 129-138. Santa Fe: Archaeological Society of New Mexico.

WORMINGTON, H. MARIE
1947 Prehistoric Indians of the Southwest. *Denver Museum of Natural History, Popular Series* 7. Denver: Denver Museum of Natural History.

Index

Abstract

This monograph focuses on the results of archaeological surveys and excavations along Los Robles Wash, a desert stream that is tributary to the Santa Cruz River in northern Pima and southern Pinal counties, Arizona. Data from these investigations are used to reconstruct patterns of prehistoric and protohistoric settlement and land use along Los Robles Wash and to illustrate that the so-called "intermediate" areas between interior deserts and the major river valleys to the north were in fact densely settled and dynamic components of the Hohokam world.

Most of the prehistoric sites discussed in this volume appear to have been organized into an extensive Hohokam community spread along the west bank of Los Robles Wash and extending westward into the Samaniego Hills. Designated as the Los Robles Community, this prehistoric settlement system apparently developed in tandem with the Marana Community, located directly across the Santa Cruz River. Dating of the decorated ceramic types indicates that the Los Robles Community spanned the late Pioneer through early Classic periods of the Hohokam cultural sequence. Prior to the early Classic, the Community's central village and organizational heart was probably a large ballcourt settlement (AZ AA:11:12 ASM). During the early Classic, the Los Robles Community evidently was reorganized around two new settlements: a village with a large earthen mound, probably a platform mound (AZ AA:11:25 ASM), and Cerro Prieto, an extensive *cerro de trincheras* (a terraced hillside site with a variety of masonry features) spread over the lower slopes of the area's most prominent volcanic hill (AZ AA:7:11 ASM). Although *cerros de trincheras* have traditionally been interpreted as short-term defensive refuges, evidence from Cerro Prieto indicates that the settlement did not serve as a fortification, but instead was a large habitation village used for multiple activities. It is suggested that some of the masonry features at Cerro Prieto, such as massive terraces, compounds, and dividing walls, were constructed to serve ceremonial and symbolic purposes.

The presence of both a mound settlement and a *cerro de trincheras* raises important questions regarding the nature of the Hohokam Sedentary to Classic period transition and the organizational structure of the Los Robles Community. It is proposed that the apparently simultaneous existence of a mound settlement and a *cerro de trincheras* reflect a time of ideological and organizational

Resumen

Esta monografía esta enfocada en los resultados de los reconocimientos de superficie y las excavaciones realizadas a lo largo del Arroyo los Robles, que es una corriente desértica tributaria del río Santa Cruz ubicada en la zona norte del Condado Pima y la zona sur del condado Pinal, Arizona. Los datos de estas investigaciones se usan para reconstruir patrones de asentamientos y de uso de la tierra a lo largo del Arroyo los Robles durante las épocas pre- y poshispánicas, y para ilustrar que las llamadas nicas "intermedias" comprendidas entre el desierto interior y los valles de los ríos mayores al norte estuvieron en realidad densamente pobladas y constituyeron un componente dinámico del mundo Hohokam.

Casi todos los sitios prehispánicos examinados en este volumen parecen haber estado organizados en una extensa comunidad Hohokam expandida sobre el margen oeste del Arroyo los Robles y que se extendió hacia el oeste dentro de los Montes Samaniegos. Este sistema de asentamiento prehispánico, designado como Comunidad de los Robles, se desarrolló a la par con la Comunidad de Marana, localizada cruzando en línea directa el río Santa Cruz. La cronología basada en los tipos cerámicos decorados indica que la Comunidad de Los Robles se desarrolló entre los períodos Pionero tardío y Clásico temprano dentro de la secuencia cultural Hohokam. Antes del periodo Clásico temprano, parece ser que la población central y corazón organizacional de la comunidad fue asentamiento caracterizado por su enorme cancha de juego de pelota (AZ AA:11:12 ASM). Durante el Clásico temprano hubo una reorganización de la Comunidad de los Robles esta vez a partir de dos nuevos asentamientos: una villa con un gran montículo de tierra, probablemente un montículo plataforma (AZ AA:11:25 ASM), y Cerro Prieto, un extenso *cerro de trincheras* (este tipo de sitios se caracterizan por el terraceado de laderas y una variedad de construcciones de manpostería) que se extendió sobre las laderas bajas del fenómeno volcánico más prominente del área (AZ AA:7:11 ASM). Si bien los *cerros de trincheras* tradicionalmente se han interpretado como refugios defensivos, las evidencias encontradas en Cerro Prieto indican que el sitio no se usó como fortificación y que por el contrario fue una extensa villa habitacional usada para múltiples actividades. Los datos sugieren que algunas de las construcciones de manpostería en Cerro Prieto, entre las que figuran conjuntos de terrazas masivas y muros divisionales, fueron hechas con propósitos simbólicos y religiosos.

flux, prompted by the demise of Preclassic Hohokam belief systems and organizational principles. Like the Marana Community, Los Robles did not survive into the late Classic period, and it is suggested that ideological and organizational changes, rather than environmental processes, were the more likely causes of abandonment. Two specialized essays discuss the environmental parameters of terrace locations at *cerros de trincheras* and the nature of enigmatic, protohistoric Pima rock cairn and talus pit sites discovered in the northwest corner of the survey area. The work concludes with a discussion of the prospects for preserving the archaeological sites of the Los Robles Community, now designated as a National Register District and a future Arizona State Park.

La existencia mutua de un asentamiento con montículo plataforma y un *cerro de trincheras* pone de manifiesto información referente a la naturaleza de la fase de transición entre los períodos Sedentario y Clásico Hohokam y sobre la estructura organizacional de la Comunidad los Robles. Se propone que la aparente coexistencia de un asentamiento con montículo plataforma y un cerro de trincheras puede significar una temporada de flujo ideológico y organizacional, incitada por el fenecimiento del sistema de creencias y principios organizacionales del Preclásico temprano. La Comunidad de los Robles, al igual que la Comunidad de Marana, no sobrevivió al período Clásico tardío, y se sugiere que las causas más probable de su abandono fueron las transformaciones en la organización y en la ideología, en vez de los cambios en los procesos ambientales. Dos ensayos especializados presentes en este volumen discuten los parámetros ambientales de la localización de terrazas en *cerros de trincheras* y la naturaleza enigmática de unos sitios Pimas de la época del contacto, descubiertos en la zona noroeste del área de estudio, caracterizados por piedras apiladas y pozos excavados en los taludes detríticos. El trabajo finaliza con una discusión sobre las espectativas de preservación de los sitios de la Comunidad de los Robles, actualmente designada como Distrito del Registro Nacional y en un futuro cercano como Parque Estatal de Arizona.